Later that night Jimmy moved his poncho farther away from mine. Ants or termites were tormenting him while he tried to sleep. Mulling over the next day's mission, I anticipated a restless night, but within moments of reclining, I performed an excellent imitation of a rock.

Kaboom! The first explosion ripped me awake. *Kaboom!* The second spun me around, and I faced the inner part of the circle. The gook trail was on the far side of our perimeter. *Kaboom!* The third explosion blinded me and took away my senses. Machine-gun and small-arms fire raged. I was living a facsimile of hell. I'd never heard such a torrent of gunfire in my life.

"My God!" I screamed. "We're being attacked!" Although disoriented, I soon discovered that most of the firing was coming from the section of the circle near the trail. In the early-morning haze, guns roared and muzzles flashed. . . .

FROM CLASSROOMS TO CLAYMORES

A Teacher at War in Vietnam

Ches Schneider

IVY BOOKS • NEW YORK

An Ivy Book
Published by The Ballantine Publishing Group
Copyright © 1999 by Ches Schneider

www.randomhouse.com/BB/

Library of Congress Catalog Card Number: 99-90017

ISBN 0-8041-1871-X

Manufactured in the United States of America

First Edition: April 1999

10 9 8 7 6 5 4 3 2 1

To:

God who watched over me and always placed good people in my path

Sharon, whose encouragement gave me the extra push I needed to see my written dream come true

Karen, who supported me throughout my time in Vietnam

My parents, Chester and Lorraine Schneider, and my brothers, Ron, Larry, and Don, who provided the emotional foundation I needed in Vietnam and afterward

My kids, Chris and Debbie Schneider and Jason and Richard Brosch, who have heard my stories so many times they could have written the book

The four to five thousand students I have taught in my lifetime as an educator; they were my first and often most critical audiences

Jason Holmes, Nancy Rathjen, Peggy Shores, Gary Wilbur, Sue Brannan, Steve Kestle, Steve Berger, Steve Warren, and Vinnie Mancusi—who helped me polish my work

Gary Linderer, who guided and counseled me—a gentleman and a scholar who best typifies what is good about Vietnam veterans

All the men I served with in Vietnam—the ones whose names I have lost in memories but with whom I share a bond as tight as brotherhood

Contents

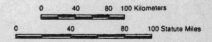

Prologue

I stood at the door of Room 601. I was back. I was back from the jungles of Vietnam. Now the room in which I had taught history and English seemed as foreign as the Viet Cong bunker complexes of Southeast Asia. In Vietnam, I had served as an infantry grunt. Like everyone in Nam, I had one dream. That was to return to the "World," as we call the United States, alive and, preferably, with all my limbs and organs in their proper places. I had been a teacher for two and a half years before being snagged in the 1968 draft, and I was returning to the life I understood. Of all my fantasies while hiding in ambush sites in Nam, little did I ever think that I would return to the exact same classroom.

Fortunately, our school had employed several other returning veterans. Our common experiences enabled us to support one another. Now, looking back to that time, I can say that of the top ten teachers I have worked with, five are Vietnam vets. The year in Vietnam did something to us: it made us builders. Vietnam vets understand the concept of mission and of teamwork. They understand sacrifice and pride in accomplishment. In our contemporary public education environment, they understand about giving their lives in what some people think is a losing battle.

Our young people need to see warriors. They need to hear real warriors' stories. Unfortunately, American kids are receiving distorted messages. They think Rambo is a true-life hero and that the American hunter is a Bambi killer.

Vietnam was a down and dirty war. It was our last great military learning experience. The Gulf War was a success because we had learned in Vietnam. It was Vietnam veterans and their families who led the way and stood at post offices to show their support for our troops in the Middle East. After an initial attempt to provide Vietnam-style journalism, the news media saw that the American public wasn't buying antiwar messages; major news organizations did a one-eighty to support the war.

Yet the Gulf wasn't like Nam. It was largely an air war and a real-time television war. Because of advanced communication capabilities, the real-time news coverage actually came from both sides of the line of combat. But watching smart bombs fly down ventilator shafts had the feel of Hollywood special effects. In a sense, the Gulf War had the aura of a *Star Wars* movie. It wasn't dirty or unpopular.

As a teacher of American history, I have never hesitated to tell stories of Vietnam in class. I have had to clean them up a little. Maybe I even embellished a story or two, but who hasn't fibbed a little on the length of a fish or the number of points on a buck. Mark Twain explained that expanding a story wasn't truly a lie, just a "stretcher." Over the years, I have earned a reputation as a storyteller and a good teacher. My students have begged to hear about Vietnam even when a test was not a prominent feature of the day's lesson. Our younger generations want to hear personal experiences from people who have been to war and lived real-life military experiences. I've always considered this passing on of oral history to be a strong component of the educational program I provide for my students. Parents have mentioned to me that my stories have been told and retold across their dinner tables for twenty-seven years. At times, I have heard my students retell my adventures to students who have not been in my class, and I have been shocked at their accuracy. I can only hope that my lessons on the Articles of Confederation and the Jacksonian Era have made half the impression.

Those of us who served in Vietnam had many things taken from us. Two years is a long time to be away from one's trade. Before going to Nam, I had always assumed that I would become a principal, but upon my return, I saw that others had been promoted in my absence. I was a step behind in my career path, and I was never able to crack the "old boy" network. Part of this was my fault; I was too stubborn to play educational politics. I had crawled though jungles in heat and rain. I had encountered fire ants and very nasty Viet Cong and North Vietnamese soldiers. I had faced AK-47 fire and claymore mines, so there was little that school principals or superintendents could do to me that would make me fear them. Some school administrators can be self-serving and petty despots. In Nam, I had served under both strong and weak officers. I knew good leadership from bad and wasn't afraid to express my views on contemporary educational issues. The educational decisions I made were based upon what was right for children, not upon my career aspirations.

But Room 601 was still a dreamworld, a classroom that should have been familiar was strange and alien. In a way, the disorientation I felt reminded me of my first days at Song Be, Vietnam. But as my mind adjusted to where I was, I noticed that the broken venetian blinds still hadn't been repaired. There was a new bulletin board. Decorating a bulletin board wasn't one of my teaching strengths, and I'd have to address that matter during my panic period the morning of opening day.

I began to circumnavigate the room, touching the teacher's desk, the blackboard, the wall map, and the student desks. On the third desk from the front, in row two, I spied a familiar marking. During my first year of teaching, one of my disaffected students had painstakingly scratched "Fuck Schneider" into the desktop with the point of a compass. I considered the engraving a badge of honor. I smiled. The memories of my first two and a half years of teaching rushed back into my mind. This was my real world, not the world of destruction and killing but the world of learning, growth, and building. I could restart my life.

CHAPTER 1

Twenty-twenty Hindsight

I don't believe that people can foretell the future, and I know for certain that I don't possess any such psychic powers. If I did, I would have had better experiences with the stock market or, when I was dating, I would have saved a good deal of dinner and movie money uselessly spent only to get a good-night kiss and nothing else.

No, I can't see into the future, but I think everyone, including myself, has inklings of things to come. Maybe it is not even a premonition of future events. Maybe it is a longing for some particular event to take place. To be more exact, it might be that we wish so hard that something good or dread so much that something bad will happen that we subconsciously guide our lives in that direction. A gambler who keeps entering the million-dollar sweepstakes wins it, and the person who has always feared cancer comes down with the "Big C." Those people have more than good or bad luck in common. They have subconscious mental processes at work shaping their future. I was the same way regarding service in the United States military.

I always seemed to feel or know that someday I would serve in the U.S. Army. That I might someday be a sailor, an airman, or a Marine never held a viable place in my mind. I'm sure that I was influenced by my brief memories of life in Tullahoma, Tennessee, where I lived with my family during World War II. My father served in the military police and guarded German prisoners of war who were brought back to the United States for safekeeping until Hitler and his men had been defeated.

I'm sure that these feelings were reinforced during my Cold War childhood in the fifties. And I suspect that 1950s television programs, such as *Combat*, played their part as well. Someday, someway, somehow, I subconsciously hoped and dreaded that I, too, would take part in mankind's time-honored tradition of warfare. I knew it in my heart, and although consciously fighting the trepidation, I still gloried in my great expectations.

This was, of course, an internal battle. Outwardly, I was like any other kid of the sixties. After high school, I went on to college to glean an education geared toward upper-middle-class employment. As an astronaut or rocket scientist, I would help America beat our economic and political adversaries, the Russians, into space. I could kill two noble birds with one educational stone. College as a draft deferment rarely crossed my mind.

Upon discovering that my gray matter didn't include a calculus section, and that astronauts couldn't be near-sighted, I redirected my goals from engineering to teaching. Following the old saying, "Those who can, do, and those who can't, teach," I decided that I would teach the astronauts of the future the history and English that they would need to beat the Russians to the moon. Besides, teaching with its job security, three-month vacation, relatively high social position, and lack of heavy, dirty labor seemed to best fit my tastes.

Like most wild and crazy college students, girls, fraternity parties, and occasional study filled my time and helped to obscure what was of national and international importance. In the early sixties, the kernel of war in Vietnam was growing, but to me, it was still small and far away. I could make my C average and still make the fraternity weekend blast or snuggle in the backseat of my '54 Plymouth with Barb, the Frito-Lay. Barb was nicknamed after her favorite snack and sport. College life was good. And as a conscientious Sigma Chi, I considered major problems—such as whom to allow to pledge our fraternity—more pressing than domestic or foreign affairs. Money was scarce, but I could earn enough working part-time at a grocery store to get by. Donations from my parents were never rejected.

College led to student teaching, and student teaching led to a full-time teaching position. The big payoff was at hand. I was hired to teach history and English in a cozy, all-white, suburban junior high school located outside of St. Louis, Missouri. I commenced to earn moderately good money and work in a challenging atmosphere. I was surrounded by young male teachers and, more important, young female teachers. "Real" life held many of the same elements as college. But I had more money to spend and was considered a pillar of the community. I was no longer a boolah-boolah college kid wet behind the ears, but "Mr. Schneider," the teacher. My ego got the best of me, and I began work on a master's degree at the University of Missouri at St. Louis. Soon I might become Mr. Schneider, the school principal or even Dr. Schneider, the district superintendent. The fact that being a teacher would also keep me draft exempt was of minor importance.

All this time, the war in Vietnam continued to grow. It had, in fact, reached a flash point both in Vietnam and the United States. Nineteen sixty-seven and -eight were tumultuous times. Bolstered by my draft deferment for teaching, I was in the forefront of the battle to defeat the powers of Communism, if not abroad, certainly at home. The domestic enemy seemed to be Jane Fonda, draft dodgers, hippies, yippies, zippies, Weathermen, and other unwelcome trash such as dopers and long-haired, weirdo freaks. But the philosophies of those types made great inroads into the teen and preteen culture, and those anti-authority, antimom, anti–apple pie, antibarber, prodrug attitudes were ruining a whole generation of kids.

Though junior high school students lacked the intellectual sophistication to understand the substance of the sixties protest movement, they enjoyed duplicating the form. A typical class discussion in social studies usually developed into . . .

"Mr. Schneider, Mr. Schneider!" In the back of the room, Frank was trying to get my attention. I was a bit conservative in my teaching. I still required the students to call me mister, and to use my last name. Many teachers, following the trend of the day, allowed students to call them by their first name or a nickname like "Aunt Dixie." Sixties teachers reasoned that educators and students were equals. I did, too, so I called each of my students mister or miss and used their last names.

"Yes, Mr. Green?" I responded.

"Vietnam is a bummer, man!" he drawled in an obvious attempt to forestall the scheduled American history test on the Jacksonian Era.

"Where is Vietnam, Mr. Green?"

"I don't know, man, somewhere over there," he stated with a vague wave of his arm at the faded world map that hung from hooks on my classroom wall.

"If you don't know where we are fighting, do you know who we are fighting? Or why we are involved in this conflict?"

"No, I don't know none of that there stuff, but I know that I want to make love, not war."

Sensing a teachable moment to discuss the Constitutional issues involved, I queried, "Why is this war different from World War I or II? Is it a Constitutional war? Which branch of government has the power to declare war?"

"I don't know, man, but I hear they got good dope in Nam!"

With this, the class erupted into the usual panic of "tee hee" laughter as if they knew some secret that I didn't. I would get revenge when I graded their tests.

The form of protest and the words were more or less correct, but the insight and the understanding of what was at stake went over the heads of the junior-high students. The late sixties was a time in our history when we shook the country right down to its foundations and found it to be strong. Watergate would do the same in the seventies. The

United States government, guided by the Constitution, survived both, and the country held together.

As I started my second year of teaching. I was getting too old to be seriously considered for military service either foreign or domestic. I was almost twenty-six. At that magic age, Uncle Sam granted to all American males who had skillfully avoided being selected from the draft pool a special dispensation—a permanent pass on being drafted to the military, an end to the annual spring reclassification process I had already undergone every June since turning eighteen: Sometime during May, I would receive a letter stating that my file had been reviewed by the local draft board and that I had been reclassified as 1A, prime meat.

I would halfheartedly talk to all the armed service recruiters about signing up with their respective branches of the service if my deferment didn't come through. But my 2A reserve classification always did, and I would be free from worry for another year. The nightmare of military service and the dream of heroic deeds would fade.

The summer of 1967, Uncle Sam almost got me. It was very close. I had even taken the Army Officers Candidate School test and the army physical. I passed both. My deferment didn't show up, and I was on the way to sign the final army enlistment papers, when in an act of desperation I called home in the futile hope that the mail would produce a reprieve. The mail at our house didn't contain a letter, but my dad, who was a postal employee at our local post office, checked the late-arriving mail, and there it was. I had my 2-A deferment for another year. If I could get one more deferment in the spring of '68, I would be home free.

Many people of that era have similar horror stories. Some missed being drafted by an equally lucky phone call. Others were fortunate enough to have been involved in an automobile accident that had caused them to be temporarily or permanently physically unfit. Really good high school and college athletes could point to knees that showed signs of cartilage removal and declare themselves draft liabilities. Some people knew members of Congress, or a local draft board member was an uncle. Some joined the FBI or the National Guard. A few people headed for Canada or foreign countries. Cassius Clay became Muhammad Ali and used a religious conversion as an excuse. Choose one. All were ways out.

It was August 1967, and I once again had my deferment. I was again enjoying life to the fullest. I would miss the war and the army. My inner voice would have been wrong, and I would live with the feeling that somehow I had cheated destiny.

Fate can be cruel. In the fall of '67, I fell in love. It was downright-honest, head-over-heels, playboy-of-the-western-world, over-the-lips-through-the-gums-look-out-stomach-here-it-comes love. Love was to change my marital, financial, social, and military status. I was a goner, in more ways than one.

Previously, while pursuing female flesh, I had always considered myself to be an honorable gentleman. I had always been truthful. During close encounters with the young women that I dated, I had always warned them of my tenuous military status.

"I could be drafted at any time," I informed them. "My life is not my own. I could face the danger of death or dismemberment very, very soon."

Southeast Asia wasn't that far away, and I was completely prepared to defend their curvaceous bodies from the domino theory and the yellow barbarians who would otherwise rape and plunder them. No, they would be safe in my hands. And wasn't I only one step away from being drafted? Why, hadn't I talked to the Marine recruiter just last summer?

Somehow, the tender, young female of the sixties confused 1A status with 2A, 4F, or 25Z. This confusion, along with the about-to-be-drafted confession, seemed to have the effect of endearing the sweet young things to me. Didn't a man about to be drafted need his morale raised as much as, if not more than, those who had already been drafted? Men who were drafted, more or less, had their future determined. Mine was still undecided.

The uncertainty of the draft greased the way for the certainty of the make-out line. The sweet, young, liberated women of the sixties were usually most comforting in my predicament.

This way of life came to an abrupt halt when a Sigma Chi brother of mine, who was teaching at our high school, introduced me, via a blind date, to his student teacher. Karen and I clicked from the start. She fell for me, and I for her.

On one December evening after our third or fourth date, I felt duty bound to warn Karen of my about-to-be-drafted military status. We had attended a Sigma Chi alumni party at the elite Missouri Athletic Club in downtown St. Louis. The more I noticed Karen's cleavage at her tailored but slightly revealing dress collar, the more I realized that for her own safety as well as my own physical well-being, I had better whip the draft status line on her right away.

The lights at the M.A.C. had been turned low. The food tasted great. The drinks were warming, and the band was mellow. The company was just the proper mixture of frat rats and respectable alumni. Karen looked good. I mean, she looked really good. Everything was A-OK, as we would-be astronauts who don't have calculus gray matter would say.

Afterward, we left the dance and parked at the local lovers' lane. Karen had nixed the idea of going back to my apartment for a drink. A nice try to avoid the inevitable, I thought. After putting my arm around her shoulders, I commenced to confess my about-to-be-drafted status. I pointed out that proof of all my misery was at my apartment, not ten minutes away.

Immediately she responded. Her eyes filled with tears, and her face showed signs of pity and remorse. I could tell that she was beginning to bend.

"Ches, that's terrible! How can you live with that uncertainty? What turmoil your life must be in!"

"Oh, it's not so bad, I guess. Just a bit lonely," I intoned, and I hung my head a little.

"One more deferment in June and you'll be set? You'll be twenty-six next January, right?"

"Yes, one more year. Actually only a few months until my present deferment is up. I'll still need one more to see me through. In fact, they could be typing up my orders in Washington, right now!"

Karen seemed to soften even more. "Then after the next deferment you will be free of all this? This summer you'll be free to make plans. That is—plans for your future?"

"Yes."

"Plans of a more permanent nature?"

"Yes."

"Plans for marriage, a house, and children?"

"Yessss . . . , I guess soooo . . ."

"What? I can't hear you."

"Yes!"

"I like you so much, and when your life is more settled, maybe we can make plans together."

"Make plans? Make plans? I've got plans right now. Let's go to my apartment. We can discuss them there in more detail!"

Maybe the tension in my voice gave me away.

"Have you always gotten your deferment?"

"Yeah!"

"Well, then you'll get another one this summer, too. Don't worry."

Obviously, my approach was failing. Since I could not dispute the validity of the line, that left only two other explanations. First, Karen didn't like me as much as she had led me to believe. Our next kiss killed that theory. Then it must be the second reason. Karen was a Communist! Or at least she was unpatriotic. Yes, that was it! There couldn't be any other answer. After all, no red-blooded American woman would let an about-to-be-drafted American male suffer so much unless she was part of a Communist conspiracy.

During the ensuing months, I found that Karen's patriotism was the only thing in question. Her morals were in excellent shape. All the persuasions known to twentieth-century man wouldn't break them down.

By then, I was lost anyway. I was in love, and as most men are sometime in their lives, I was being sucked down the drain of matrimony. I was naive enough to think that I was the moving force, but in reality, I wasn't.

Karen's classic Italian looks, charming personality, and interest in fishing and hunting had captured me. In addition, her family had money. Her father owned a local night-club where I could get free booze, and she could type forty words per minute. I hadn't checked her teeth closely, but I assumed that they were in good condition.

In July, we set the date for our nuptials. We would be married during the 1968 Christmas break from school. That summer, I started going through the motions of being drafted. I knew full well that August or September would produce the final 2A draft deferment.

August came and went—no deferment. The local draft boards were now clearing out all the loopholes and untidy corners that had accumulated over the years. Teachers were being drafted. I was one of them. During the period between September 1968 and June 1969, I was both married and drafted. Both presented new horizons and challenges. Both were a step toward manhood. Both could be a definite pain in the ass.

In October, I appealed to my local draft board. I cannot think of a more degrading experience than when I went to the Mart Building for a personal appeal. The draft board consisted of three elderly gentlemen appointed to judge whose tale of woe merited exemption and whose did not. My five-minute interview didn't go well.

"Do you have any special reasons for requesting an exemption?" the chairman asked.

"Well, I'm a teacher, and I feel that I can do more to help the country in that capacity than I can in any other."

Silence followed for about four minutes. I waited, and they waited. Finally, I asked, "Should I be asking or answering questions, or something?"

"No" was the reply. We sat there in more silence.

Finally, the chairman asked, "Anything else?"

"No, I guess not," I replied. I was now resigned to my fate. The board hearing had been a farce. The decision had been made long before I entered the meeting. It had been made by forces that weren't even present in the room.

The chairman stated in a businesslike monotone, "You will be informed of our decision within two weeks. Thank you."

"Thank you," I dutifully replied.

As I left, I hated myself. It had been humiliating. I had seemed to be begging for something, and begging left a bitter taste in my mouth. This may have been the most disgraceful experience of my life. I told myself that I hadn't pleaded or groveled, but a small voice inside of me said, "But you did ask!" Was there shame in that?

The appeal was rejected, but I was told that I could finish teaching the present school year. Then I should report for duty on July 1, 1969. Karen and I were married during Christmas break on December 28, 1968, and the six months between January and June of 1969 were a nonstop, sweet-sour holiday. Life was one of those picnics with a persistent storm cloud over it.

On July 1, I reported to Fort Leonard Wood, Missouri, for eight weeks of basic training. The Ozarks, which had always represented freedom for me as I hunted, fished, and spelunked, now became a prison. My drill instructor, or DI, was promotion bound. He damn near killed us with the combination of traditional army physical training plus split-and-polish inspections.

It didn't take him long to find out that I had been a schoolteacher in real life. "Schneider, what grade did you teach?" He asked as he ran beside me on the three-mile jog we used to work up an appetite for breakfast each morning.

"Eighth grade, Drill Sergeant," I huffed. I was just a little out of shape.

"I hated my eighth grade teacher!" he barked into my ear. "She was the last teacher I ever had in school. I hated her ass then, and I hate your sorry ass now!"

He made me his pet project. Even though I understood the psychology and motivation behind his every torment, I couldn't avoid becoming the object of his every character-building experience. Through his guidance, I lost weight, transformed into top physical condition, and learned to hate the army. If nothing else, I was normal. Only Karen's conjugal weekend visits and daily letters kept me from going insane.

After the torture of basic training, I was assigned to Fort Gordon, Georgia, for Advanced Individual Training (AIT). My MOS, or military occupational specialty, was to be 11Bravo20—infantry soldier. I had known that I would be assigned to infantry way back at the induction center at Fort Leonard Wood when we took our Army Entrance and Placement Tests.

Some of the test questions were:

Question 46: Do you enjoy walking as a form of exercise?
  I answered: Yes
Question 48: Are you afraid of loud noises?
  I answered: No
Question 50: Do you enjoy the outdoors?
  I answered: Yes
Question 54: Do you enjoy camping?
  I answered: Yes
Question 58: Do you feel comfortable walking through the woods at night?
  I answered: Yes
Question 68: Have you ever fired a firearm?
  I answered: Yes

I knew what answers to give to avoid assignment to the infantry. I knew, but I could not and would not give them.

Still another chance for escape from the infantry presented itself when the NCO in charge of new recruit reception asked, "Does anyone want to be a chaplain's assistant?" Suddenly, I, too, saw a light at the end of the Vietnamese tunnel. The solution to the maze was obvious. I was as religious as anyone else. Why not volunteer?

I slammed the door on my own fingers by not volunteering. I was helping the army fulfill my lifetime premonition. I was consciously and subconsciously guiding my own fate. I was infantry bound, come hell or high water.

After the grueling basic training at Fort Leonard Wood, life at Fort Gordon was nice. AIT was hard, but the work was evenly distributed, and the personal harassment was minimal. I was far away from Karen, but on the second weekend of AIT, she and my brother Ron brought down my Camaro, and I had transportation to use in off-duty hours. The United States Army and I made a temporary truce, and for the next six weeks I coasted. Other than a badly sprained right ankle that I suffered during escape and evasion training, everything went A-OK.

The main concern of each of the soldiers in my training company was permanent duty reassignment. Our drill instructor and company cadre swore that the infantry recruits from our training cycle were bound for Germany. This was only one of the many lies army personnel told us. It kept people from going AWOL. When the company clerk took our heavy overcoats, and the medic gave us tropical disease shots, we knew we were not headed for *das Vaterland*. No, we were going to RVN, the Republic of Vietnam.

I finished my AIT and was given three things: a two-week leave, my orders for Nam, and a case of army food poisoning. I had two reasons to barf all the way back to St. Louis.

CHAPTER 2

Into the Tunnel

After AIT, the army granted me a fourteen-day leave, and I took three extra AWOL days. Karen and I lived for the moment. This was a radical departure from my German, save-for-tomorrow upbringing. "To hell with tomorrow" became our hedonistic cry. But tomorrows, as Orphan Annie says, "are only a day away."

Karen obtained some personal leave time from her teaching position to help me paint San Francisco, my port of embarkation, red. That was why I ended up being AWOL. I had been unofficially told when I left AIT that I could report up to five days late without penalty or punishment. Since I was to report to Oakland Transit Terminal the day before Thanksgiving, I boldly declared to my family and friends that the U.S. Army could have me after Thanksgiving and not before. Karen and I used the AWOL days to do the City by the Bay, and each other, up in style.

I reported late. The army punished me with an Article 15, which was the equivalent of a slap on the wrist or after-school detention back at junior high school. I was reduced in rank to E-2. I grinned inwardly whenever I thought of the shameful way Karen and I had spent money and enjoyed each other. The Vietnam War wasn't going anywhere. It could wait three days for me. It did.

On the morning of November 27, 1969, I kissed Karen good-bye outside the Transit Terminal and turned my back on her and the real world. I remember facing those green, paint-chipped double doors, taking a deep breath,

and stepping through them into oblivion. How I got
through those doors and the next few days of waiting, I'll
never know. President Nixon had talked about a light at
the end of the tunnel. I saw no light; for me, the Vietnam
War was just starting.

In other wars, units had gone over en masse, and soldiers were together with people they knew and with whom
they had trained. Maybe that method would have helped.
One man could take heart from the courage of his buddies.
However, that was not the case with soldiers shipping out
to Nam. Even though in a crowd of several thousand individuals who felt exactly same way, each man was on his
own. Each man was an island. Each man had to face the
future using his own inner strengths and dealing with his
own inner weaknesses. I owned plenty of both.

The ever-present KP helped kill some time. Somehow, I
seemed to be a natural for getting picked, but I could then
cuss the army and some cook. It was therapeutic swearing.
While I waited for overseas transportation, I ran into Joe
MacCord, a buddy from basic training. He had been with
me at AIT at Fort Gordon as well.

Joe MacCord was a gentle, good-natured farm boy
from Kansas. He had arrived three days AWOL, too. He
had elected to stay with his family and girlfriend over the
Thanksgiving holiday, so we in-processed together. Thank
God for a familiar face. We talked of old times and adventures during the last four months of training and worried
about our next twelve months. When facing extreme adversity, the human heart loves to have a kindred spirit. Joe
and I were just trying to muddle our way through the
limbo in which we found ourselves mired.

At the Oakland Transit Barracks, we waited for orders.
There we were outfitted with new jungle fatigues and
boots. Army personnel misled us again. A little lie but a lie
all the same. The army told us to turn in our dress uniforms
and Stateside clothes. As we stripped and threw them
into big bins, the supply clerks told us not to worry, that
we would be given "credit" for them. Upon our return, we
would be issued new ones. I looked across the warehouse

floor and saw returnees from Nam paying for their "lost" uniforms, but I didn't understand the army quartermaster system at that time.

One sergeant E-7, on permanent duty at Oakland, explained, "You won't need these clothes where you're going. It's too damn hot over there. If you return, you'll weigh a whole lot less than you do now, and these uniforms won't fit. Why, I know a guy who lost thirty-five pounds over there." He paused and grinned. "Yep, he lost his left leg and part of his right arm when he stepped on a land mine! Ha! Ha! Ha! Step along now, through that door. Don't hold up this line."

It takes twenty-two hours to fly from Oakland to Saigon, RVN, via Anchorage, Alaska, and Yokota, Japan. I left on December 2, 1969. I read. I slept. I reviewed the high and low points of my life. During the previous twenty-six years, nothing had prepared me for that experience. Nothing equaled this ordeal either.

At Anchorage and Yokota we were confined to the airport terminal. I did not get to do any sightseeing. It was night, and I couldn't distinguish what was outside the airport terminal windows very well. Alaska seemed very frigid. My only impression of Japan was that the toilets seemed too high. I thought the Japanese were little tykes. How did they crawl way up on these? My feet didn't reach the floor when I sat down.

The airplane droned on and on and on. I killed time by composing a humorous postcard to send home at each stop. I told myself that I was not homesick and that the postcards were to keep the folks at home happy. I tried to imagine what other soldiers in other wars must have felt. All soldiers in all wars must have experienced similar feelings. But I wasn't all soldiers in all other wars. I was me, in this war, and although, as a history teacher, I could attempt to understand the historical perspective, war close up was a very personal experience.

When our pilot announced that we were over Vietnam, there was a general rush to the windows. After a minute of staring at the clouds and ground and not seeing anything of importance, all the other passengers lost interest and returned to their seats. I was already seated next to a window. In a morose manner, I continued to stare at the ground. It was daylight, and all I could see through the clouds were patches of green and brown, broken at times by the blue of a stream or river.

Suddenly the muzzle flash of a large gun caught my eye. Fright shot through me. With a moan, I cried, "Oh God, they're shooting at the plane." Either no one heard me, or they refused to believe that was true. The other soldiers were too engrossed in their own thoughts. Some may have heard me and envied me my good start at a Section 8 insanity plea. Maybe they thought that they would reserve that trick for a later date.

Actually, it was better that no one paid attention to my raving. We weren't receiving fire. The enemy was not trying to shoot down a troop transport. American artillery was shooting a fire mission against a VC position somewhere out in the bush. Of course, I only understood that sometime later, when I knew more about the art of war. As a neophyte, my honest opinion was that we were the object of enemy antiaircraft fire.

This was the start of a theme that would dominate my entire tour in Nam. I would never really know or fully understand what was happening. I often wouldn't understand until sometime after the actual event was well over. Sometimes, I would reflect upon an incident for days or weeks to comprehend what had taken place. Sometimes, I asked others to explain what I had just seen or experienced. It was as if I didn't trust my own judgment or senses. War is too big to know it all, or even learn about it quickly. A person needs to comprehend a little piece at a time. It takes time and experience. I was off to a good start.

Although I didn't know it then, the pilot was following standard procedure and was flying high and well out of range of most enemy small-arms fire. My fright didn't improve when the plane abruptly banked and headed down at a steeper than normal angle. This was to avoid giving enemy gunners a prolonged target to shoot at as we approached the airport runway.

My imagination was in high gear. I had heard and believed all the war stories told by Vietnam returnees during basic and advanced infantry training. Our steep dive toward the runway must indicate that our aircraft might be hit by VC gunfire. As we descended into Tan Son Nhut, Saigon's military airport, I saw columns of smoke encircling the airfield. I was firmly convinced that the Viet Cong were attempting to blow us out of the sky and that the entire airport was under attack. And here we were, heading straight into the carnage.

The plane landed and taxied to an abrupt halt. I assumed that everyone would mob the exit doors and run or low crawl for cover. To my surprise, no one did. In an orderly fashion and much to my disbelief, the officers and senior NCOs calmly disembarked the plane. The rest of us followed into the stifling heat. Outside the plane, we assembled and marched to the tin shed that served as the Tan Son Nhut airport terminal. It was a calm and cool military march. No mass panic took place.

Only five minutes in Nam, and I was already seeing myself through different eyes. Even though I was certain that the plane and the airfield were under enemy attack and that I would probably be killed at any moment, I sedately followed the others.

Why didn't I run or duck or crawl? Because I was a coward! I didn't want to stand out. Frightened as I was, I did not want to appear to be different from the other soldiers. I didn't want to break a mysterious norm that was forming. In a wave of recognition, I realized why I had not gone to NCO or to Officers Candidate School. At that instant, I understood why I was in Nam rather than in Canada. Why I was walking instead of running. Why I would do whatever the army told me to do when they told me to do it—no matter what. I realized that I was a lemming.

Once off the airport runway, a grizzled, second-tour veteran explained the fearsome columns of smoke that ringed the airfield. They were not exploding enemy artillery shells? No, and telling this, I feel a bit foolish. In Vietnam, I was to learn, at 1000 hours every morning, some poor sucker, usually the lowest-ranking private, took the human feces from the outhouses and burned it in cut-off fifty-five-gallon oil drums. In Vietnam, there simply was not a sewage system present to dispose of human waste in a sanitary manner. Fecal waste was mixed with crude oil and gasoline and then ignited. The trooper on the detail had the privilege of stirring the mixture until it was completely gone.

When lighted, the concoction produced a pungent odor and thick, dark smoke. What I had seen and mistaken for enemy shelling when we landed was actually the daily ritual of "burning the shit." I didn't know this until several days later when I was allowed to give it a turn, so to speak, myself.

A tin shed served as the airport terminal for Tan Son Nhut. This terminal was the main corridor to the war in the southern part of Vietnam. An army guide greeted our group with a welcoming speech. He apologized for the shed, but assured us that by the time we left, Tan Son Nhut and Saigon would have an airport facility to rival that of most major American cities. It was under construction just then. His greeting helped quash any hopes we had for an early end to the war. It simply wouldn't make economic sense to end a war before the United States extracted its money's worth from the new airport terminal.

We were FNGs, fucking new guys, and sat in the FNG section of the shed. A roar went up from a group of soldiers that equaled our number. They sat in a section marked DEROS. I realized that DEROS must mean, "going home," or something to that effect. I fully understood why they were happy to be going home, and of course, I envied them. But I couldn't comprehend the meaning of the insult they hurled in our direction. "Short!" they yelled. "Short!"

"Beaucoup short!" they screamed, and made a sign with their index finger and thumb to indicate just how short they meant. They were a rowdy, unkempt, and undis-

ciplined group. Some carried souvenirs, weapons captured from the enemy. All wore smiles that couldn't be
ripped from their faces. They were going home, and we
were just starting.

It seemed so unfair. It was very depressing. As we
marched out to the buses that would transport us to our
next destination, I turned to see that undisciplined herd
stampede toward *our* plane. They didn't march. They
didn't even walk fast. The undignified, unmilitary, obnoxious rabble stormed our airplane. It was then that I made
the most solemn vow I would ever make in my life.
Standing there watching those returnees rush the plane, I
vowed, "If and when I ever leave for home on some plane
like that, I will never sink to that level of behavior. I will
hold my head up high and walk, not run, to the plane. I
don't know what the U.S. Army, the Viet Cong, and North
Vietnam can throw at me for the next 365 days, but I know
I will leave this goddamn country with dignity!"

We in-processed at the 93d Replacement Battalion.
Rumor had it that the bus in front of us had received sniper
fire as it passed through the crowded streets. Rumor had it
that our bus had been the target, because we had officers
on it. Rumor also had it that we would be going home
soon. Rumor had it that we wouldn't stay the mandatory
365 days. Rumors are a staple of the army diet, and like
the army chow, should be ingested with care and prudence.

We were given malaria pills and an orientation. Orientation included exchanging our green U.S. dollars for
military payment certificates (MPC). I had never thought
an entirely new money system would have to be constructed for a war. I had never heard about "scrip." Scrip,
MPC, wasn't Vietnamese money.

The South Vietnamese use piasters. The value of the pi-
aster fluctuated wildly. This new MPC money system took
time to get used to. This was because of the different col-
oring and due to the fact that the new MPC money was the
size and shape of Monopoly money. MPC just did not
seem real. Because MPC seemed like play money, I was
worried, so I hid a ten-dollar, US of A greenback in one of

those semisecret compartments in the back of my wallet. I think this was to somehow get me home in case of an emergency. It was a silly, useless act, but it wasn't the only silly, useless, or even illegal act that I would perform while in Nam.

Another part of the orientation included the VD films. Along with these films came the required hygiene lecture. There was a hint that there was a Vietnamese brand-X type of venereal disease that had mutated to form a strain that couldn't be cured. Somewhere on an island off the coast was a colony of hopeless, brand-X-infected GIs, doomed forever. I believed this story! Any country that could develop three- to four-inch cockroaches could easily produce a brand-X type of syphilis. I didn't ever intend to end up on that island, watching my short arm rot off.

In-processing included dividing us into groups and eventually assigning us to units. MacCord and I were separated. He went to the 1st Air Cavalry. I went to the 1st Infantry Division, the Big Red One. My stay at in-processing took four days. Once again, I was given the opportunity to do KP—Vietnam style. Not surprisingly, there was little difference from Stateside KP.

After I left the 93d Replacement Depot, I was transported to the 1st Infantry Division base camp at Di An (pronounced Ze On). Here, I received a refresher course in patrolling and small-unit jungle fighting. After a few days at Di An, I was sent to Lai Khe (pronounced Lie Kay). Lai Khe was the rear area for Company D, 2d Battalion, 16th Infantry, of 1st Infantry Division. This was my new unit. I would be stationed in the central section of Vietnam, about forty or fifty miles north of Saigon. I would be fighting in an area called the Central Highlands. Fighting in this area was no pushover, but if one were grasping for straws, he could argue that the contact with the Viet Cong was said to be less serious than up north with the North Vietnamese regulars, and that the weather and terrain were more desirable than the rice paddies down south in the Delta country.

Despite having contracted a head cold, I was getting acclimated. The period between December 3 and December

11 that I spent in training, transition, and transport was "good time," safe time.

I felt good about arriving at Lai Khe, my new home base. It would be with those people and that company that I would spend the remainder of my tour. Those would be the people with whom I would fight the Communist menace. I would depend on them, trust them, and eventually need to be trusted by them. They were to be my new family.

Lai Khe was a military outpost located outside a sizable Vietnamese town located in the rubber-tree country, and I was enthralled by the scenery as our C-47 landed at the airstrip outside of the base. Rubber trees in exact neat rows stretched endlessly to the north, south, and west. The rubber-tree groves were only cut by roads. Also surprising was the fact that the Vietnamese town was so close to the U.S. Army base. Only barbed wire separated the town from the military base.

At the airport, the company clerk greeted a fellow new guy and me with, "You the FNGs for Delta Company?"

We nodded in the affirmative. My dreams of Dr. Schneider or Professor Schneider had faded, and now I accepted FNG Schneider without a blink.

"I'm Murphy," he added. "And don't believe what you hear about Lai Khe. It's not that bad."

Startled, we both turned to face Murphy for an explanation. The other new guy stammered, "What do you mean? I haven't heard anything!"

Murphy's face seemed to gleam. He loaded our gear into his jeep and started the trip to headquarters. He began his orientation.

"Lai Khe is called Rocket City," he yelled as the jeep bounced over the dirt road, kicking up a red rooster tail of dust as we sped along. "The Viet Cong have been hitting us with rocket fire. It's also called Dr Pepper Land. The rockets usually come in around the clock at ten, two, and four. Charlie likes to aim at the medical station, the chopper pad, and, at four o'clock, the mess hall. He thinks he'll get lots of dead meat if he hits the mess hall." I quickly checked my watch. It was ten after three.

"The company is in the field," he continued, "and I can't get you transportation out to them until tomorrow, so you'll have to stay here tonight."

Murphy and I passed the next few minutes in general small talk about where we came from in the States. The other FNG sat quietly in the back of the jeep with the duffel bags.

When we arrived at the hut that served as the Delta Company headquarters, we unloaded. Murphy turned to me and said, "I've already assigned you my perimeter guard position on the bunker line tonight. I've got a lot of paperwork to do. You go over to the mess tent and eat some supper. If the gooks hit us with any stuff, run out to a bunker. They're located just outside the mess hall. Follow the others. Eat supper, and I'll get you a rifle, ammo, and a blanket for tonight. You'll be on guard from 2000 hours until 0600 hours tomorrow morning."

"I've never really been on this kind of guard duty before," I said. "What do I do?"

"It's easy," he replied with a gleam in his eye again. "All you do is watch the outside of the perimeter of the base. Look for movement or VC. If you see anything, call the command post and ask for permission to shoot. If the gooks shoot at you first or if they shoot at you before you get permission to fire—sometimes that takes a long time—then you may blow the suckers away. Don't initiate fire. Only return it. There are a lot of friendly Vietnamese out there who leave early for work, so be especially careful in the morning right before dawn."

"How do I know if they are the friendly guys going to work, or VC returning from a night ambush?"

"Well, that is a problem."

"Listen," I said, "I'm sorry, but I don't feel very confident about this whole perimeter guard thing."

"Hey, that's okay. None of us do."

"Will I have some relief? All-night guard duty is really

tough. I'm not sure I could do it by myself. Will there be anyone else on duty to relieve me?"

"Why sure! You aren't expected to stay up all night. There will be two of you on duty. You won't be alone. Take turns sleeping and guarding. Two hours on, two hours off."

"Oh, good! I'm glad that I'll have someone with me. I sure hope he'll know what he's doing. Who will it be?" I sighed.

"Well, I don't know," Murphy said, looking away from me at some point over the horizon. "You'll be with that other new guy. That field commo wireman that you came in with," and he pointed at the other FNG who was sitting on his duffel bag, grumbling and alternately glaring at us and the ground.

We placed our gear outside the door of the company HQ, and Murphy continued, "Don't worry about not having done this before, neither has he. I've got to run. Meet me back here at 1945. I'll give you your stuff, and I'll show you the way to the defense perimeter. It's almost chow time, so go and eat. Take the wire guy with you. He's looking for the mess hall, too. Follow your noses. Go find it together."

"Thanks for the help!" I said sarcastically.

"Hey, no problem. Don't even mention it," he replied and vanished into the company tent.

Supper was uneventful, although I choked on my food at every loud noise. Charlie must have had a light supply of rockets that afternoon. At 2000 hours, Murphy, the commo guy, and I walked to the bunker line, or "green line" as it is also called. I guess it was called the green line because there were no trees or grass inside the area, and there were trees and grass on the far side of the cleared area outside the bunker line.

A bunker line or green line was a raised earthen mound of dirt that formed a berm. Bulldozers had raised earth inside the line to make a permanent saucer surrounded by a ten-to-twelve-foot mud dike or wall. The raised dike or wall extended around the whole installation and provided some means of protection against direct-fire weapons from outside the berm. A kill zone or cleared area extended for several hundred yards outside the berm. This meant that anyone or anything crossing the area would be exposed to sight from the bunker line. Inserted in the berm were protected fighting positions called bunkers. They were evenly spaced along the berm and between every five or so bunkers there was a raised watchtower.

The bunkers looked as if they would be havens in times of trouble. They were constructed of corrugated metal and sandbags. Each bunker provided overhead protection from rain and mortar shells. Openings or gun ports faced the kill zone outside the perimeter. Barbed wire, both the traditional kind used in the American West and the new, improved, circular concertina wire, was arranged outside the perimeter. The barbed wire was to stop or slow down enemy soldiers as they charged the position. Large fences similar to those used as baseball backstops were placed directly in front of each bunker about twenty feet out. The baseball backstops were to deflect hand grenades or rocket-propelled grenades (RPGs) from reaching the bunkers. All in all, the bunker line seemed to provide a formidable obstacle to any would-be attackers.

At night, two-to-six-man units were assigned to each fighting position. The individual companies provided guards for their own assigned bunkers. The company clerks, cooks, barbers, postmen, and other rear echelon personnel, affectionately referred to by the 11Bravo20 infantrymen as rear echelon motherfuckers, or REMFs, would pull guard duty at night after performing their various tasks all day. When FNGs appeared, the FNG would be assigned to guard duty, and the REMF could take the night off. Company clerks were always looking for warm bodies to stand their guard duty. Anyone would do!

I was never quite sure of the ethnic origin of my fellow guard, the commo wireman. He had a dark complexion and dark brown eyes and hair. He might have been Hispanic, American Indian, or Italian. To a white midwesterner, all other nationalities look the same. My wife,

Karen, was Italian, but when she had been in the sun and her skin had darkened, she could pass for a variety of nationalities.

The commo guy and I had trouble communicating. It was obvious from the start of our relationship that we weren't going to form a long-lasting buddy bond. Neither of us seemed to like the other. The commo guy had a negative, antieverything personality. Most of all, he was vehemently disgruntled with Delta Company, the U.S. Army, and the world. Since I somehow seemed to represent all three, he didn't like me either.

He wasn't Mr. Personality either. On the other hand, I had been voted Most Congenial Brother for 1964 in my college fraternity. Under the best of circumstances, we wouldn't have been good friends or even friends. During our night together, we were barely civil.

He explained part of the problem in one of our rare exchanges of conversation. "I'm a field wireman. That's my MOS. I reenlisted for an extra year to get out of the infantry. According to my military job description, I should string commo wires between a command post and bunkers or answer the telephone in a CP (command post), but these SOBs are going to send me to the jungle. I'm going to hump the boonies with you goddamn infantry grunts!"

Naively, I tendered a suggestion. "Can't you complain to someone? The inspector general? Or someone?"

"Hell, yeah! I did. It didn't do any good. The muddafuckers said that if I complained, they would give me a wire to carry, a roll of claymore wire."

"Yeah! I know. Sounds like you have been screwed."

"Well, that's not all either. If I still object, they'll make me carry the captain's radio. The gooks look for the captain and his radioman. They spot the antenna. They know the bastard is surrounded by radios, and the best way to fuck up a unit is to blow away the captain and his RTO. Goddamned army! To think I re-upped for this."

"You've been had."

"Yeah, what about you? What's your MOS?" he sneered revengefully.

"Oh, I'm just an 11Bravo20. I'm infantry," I replied sheepishly.

"You volunteer?"

"No, not really." I laughed. "I was drafted."

"What did you do back in the World before you were drafted?"

"I was a schoolteacher."

Now someone must have whispered a joke in his ear, because he fell into a fit of laughter. When I asked him what was so funny about my having taught junior high school, he became hysterical. After a while, he seemed to calm down, and it was my turn to become disgruntled. My former employment seemed to cheer him up, and finally he crooned, "Ha! Ha! Ha! If you think that I got screwed, what about you? What about you? What's a guy with all your education doing headed for the boonies? A school-teacher, a grunt. Ha! Ha! Ha! Ha!"

By now, I was hot! He had hit a particularly sensitive nerve. In a voice well practiced at reprimanding wayward kids, I ripped him.

"Listen, I didn't ask to be sent here, and I'm tired of hearing that 'all that education' crap. That's all I've heard since I've been in this army. In basic training it was, 'A guy with all your education will never be put in the infantry.' In AIT it was, 'A guy with all your education will never go to Nam.' On the plane coming over here people said that with all my education I would never hump the boonies. 'You'll get a desk job.' Now look at where I am with all my education. In twelve hours, I'll be humpin' with you and all the other dummies. My superior education doesn't mean shit!"

Our relationship was over. It had its high-water mark somewhere back when we both agreed the army had shafted him. Despite my outburst, I could still see he thought my situation a bit humorous so I gave him one last blast. "Well, my education did one thing for me."

"Yeah, what?" he smirked.

"I was smart enough not to reenlist to be a commo man and get blown away walking next to an officer. This army has me for two years. Two years, sucker! That's all! Let them do their damnedest with me or to me. I don't care! I'll be out before you, and you'll still be G.I. Joe. 'Ha ha' that!"

Abruptly, I changed the subject. "I'll take the first watch from eight to ten. You take it from ten to twelve, and we'll rotate every two hours after that. Okay?" I had slipped back to my civilian frame of mind and so did not convert the time to proper army jargon.

"Yeah! Okay," he answered and went into our bunker. I think he was sullen again, and that put our relationship back to where we had started, so there wasn't any ground lost.

About eight-thirty (twenty-thirty hours in armyese), the captain of the guard on duty that night came by. "Hey, bunker thirty-two," he shouted from his jeep.

"Yeah!" I replied, not noticing that he was an officer.

"You got all your equipment?"

Upon recognizing his officer's insignia, I came up with some "sir" stuff. "Yes, sir, but I'm not really clear about our instructions. Is there a password or something?"

"Use the same one as last night," he ordered. Then, in recognition of where he was, "That's right, this is bunker thirty-two. You're the FNG. Didn't your company clerk explain your duties to you?"

I didn't want to get Murphy in trouble, so I hedged, "Well, vaguely, sir."

"Well, if you don't know what to do, ask the guy in the bunker with you."

"He's new too, sir."

"Ha! Ha! Ha! Two FNGs in the same bunker." He seemed to see some humor in the situation that I didn't. "Where's the other guy?"

"He's in the bunker sleeping," I replied.

"No need to wake him. Here, take this field telephone and hook it up to those commo wires by the right side of the bunker. If you have any questions, call the CP. Understand?"

"Yes, sir!"

"Above everything else, don't do anything unless you call the CP first. Don't fire your weapon. Don't blow your claymores. Don't do anything until you check with us. Okay?"

"Yes, sir!" I barked and snapped him a right smart salute.

"Don't fall asleep either; if the gooks don't get you, I will. Now hook up the landline and check in. Have a good night." He returned the salute and drove on.

Fastening the landlines to the terminals on the phone was easy, SOP. But what wasn't standard operating procedure was making the damn phone work. The darn thing just would not produce sound.

"Luckily, I have an expert at my fingertips." I chuckled to myself.

"Hey, uh you, in the bunker, Commo. Sparkie, wake up," I gleefully called into the bunker. Waking the guy wouldn't be the most unpleasant task I had performed in the army. "Hey, we got a landline, but it won't work. Can you fix it?" I queried.

He crawled out of the bunker and glared at me and then at the phone. After examining the phone and the wires and after connecting and reconnecting the wires about a dozen times, he stated that the phone wasn't working. His final diagnosis was, "If this phone isn't broken, then the wires between here and the CP must be cut or broken."

It didn't take a genius to figure that out. In good faith I asked, "Can you fix it?"

"Not tonight. It's too dark," he said in a resigned voice and then as an afterthought, "This is exactly the kind of problem I could work on tomorrow instead of humpin'."

"How will we contact the CP if we're attacked?" I mused aloud.

He had the answer. "I guess I'll have to run over and tell them if that happens. Where do you think the CP is?"

"I don't know. Anyway, we are worrying about nothing. There hasn't been a ground assault on Lai Khe in months. Just rockets," I hoped without much conviction.

He was a bit more pessimistic. "Well, with the way my luck has been running, this will be the night." He went back inside the bunker and started snoring.

When I started my guard duty, I was full of apprehension, but after two hours of staring into blackness with nothing happening, my confidence began to grow. Soon, my watch was over, and it was the wireman's turn to worry us through the next two hours. I woke him, and we exchanged places. I settled down in the bunker for some sleep.

Shortly before midnight it happened. Shots rang out from the watchtower to our right. Commo guy immediately crawled into the bunker to tell me the obvious. I was already wide awake and terrified. We both crawled to the front of the bunker and prepared to fire at the impending enemy ground assault.

Actually, we could see little. It was pitch-black. Occasionally, a shot would ring out and a flare would light up the sky, but no masses of charging bodies appeared. Communication with the CP was nonexistent. We had no knowledge of what was taking place. Commo once again volunteered to try to find the CP and see what course of action we should take, but I threatened him sufficiently, and he elected to stay in the bunker. I wanted him to share the misery with me. He probably would have gone despite my objections, except that I mentioned that he could be mistaken for a Viet Cong due to his size and that it was not very safe walking around under such circumstances. He grudgingly agreed.

"Your rifle loaded?" he asked.

"Sure, is yours?" I replied.

"Yes."

"I didn't zero mine in," I confessed. "Did you?"

"No, they just handed it to me."

"Me, too."

About ten to fifteen more shots rang out from the watchtower. This was the most sustained firing up to that time. Our nerves worked overtime. Maybe our M-16s wouldn't be enough.

"Listen," I offered, "load the machine gun Murphy left us. Just in case."

I was assuming command there just as I had in class-rooms back in the States. It was an unconscious action.

"I don't know how to," he replied.

"What? What are you talking about? Everyone knows how to load an M-60. That's something we all learned in basic, remember?" I growled in disbelief and disgust.

"Well, maybe I was thinking about something else that day. Maybe I was thinking about reenlisting or something. Anyway, I didn't pay attention to a lot of that stuff. I wasn't really good in school. A lot of that stuff was boring. You know how to load it? Load it! And if you fire it, take it over on the right side of the bunker. I don't want those tracer bullets marking my place."

"Well, shit!" I exclaimed as I lifted the breech and in-serted the chain-linked belt of bullets. I cocked the gun, checked the safety, and got ready for business.

Nothing much happened, and wire guy retired to the back of the bunker to sleep. He reasoned that since nothing much was taking place that one of us should sleep and remain fresh. There was no use both of us being bleary-eyed. I agreed somewhat reluctantly.

Once in a while, a flare would light up the area outside the berm or a shot or two would ring out. We didn't seem to be in immediate danger, and I was fairly sure we hadn't received any enemy fire at our position. As best I could tell, all the firing seemed to be from inside the perimeter directed out. I spent the next two hours sitting and aging. Finally, 0200 rolled around, and my turn at guard was over. Thank God!

I rousted Commo. He crawled to the front of the bunker, and I took his place in the rear. I was really bushed. The late hour and the excitement and worry had taken their toll. I did not fall asleep; I passed out.

Commo wasn't on guard more then fifteen minutes when he jostled me awake. He whispered, "I heard some-thing. Come out here quick!"

His voice was so shaken and full of excitement that I lost no time in returning to the front of our position. "What was it?" I said in a hushed tone.

"Shhhhhh, listen!"

After about ten minutes of silence, I asked again. "What did you hear?"

"I'm not sure! Listen!"

We listened again for about twenty minutes. Nothing. Occasionally a shot or two would break the silence and make us jump. But this was only what had been taking place off and on all night. Eventually four o'clock rolled around and Commo announced that he was off duty and crawled back into the bunker to sleep. I took over guard and began to realize that "we" stood his guard, while "I" stood mine. I was exhausted, and during the next two hours, I faced the blackness and stared out through sleepy eyes. Sometimes a shot or two would ring out. Sometimes a flare from the mortars would illuminate the sky. During those brief periods of daylight, I would frantically search the area immediately in front of our position. Nothing ever seemed to be there. I can't say I really knew what to look for or what to do if I saw something.

As dawn approached, the friendly Vietnamese came out. I just sat on the berm and looked out over their world as they started another day. During this time, I sat in grim resignation. I had assumed that during the night I would be killed. If I had been killed, I would never really have understood what was taking place in the war or even in my bunker area. I had spent a lost night in nowhere. With dawn, this grim resignation turned to thoughts of home and family. Karen and our future filled my time and mind. It had been a miserable night, the first of many.

On the brighter side, the night had ended. They usually do. I was alive. I was sleepy, but alive. I could feel my internal body clock start to take over. Commo was alive also. And I bet the Viet Cong were alive. I know Commo and I hadn't done anything to ruin their plans for the day.

At 0600 hours, the captain of the guard sped up in a jeep and skidded to a halt. I gave him the useless field phone, and before I could ask him questions about the shooting from the watchtower, or tell him about the phone being broken, he raced off.

I never did know what all the ruckus had been about. Two stories accompanied breakfast in the mess hall. One story was that sappers, Viet Cong who sneak through the wire and bunker defenses to secretly plant demolition charges under aircraft and in CPs, had been spotted at the trash dump. They had been detected and repulsed.

A second story told of the initiation of two FNGs. This story emphasized how frightened these guys must have been all night.

Both stories were true.

I spent the rest of the morning getting ready to join the main body of our company when they flew in from their present AO (area of operation). We would be trucked through Ben Cat to a new AO. I would join them at 1500 hours, or three P.M., whichever came first. I still hadn't been given an opportunity to zero in my M-16. During the morning hours, I snoozed and wrote a letter home. Now that I had a permanent mailing address, I could start receiving mail from Karen and my folks. I looked forward to return correspondence with great anticipation.

When the jeep came to take Commo and me to the chopper pad, I couldn't believe how heavy my rucksack had become with the few items I had put in it. Later, I would learn that I had packed at least ten pounds of unnecessary material, but at the time, I thought such items as a spare pair of fatigue pants and three pairs of olive-drab underwear were necessities. In addition to my own personal gear, I had about forty pounds of food, water, ammunition, a blanket, a poncho and poncho liner, a claymore and claymore wires, and assorted military hardware.

As I mounted the jeep, I tested my right ankle. It was my ace in the hole. I had dislocated it playing basketball in the alley behind our house in St. Louis when I was seventeen. I had reinjured it during escape and evasion training at Fort Gordon. Most recently, I had slipped on some ice while deplaning at Yokota, Japan, on the way to Nam. The ankle had always been a little sore and weak. My plan was to nurse it along until life in the field got really bad. Then I would demand to have it X-rayed. With a little playacting,

I might be able to parlay this affliction and my twenty-five-words-per-minute typing ability into a rear job in Di An or Lai Khe. I savored the slight pain it provided when I stepped on it.

Someday, I thought, someday it will give out. It might go in a day or a week or a month. I chuckled inwardly. I'll beat this Nam thing yet!

CHAPTER 3

First Mission, and There's Hope

Our jeep raced toward the red dirt chopper pad where I saw the men of Delta Company. The company was divided into three distinct groups of twenty-five to thirty men each. A fourth, smaller group, stood to one side. The three large groups were the line platoons—designated Lima, Mike, and November. The smaller group was the headquarters unit, consisting of the captain, his entourage of radiomen (RTOs), an artillery forward observer (FO) with his RTO, an E-7 top sergeant, a medic, and other assorted personnel.

Upon our arrival, there was a general rush to our jeep. At first I was flattered by the attention, but then I realized that the object of the general clamor was to get the sundry packs. Sundry packs contained candy, cigarettes, soap, and other necessary and valuable items.

After the CP packets, C rations, and mail had been distributed, attention was turned to the other FNG and me. Since there were only two replacements and there were three platoons, one of the platoons was sure to lose. I felt like a slave girl on the auction block. Finally, it was decided that the wireman would go with the captain, and I was left to be chosen by one of the line platoons. After much haggling, Mike platoon won me.

A twenty-year-old, blond-haired, blue-eyed E-5 sergeant came over to claim his prize. He introduced himself as Sergeant Krueger, but added, "Call me Karate. I'm in charge of Mike platoon. We'll get an E-6 someday, but 'til then, I'm in charge.''

Oh, boy, I thought, Kid Karate. This guy must be bad news. It was apparent from the start that Karate relished his position. He obviously enjoyed playing war.

"You'll be a rifleman, walking rear security for a week or two, until you get used to carrying the weight of your pack in this heat. Then you'll get the ammo cans for the M-60 machine gun. They weigh about twenty-five pounds. When we get another FNG in the platoon, then he'll get the cans, and we'll teach you to walk point. After a while, you'll get more and more duties and responsibilities as other FNGs come into the company. In a few months, if you're any good, you'll make E-5 and take my place. I'm getting short. Five more months, and I'll be on a Freedom Bird winging its way back to the World. Go meet the other guys and rest up. We'll be trucked through Ben Cat to our next AO, and then we'll hump a bit. This is a good area. Don't worry. We'll take care of you until you catch on. That's our group over there.'' He pointed to a group of people and then busied himself with sergeant-type chores.

I ambled over to Mike Platoon. They weren't unfriendly, just preoccupied with the division of food, water, and equipment. They introduced themselves to me at breaks in their preparation. I could see that they had put me on the back burner, so I put my pack down, sat down, and leaned back against it. I started a letter to Karen. Usually, writing to her straightened out my mind and cut through the loneliness.

It was Monday, December 15, 1969, and I was about to start my first real combat mission. That mission was what all the training and "army stuff" had been all about. It was about to be for real—no drills, no contrived situations, and no chance to rectify mistakes. That was as real as it got.

That afternoon at 1400 hours, a red cloud appeared and it was heading for the chopper pad. In front of the cloud were the trucks that would take us northeast of Ben Cat. The grunts groaned and muttered as they prepared to get "off and on"—off their butts and on their feet. As we stood up and shouldered our rucksacks, I noticed that everyone seemed to carry a terrific amount of equipment. In addition to personal survival gear needed for living in the jungle, each soldier had pounds and pounds of equipment for killing. Some of the rucksacks must have weighed fifty to sixty pounds. Carrying such weight didn't allow fast movement. Each man shuffled his way over to the waiting trucks. Following their lead, I got off and on, too. I hoisted my rucksack onto my shoulders and staggered under its weight. Taking the deepest breath I have ever taken, I faced the trucks and whispered to myself, "Well, here we go! God, please watch over me!" I exhaled and started toward the trucks.

I guess I wasn't accustomed to walking while carrying such a heavy load on my back, or maybe my mind was preoccupied with thoughts of my first combat mission. Somehow, I didn't see a shallow indentation in the tarmac of the chopper pad. I stepped into it and twisted my weak right ankle, the same one that I had injured in AIT. Pain shot through my ankle and up my leg. I stumbled and fell to my knees. Oh, God, not now! Not now! I prayed silently.

No one paid attention. A few people looked my way, but they said nothing. They probably didn't want to embarrass the FNG. Maybe they were choking back a laugh. In any case, we all looked as if we were a bunch of camels getting up with heavy burdens. No one came to my assistance. No one even cared that I was down. I realized my predicament in a flash. Sure, I had a sore ankle, but who would believe that. Ten steps into my first mission, and I was "supposedly" injured. Everyone would think that I was faking. Everyone would remember forever, and I would be the goon of the unit. I would be disgraced. Even before I regained my footing and tested my foot to assess the damage, I knew the answer. I had known the answer at the first twinge of pain on the way down during my fall.

I had to walk! I had to get up! I just had to walk! As I tested my ankle, it hurt, and hurt badly, but I also knew that I could make it to the truck. Thank you, God! I thought, Thank you!

On the way to the deuce-and-a-half truck, I considered my plight. Nobody was talking; premission jitters, combined with immense quantities of red dust, kept everyone's mouth closed. Once in the truck, I rubbed my ankle through my boot as best I could without letting it be evident that something was amiss. What had I to be ashamed of? The injury was real, not faked. But would others in the platoon see it that way? Or would they assume that this was a phony attempt to avoid my first combat mission? I definitely didn't want them to doubt me. I wanted their respect.

The lemming condition struck again; more than pain and injury, I feared social disgrace and the condemnation of others. I feared condemnation more than death. I noted this as a weakness and vowed not to allow that new discovery regarding my personality to influence me strongly in the future. There would be times when I would have to do what I judged to be best and to hell with the others or what they thought. I would have to learn to control the social animal inside me and learn to survive. As for the more pressing problem of the ankle, I decided to walk or limp as far as I could. Then, when I couldn't walk any farther, I would be the army's problem, not my own.

With my decision made and off my mind, I studied the surroundings as we passed through. On a semipaved road, we entered the town of Ben Cat, proceeding through on its main street. Vietnamese people congested the streets. Traffic and pedestrians competed for the same road space. The only traffic rule was that whoever could outbluff the other party got the right of way. The traffic included not only the trucks in our convoy but Vietnamese Lambrettas, buses, cows, dogs, and kids.

The Vietnamese watched us as we rolled through. I couldn't read their feelings by their facial expressions. Adults masked their emotions, if they had any. Kids greeted the trucks by forming a V-for-victory sign with their fingers and begging for food. The GIs threw the little tykes unwanted and undesirable C-ration cans, usually powdered eggs. Sometimes they threw unwanted CP candy. The GIs were nice in a guarded way. On the other hand, one VC hand grenade thrown into an open truck would have ruined everyone's day.

One minor incident did take place when a GI in the lead truck tossed a purple smoke grenade into one of the Vietnamese shops. It was a mean thing to do, but we all laughed as the locals poured out of the goofy grape cloud, shouting and shaking their fists at us.

We reached the countryside after passing woodcutters and naked little kids bathing in streams beside the road. The trucks stopped, and we off-loaded. Adrenaline was pumping through my system so fast that I could have walked on my ankle if it had been cut off. I barely felt the pain. In routine fashion, the platoon lined up. I was assigned the position of second from the last man in a line of twenty-five or so people. My assignment was to help watch the rear and to observe how the man on rear security guard operated. My eyes must have been as wide as extra-large, AAA-grade eggs as we started across the field. What was routine to each of these men was tremendously unique for me.

I am sure that we weren't dumped off just anywhere and that it wasn't just any field, but I wasn't privy to the strategy or tactics that were being employed. I knew nothing of our grand mission to liberate that section of Vietnam from the Communist aggressors from the North. All I was told was "Follow the guy in front of you and look backward periodically."

At the far side of the grassy field was a creek drainage ditch, measuring twelve feet wide by ten feet deep. Water in the bottom amounted to little or nothing. It was the dry season, though, so maybe during the monsoon season, the ditch would fill.

Our point man stopped the column. He stepped into the ditch and disappeared over the edge. It dawned on me that he was checking the culvert covering the ditch for booby traps. Simultaneously, I was awed and assured by his action. Many times in training, we had been told to do the very same thing, and we had made a halfhearted effort to search. We had been more interested in avoiding the anger of a drill sergeant than in really finding a concealed booby trap. But our point man was actually checking for something that could kill. Again I hammered the point into my head that the patrol was for real; it wasn't a dream, a TV show, or a training exercise after which we would go back to an army cot in some barracks. This was for keeps. This point man cared about himself and those behind him. I was impressed.

Then I was alarmed again. Several hundred meters farther across the field, we entered a lane that cut through a forest. All heads glanced to their left as each member entered the pathway between the trees. We walked single file with intervals of about fifteen to twenty feet. Most of the platoon was well down the lane before I entered it. I then saw what the men were looking at. There, nailed to a fence post and also affixed to the barbed wire, were signs in various languages and colors that read MINE.

Why the hell were we walking here? Why enter a mined area? I thought. I turned wide-eyed again toward Denny, our rear security. He consoled me before I spoke.

"It's okay. We've been here before," Denny said in a subdued tone. It was not much in the way of an explanation, but my lemming tendency encouraged me to continue on down the path. Three thousand meters down the path, we divided the platoon in half. Each group of ten or twelve men plunged into the thick undergrowth of the jungle to set up an ambush on a part of the trail. About 1800 hours in the evening, some of the squad members started to prepare the ground for sleeping. Leaves and debris were scraped away from the places they had chosen as their sleeping area for the night. Without speaking above a whisper, they formed a defense perimeter in the form of a circle among the roots and trees that formed a barrier around us. One group left the ambush site to set up claymores. I was selected to accompany it. My on-the-job training had started.

We hid the claymore mines on both the north and the south side of the trail. We rigged trip wires to cross the trail. The trip wire was attached to a plastic spoon that separated two terminals of a small battery. If the trip wire was moved, the spoon would be pulled from between the contacts, they would close, and an electric charge would travel through the wire to the claymores. The ensuing explosion would devastate anyone in the killing zone of the claymore. Of course, that would mean that one or more of the enemy had walked down the trail and had stepped into our "automatic ambush," the GI term for a booby trap. Locals who were good guys wouldn't normally be wandering around the countryside at night; they were instructed to stay within a prescribed zone by their village.

Since I knew that we would have to pick up the claymores in the morning before the local woodcutters came out, I watched intently as the claymores were placed. Again, I was impressed by the care with which the squad members carried out the deadly task.

Upon return to the ambush site, I ate some C rations and received instructions for my turn at night guard duty. At 0100 hours, I was to sit by the radio and, while watching for the enemy, guard my sleeping companions. I would also listen to the messages being received over the radio. At times during the night, the command-and-control units would call us and, in a whisper, ask for a situation report, a "sitrep." If everything was okay, whoever was on watch would squeeze the talk button on the mike two times. This would break the squelch sound twice and would indicate two things: that we were safe and that there was no activity in our area; the guy on duty was awake and watchful.

I thought I understood the instructions and our call sign, so I went to sleep. Needless to say, after spending the night before on bunker-line guard with the wireman and the real or imagined sappers and after the patrolling and other activities of the day, I was a candidate for some real shut-eye. At 0100 hours, I stood my night guard duty. I hoped I did the sitrep thing correctly. It was all so new to me. If I did mess up, no one embarrassed me by saying anything about it.

Dawn broke, and our squad came to life. The morning was cool compared to the heat of the day past and the heat of the day to come. The sun was up, and everyone in the platoon started the day on a high note. We disassembled the claymores, then sat around the ambush site until noon. We talked in hushed voices and whispers. While on ambush, loud talk and sounds were discouraged. It took some time getting used to this manner of communication, and I was "shhhhhhed" several times. Sooner or later, each man in the unit came over to talk to me to find out where was I from, where had I been for basic training and AIT, did I have a girl, or a wife, what did she look like, what did I do back in the World, and a hundred other assorted questions. Each man, in turn, gave me the same kind of information and added how short he was in Nam, how much longer he had until he was discharged, what the company, platoon, squad was like, or what he personally had done to win the war lately, and how he felt about the army, the captain, the lieutenant, and Karate.

Sergeant Karate and six men had recently made contact, and I heard seven different versions of the adventure. About a month earlier Karate and his squad had been on ambush beside a trail when two NVA walked up on them. They had killed one of the soldiers and wounded the other, but the machine gun had jammed, and the wounded NVA had left in a great hurry, or as we multilinguistic grunts would say, "*didi mau*'d." By this time, I was beginning to respect showboat Karate more than I had when we first met. He did act for the back row at times, but he seemed to know his stuff. I decided that he would be a good model from whom to learn the finer points about the proper conduct of war games. I would overlook his penchant for theatrics.

Nothing happened either the next day or the day after that. We were evidently not in a high-crime area. The lack of action made life dull. We would move, sweating and straining, to a new ambush site every day or so. We would set up the claymores and settle down to wait off the main trail. One person remained alert and on guard while the rest dozed, read, played cards, or used a radio earplug to listen to music from the American military radio station in Saigon. The mission was like an extended camp-out. I read borrowed paperback books and wrote letters to be mailed at a later date. No one complained. The duller the day, the better the GIs liked it. "No one ever died of boredom," one of them explained. I agreed.

After my three-day acclimation period, I was awarded the cans. Each new guy received the dubious privilege of carrying ammunition for the M-60 machine gun. This weight was in addition to my original pack. Each of the two cans weighed about thirteen pounds and was attached to a set of web gear or suspenders. Each can swung freely on each side of me as I walked. At no time did the cans ever swing in the same direction at once, nor did they ever seem to be going in the same direction that I was. Each can had a mind and a will of its own.

Never did they cooperate. If I was walking up a hill, they wanted to stay downhill, and hung back. If I was going downhill, they wanted to race to the bottom whenever I leaned over. On level ground, they hung obediently by my sides. Their weight dug the suspenders of the web gear deep into my shoulders and rubbed the skin off my neck and back. The corners of the cans were pointed and unyielding. Like gremlins, they loved to poke the thigh as a reminder of their whereabouts. I knew that the cans looked forward to the next hill to be scaled, or the next log to be crawled over, or the next stream filled with slippery rocks to be crossed. It was at those times that they were especially wayward.

At first, carrying the cans was bothersome. Then the task became irksome. Then it became unbearable. Finally, it became hilarious. Laugh, cry, or cuss—the cans hung there. I had to carry them. I had to look after their needs. The M-60 cans were mine until that distant and undefined time when I would turn them over to some new guy, and say with almost a straight face as I had been told, "Here are the ammo cans. They're not so bad."

Three days after I started carrying the cans, we crossed a marshy area. Although not officially proclaimed a swamp on the map, water was sometimes knee deep. In an effort to keep the cans dry, I carried them extra high on the web gear. I hadn't even been able to set them down on breaks in our walking.

At one particular stop, I couldn't sit down because of the ankle-deep water. I was so exhausted and overcome by the oppressive heat that I stood with my legs spread apart and placed the butt of my M-16 rifle on the ground in front of me. Water covered the bottom three or four inches of the stock. I leaned forward and placed my forehead on the muzzle of my rifle, using the front of my steel helmet as a cushion between my forehead and the barrel of the gun. The tripod thus formed helped to support the weight of the cans. Of course, that was a really stupid position to stand in; if the M-16 had fired, I would have shot myself in the forehead. But at that point, it was so hot, the march had been so long, and the marsh was so miserable that I simply didn't care anymore. I knew that, if I sat down, I would get soaked with water and that leeches would crawl up the legs of my pants and head for the private parts of my body. And I was also afraid that if I sat down I just wouldn't get up. Using the muzzle of the gun as a support was a minor personal protest. It was a time-out from sanity and gun safety.

When we started to move again, my mind reasoned that I hadn't died doing that dumb stunt, so I would be able to finish the mission. It was crazy reasoning, but it worked. Somehow, I made it to our next objective.

On the morning of December 21, good news arrived with the sun. Our platoon's six-day mission was over. Our unit would be taken out of the field to guard an artillery base for a day or two while another platoon took our place in the boonies. That was to be our 1969 Christmas present from Uncle Sam. The fire support base afforded all the comforts of fifteenth-century living, including open-air shelters, cold showers, and hot meals. In addition to letters from home and time to sleep and relax. All that luxury was provided us. And all we had to do was to guard a few artillery pieces from ground assault by the VC. A cheap vacation at double the price. We broke camp and headed back into the marsh. At noon, the choppers sat down lightly or hovered while we climbed aboard for a picturesque ride to Firebase Dominant.

So far, in my limited exposure to Vietnam, I hadn't been to a fire support base. I was curious to see one. Our helicopter flew over the jungle and closed in on an area to the north of our AO. There I saw a berm containing a circle of bunkers much like those back at Lai Khe. The same type of barbed wire was strung outside the circle. A chopper pad was cleared at one end. One-o-five artillery pieces were arranged inside the center of protective boxes and earthworks. The artillery on the firebase was situated to provide support for infantry units in the field. Along with this function, if a spotter plane or a helicopter observed enemy troops or an enemy storage area, the artillery would shoot at that, too. Sometimes the artillery fired at predesignated targets such as known trails, trail intersections, or old unused enemy bunker complexes. While that type of harassment and interdiction ("H & I") fire was expensive in shells, the cost was cheap in American lives.

Fire support bases were the subject of periodic attacks by the enemy. Sometimes they would try sapper attacks, as had been the case back in Lai Khe the first night that I had guard duty. Sometimes the VC would hide a sniper in a tree outside the perimeter to try to pick off one GI at a time. Sometimes, when they acquired a few extra mortar rounds and a mortar tube, they would chuck them into the fire support base to practice their own form of harassment and interdiction.

Firebase Dominant had not been attacked in a long time, and as in most of the Big Red One's area of operation, the VC and their Commie brothers from the North Vietnamese Army (NVA) were on the defensive. Most grunts like firebase (or, as some units called them, LZ) duty. Far more comfortable than the jungle, it was usually safer. Often there was a piano-crate PX available, where we could buy sodas and, sometimes, beer. Duty was usually light and included night guard and general house-keeping chores such as filling sandbags and burning the shit. This was the U.S. Army, so the tranquillity of this kind of life was often interrupted by the command-and-control sections of the army. In slack periods, C & C lifers looked for someone or something to command and control. The boisterous, often cocky, unshaven grunts who had just returned from a mission were prime meat.

An 11Bravo20 grunt returning from the field is not a pretty sight to see or to smell. He needs a shave and a shower, clean clothes, as well as a beer, hot meal, and mail from home. Somehow the last three items always seemed to conflict with the first three items in priority. The command-and-control section of the United States Army consisted of first sergeants and other lifers who never quite seemed to make it as far as the field for a mission. Instead, they felt that it was their mission to badger the grunt just in from the field into a proper military appearance. Harassing field soldiers seemed to be their major contribution to the war effort. Once a grunt had completed the required amenities, his time was his own. Personally, I spoiled myself rotten. I took off my shoes, opened a Coke, propped up my feet on a bunker, and opened my first mail from home. This was the first mail I had received since I had come to Nam. I read and reread each letter until the light failed and it was time for bunker guard. I was looking forward to the next day when I would write an answer to each and every question asked of me by Karen and my parents. I now felt that mail was an umbilical cord to real life and the World.

"Off and on," Karate called the next morning about 0700 hours. "The Bob Hope show is on its way to Lai Khe, and so are we!"

The news hit like a VC B-40 rocket. In disbelief I squealed, "We're going to see the Bob Hope show? Wow!

I've seen every one of his Christmas specials on TV, and now he has come personally to Nam to entertain me!"

"Not even, Professor!" Killjoy Karate grinned. "He has come to entertain the brass and the REMFs, not us. Lai Khe will be choked with helicopters. They will be double-parked on the chopper pad. Anyone who is anyone will be there. But you aren't anybody, so you, and I, and the rest of this platoon will be keeping the gooks from popping a few mortar rounds in a tube and ruining everyone's good time. We will run sweeps outside Lai Khe to keep Mr. Charles from setting up. If you think the crowd at the show will be big, it will be about one-fifth the size of the people working the perimeter. You'll need damn good vision to see Hope or any of his lovely ladies."

Good old Karate had set me up. Everyone groaned about the REMFs being the ones who least deserved to see the show. Jimmy, our black machine gunner, concluded, "Let the REMFs run security, and let the grunts see the show. We're the only ones doing anything in this damn place anyway!" He was right. Ask any infantry soldier. Don't ask a REMF. They sometimes exaggerate their importance.

About noon, Echo Company staggered in from the chopper pad, just as dirty and tired as we had been the day before. They took our place on the bunker line, and the command-and-control people went into a feeding frenzy. They also had to go through the clean-up, shape-up and get-military routine. Our unit was headed out to the chopper pad and a lift to the jungle slightly west of Lai Khe.

The flight was routine. From the air, Vietnam was always beautiful. The closer we got to Lai Khe, the more signs of civilization appeared. Jungle gave way to rubber trees and fields. One could see the white cone hats of the farmers and their families as they worked the farms and the plantations. The tranquillity of this placid scene was broken by the portside door gunner. In a flurry of motion, he quickly locked and loaded the chopper-mounted M-60 in front of him. He gave my inquiring stare a quick look of panic and started to yell in an animated fashion into the mouthpiece attached to his fighting helmet. At the same time, our chopper, the two ahead of us, and the one behind us made a steep bank to the left and headed down. Something was wrong.

Jimmy was sitting close enough to the door gunner on our side of the chopper to catch snatches of conversation over the sound of the engines. He relayed the bad news to us. "The LZ is hot! Get ready! We're going into a hot LZ!"

All ears turned to Jimmy and the door gunner for any piece of information. Jimmy continued to eavesdrop on the conversation between the door gunner and the pilot. He relayed, "Alpha Company has made contact. They have some gooks on the run!" He paused and leaned closer to the gunner to hear more. In a moment, he turned back to us. "The VC were trying to set up some rockets when Alpha walked up on them. Alpha is in pursuit. We're gonna set down ahead of the gooks. Alpha will try and run them into us. The pilot is looking for an LZ close ahead of them to set us into."

Once again he paused and listened in on what the door gunner was saying. Then he transferred the scraps of information to us. "They are afraid that they will find an LZ either too close or too far away from where the gooks are."

We banked again. From our angle of descent, it was apparent that we were headed toward a small clearing surrounded by thick jungle. I was sitting on the chopper's floor with my feet hanging out of the door. Held in the helicopter by my sixty-pound pack, I liked the thrill of riding like that. Looking down at the countryside a couple of thousand feet below through my boots was far more exciting than pounding ground with ammo cans. As the earth rushed up to meet us, I realized that I and the ammo cans would be the first out the door. Karate leaned forward and yelled into my ear to confirm this. "You're first out! Jump, when we get close to the ground! Jump! Don't wait for the slick to land. Jump when I tap you!"

I nodded in understanding and agreement. I could see our intended landing zone. It was barely big enough for all the choppers to land at the same time on line. A Cobra gun-ship appeared to escort us in and protect us as needed. The Cobra would work out on a tree line with miniguns and its grenade launcher to give us time to unass a chopper and find cover. The sight of the gunship raining death on would-be assassins would be reassuring. Our own ship came in for a landing like a goose landing on water, nose pointed up, skids outstretched in front. Our door gunners prepared to open up with their M-60s on the tree line. The pilot leveled the craft and hovered six to eight feet above the ground. I waited for him to close the gap between the ground and the skids, but he never did.

"Jump!" Karate screamed. "Jump! Damn it!" His tap quickly became a more than generous shove. Out I went, feetfirst and free-falling. My rucksack and the twenty-six pounds of M-60 ammo provided additional weight. Impact with the ground rattled my teeth and stunned me. Every joint in my body was in pain. I looked down. I couldn't see or feel my legs. They weren't in their accustomed spot below my hips. In the same instant I realized that the others would be piling out of the chopper in the same fashion. I grabbed the back of my head and bent over forward, expecting to feel the full force of someone landing on top of me. For the next few seconds, nothing fell from above, so I lifted my head to see why. I half suspected that the others may not have jumped and that I was the only one out. This proved to be wrong. The sideways motion of the aircraft had deposited each person at a slightly different point below the helicopter.

I took an inventory of my body parts. The center of the pain seemed to be located in my legs. Surely, I reasoned, I had broken both legs. This theory seemed to be borne out by the fact that I not only felt pain in my lower extremities but that my legs were AWOL from their anatomically assigned place. My mind flashed "an honorable way home," and I was almost full of glee. I couldn't be blamed for broken legs. Let's see how broken they are, was my next thought. I tried to move my left leg and it answered all its commands. A wave of disappointment surged through me.

Well, at least the right one . . . but in the same instant that leg worked properly, too. I was filled with dismay. It was evident that I hadn't broken either leg. In fact, my ankle even felt okay.

"Mud!" Jimmy yelled as the chopper cleared off. "Help me! I'm stuck in mud!" In amazement, I looked at him and then down at myself. The reason I could feel but not see my legs was that we had landed in very thick, hard-packed mud. Movement in the ooze was virtually impossible. My legs were okay. They were just stuck down there somewhere in the muck. So were everyone else's.

The battle to extract ourselves from the quagmire was time consuming and exhausting. Karate, one of the first to free himself from the mess, came back to help pull me and my equipment out. Then we both went after Jimmy and the machine gun. It took at least forty-five minutes to get out of the bog and reassemble. Thank God our LZ had not been hot. We would have all been killed and planted at the same time.

Eventually, we got down to the work of setting up ambushes. The VC either had not come our way, or had come our way and seen our problem with the mud and were laughing at us back in their village. They may have mistaken us for the Hope comedy troupe.

Alpha Company did receive a special honor for its efforts. The next day, command and control airlifted Alpha Company into Lai Khe, and the men were given front-row seats to the Hope show. During his performance, Bob quipped, "Here we are in beautiful Lai Khe. We are so close to the action that we had to save the back-row seats for the VC!" The REMFs and the brass howled with laughter. Bob introduced November Platoon, Alpha Company, 2d of the 16th Infantry, 1st Infantry Division, and they waved to the TV cameras.

As for our company, Delta, we set off on a hike through the jungle for the next two days. Nothing of great importance happened, so the command-and-control guys extracted us and sent us to another area to sit out the Christmas truce. On December 25, we were in squad-size (groups of six to eight people) ambushes. The Christmas truce had been called, but that did not really mean anything. Maybe it meant something back in the World or at the peace negotiation table, but in the field, we set out our automatic ambushes, and so did the VC. Neither side wanted to be caught with its pants down during the truce. There was no glory in being a Christmas casualty.

Christmas Eve was the pits. Hiding in a thicket of dense bamboo on ambush and surrounded by claymores, I just knew that Santa wouldn't find me. And he didn't, either. I am not sure he even tried. I ate a can of C-ration pork and beans as my Christmas meal, then poured out my troubles in a depressing letter to Karen.

The letter was a gem. I bemoaned the fact that I hadn't thought to buy her a Christmas present to leave for a relative to put under her Christmas tree. I admonished the Vietnamese for being at home with their families while I was away from mine hiding in their damn jungle and fighting their damn war. Our first wedding anniversary was December 28. I pointed out that I wouldn't be there for that either and that she had been wrong to marry me. I hinted that I might be killed or crippled. If I were terribly injured, I told her, I would divorce her so she wouldn't have to live her life with half a man. I ran on about how I had ruined her life and that she would have been better off if she had never met me. I told her that I was resolved to be faithful to her, and I hoped that she could remain faithful to me. If she couldn't, I would understand. I carped that a private first class, pay grade E-3, didn't make a lot of money and that I couldn't buy the fine clothes and household items to which she was accustomed. I told her to buy the forty-dollar lamp we had argued over a few months earlier. At that time, I had thought that forty dollars for a lamp was extravagant. Now, it could serve as a memorial for me if I didn't return. I pleaded with her not to drive too fast, not to eat too much, and not to forget to brush her teeth. In conclusion, after pouring out four pages of depression, gloom and doom, I ended it with the closing:

It's starting to rain now . . .
I love you.
Merry Christmas—
Ches

The letter was a real tearjerker. From my C rations, I took three cans. One was peanut butter, and one was grape jelly. I mixed them to form a purple paste that I put on my canned C-ration pound cake. I ate the treat as my Christmas dessert. Morose, I then rolled up in my poncho and poncho liner and went to sleep. In the morning, I felt considerably better. I had poured out my sorrows on a sympathetic but distant ear, and I was ready to get on with another day in Nam. Maybe I shouldn't have, but I still sent the letter to Karen. Needless to say, when she received it some weeks later, it didn't brighten her day.

Of course, by then, I was feeling fine.

CHAPTER 4

Cache

After the Bob Hope show, it took the army a few days to sort itself out again. I guess the lifers had to sleep off hangovers. The command-and-control units had to relocate each of the infantry units, and then dream up somewhere for them to go. We stayed on Palace Guard outside of the Lai Khe area until December 29.

Eventually, it was off and on again. We were off the ground and on the choppers. This time, we headed for VC territory northwest of Lai Khe.

I never knew exactly what part of the Central Highlands the army intended us to search and destroy. I didn't really care that much. Searching and destroying one part of Nam was as good as searching and destroying another part. One piece of jungle was like all the others. All the open fields were the same, and all the streams seemed to be alike. I just got on the helicopters and rode until they dumped me off. Then I followed the guy in front of me through the bush. I had no idea of the grand plan to win the war.

We measured where we were by the amount of danger we anticipated. Guarding Lai Khe during the Bob Hope show was a nice stint, because we reasoned that the gooks would be few and far between. That area had been worked so much and the military base and village were so close that there would be few if any gooks. Alpha Company had just chased a few VC trying to make a name for themselves in showbiz.

We now ventured deeper into the jungle. The farther

away from civilization we got, the more threatened we felt. The basic pattern of each mission remained the same. Mike Platoon would air assault into an open area, move into the jungle, break down into smaller groups, and set up ambushes. Once in the ambush site, we would set out trip-wire claymore mines and then post one or two guards. The grunts not on guard read, slept, played cards, or wrote letters home. I was a lucky charm for the platoon. Since I had joined them, we had experienced no contact with the enemy. We had walked through enemy bunker complexes, but they were most often old and always abandoned. Many had been used to fight the French in the fifties.

But during the first week of January, one of our squads located an old VC base camp that showed signs of recent use. This was enough to inspire the entire platoon to hump over to the position for a look. Karate thought that VC might have used the camp the night before we arrived. Remembering the hazing I endured during my first night of guard duty in Lai Khe, I took that information with a grain of salt. On the other hand, even though I am from Missouri, you didn't have to "show me" too much in Nam to make a believer out of me.

First Squad entered the camp, and our squad set up a perimeter defense around the outside of the camp. VC and NVA had been present, so the 1st Squad started to search the bunkers and spider holes inside our perimeter. Karate placed our machine gun on an obvious trail leading into the complex from the north. He instructed me to watch the trail just in case the VC came back home.

About two months before I had joined the company, the platoon had found the same type of area, and during the ensuing search, a grunt named Red had been wounded slightly by a booby trap as had several other GIs. All had received Purple Hearts, and two of the GIs had earned a trip home. No one had been killed, but one of the South Vietnamese scouts that was with them at the time had his legs badly mangled. Red was still recovering from his wounds but rejoined us later. The veteran grunts were understandably nervous.

There was an edge in Karate's voice as he made eye contact with me and gave me my instructions. "You watch down this trail. Don't take your eyes off of it! If you see a gook, shoot. This is a free-fire zone. Anyone out here is either VC or NVA. We'll search the bunkers. You stay put. You stay here and watch the trail." He started to walk away, but returned with additional words of caution. "This place could be booby-trapped. Don't touch anything. Don't wander around. Repeat—don't touch anything! Stay here and watch the trail. Got it?" I nodded, and he carefully walked off toward the center of the VC base camp.

Karate's orders served a dual purpose. He was attempting to protect me from injuring myself, and to keep me from blundering into something and injuring someone else. I was mildly disappointed about being excluded from the main search team. But what the hell, I could get blown away, too, so I decided that he was right to stick the rookie in a safe, out-of-the-way spot. My teacher education courses hadn't included VC Bunker Searching 102. I still had ten months left in Nam, and I could learn the fine art of probing bunkers for enemy stuff sometime in the future.

Even though I'd been accepted by the platoon in some ways, I was still an unknown entity in other ways. How I would react to the extreme pressure of contact and danger was yet to be determined by those around me. I confess that I wondered about that myself. I wrestled with self-doubt as I sat facing the trail, so I pretended that I saw gooks and game-planned how I would handle them. I was alone, and I took that guard duty very seriously. There are only a thousand ways to imagine that a VC soldier is coming down the trail, and I had mentally exhausted all possibilities.

Meanwhile, in the base camp, no one could find anything of any value. The camp, despite some signs of recent activity, was a dry hole. Every once in a while, someone wandered by my position to give me an update. The bunkers were clean. After the one thousand ways of imagining a gook walking down a trail passed from my mind, I turned to 947 ways to imagine making love with Karen.

After a while, I had exhausted even those. Boredom replaced daydreaming, and I began to look a little less down the trail and a little more around my immediate area. After spending some time watching red ants crawling up and down the tree that semiobscured me from the trail, I began to notice something very unusual about the base of the tree. A piece of rubber poncho about two inches square was exposed to the left of the trunk and the right bipod leg of the M-60 was sitting on it. The piece of poncho didn't fit into the surroundings. Curiosity started to gnaw at me. Why would there be a scrap of poncho this far outside the perimeter of the base camp? Was the poncho U.S. or North Vietnamese?

I was alone, so no one could ridicule me if the poncho was nothing, so I started to investigate it more closely. I lifted the machine gun and moved it to a more exposed position to my left and looked intently at the poncho. It seemed to be just a piece of dirty old rubber covered by jungle debris. I began to pick leaves and twigs and soil off it. As a kid, I had seen Vic Morrow do the same thing on the TV show *Combat* when he unearthed German mines. Slowly, the small patch of poncho began to take on the dimensions of a square about two feet wide on each side. When the entire poncho was free of jungle debris, I decided that it was time to take a look under it. I slowly peeled back the plastic. It covered a board that, in turn, covered a hole in the ground. I cannot describe the terror in my mind as I lifted the board off the hole. No one gets used to real terror no matter who he is or how accustomed he may say he is to it. Each new terror is simply that—a new terror.

A peek into the hole sent chills through my body. There it was—the whole candy store. The poncho covered a hole full of enemy munitions the likes of which I had never seen. Here was a hole about two feet square and four or five feet deep just chock-full of enemy hand grenades, mortar rounds, bullets, claymore mines, and several large rocket-propelled grenades called RPGs or B-40s. Of course, I gasped in wonder. My mind refused to accept what my eyes were seeing. I really didn't know what I'd expected to find under the poncho, but the reality of what I was actually viewing boggled my mind. I had been sitting on a cache of enemy ammunition!

Joy replaced my astonishment. I had found some *real stuff*! My self-esteem soared. I would now be somebody in the eyes of the guys in the platoon. That I had done all this without assistance or experience caused my ego to continue to inflate. But wait! Who had been the dumb son of a bitch who had set me up literally on top of that stuff? That damn fool Karate had been the one. Why, I had assumed that he was an expert at spotting caches. Hell, *I* was better! He had been in such a hurry to dump me off and start searching the main part of the bunker complex that he had overlooked it.

Now what should I do with this matériel? crossed my mind. In my loudest whisper I called to the first person who ambled my way. It was Jimmy, who was normally in charge of the machine gun.

"Hey, Jimmy, come here!" I demanded.

He wandered over, but froze. His eyes enlarged to the size of saucers as he spied the hole and its contents. "Look at that!" I boldly commanded.

"Not fucking even . . ." he started in disbelief, but I interrupted him.

"It was right here under the leg of the gun!" I explained. "I uncovered it. Watch the gun. I'm taking this stuff to the lieutenant. With that I reached down into the hole, never considering that the munitions might be booby-trapped, and extracted a mortar round and a rocket-propelled grenade.

Jimmy was a sergeant, E-5, and the leader of the gun team. Normally he ordered me around, but his surprise coupled with my assertive bearing justified our temporary change in status. I strapped on my rifle, and taking the miniature bombs, I headed for the center of the complex to find the lieutenant.

I found him sitting against a tree with his back to me. He

was inventorying a small pile of claymore wire, canteens, enemy clothing, and yarn. It was definitely a meager haul.

"Lieutenant James," I called in too loud a whisper. "Look at what I found!" and as he whirled to face me, I continued, "And there's a whole hell of a lot more!"

Shock, surprise, and relief took turns registering on his face. Now he could make a real report! The lieutenant congratulated me. He then called Karate and showed him. Karate was 40 percent jealous and 60 percent sincere in his praise. He was getting hard not to like. Together, we walked back to my cache. The ell-tee and Karate took time to explain exactly what I had found and how each kind of ordnance functioned. I could sense that a bond of mutual respect was growing among the three of us.

Just that suddenly, I was unanimously accepted as a working member of the platoon. A veil had been lifted away from me, and I was found not to be a nerd. Strangely and without fanfare, I had passed the first part of some tribal ritual and become one of the warriors. Jimmy took over duties on the machine gun, and the ell-tee and Karate cataloged the munitions in the hole as I took them out. The cache contained five RPG rounds, seven mortar rounds, a dozen or so VC potato-masher hand grenades with the firing device in the handle, and an assortment of SKS and AK-47 small-arms ammunition. We were very proud of our modest find.

I could now wander the VC bunker complex. Not that anyone officially granted me specific authority or anything. It was just that I decided that with Jimmy on the gun I would rather search than guard. Social forces were at work, and no one had the gumption to stop me. I had already put the more experienced men to shame, and if anyone had chided me, it would have looked as if he were jealous of me and my success. Besides, the central core of the complex had already been searched and nothing had been found of any great value.

I couldn't get into any trouble, they reasoned, so everyone's attention shifted to searching the area around the machine gun and farther down the trail. With no one to restrict my movement, I took my M-16 and headed for the far side of the complex.

I decided that I would search the area directly opposite where I'd found the cache. Maybe the VC had a cache of munitions set at opposite ends of the camp. I poked my head into several bunkers around the perimeter and found nothing. Then I started going down into the bunkers to see how they were constructed. I was amazed at how well the VC had been able to build the fighting positions using just bamboo, logs, and soil. I marveled at some of the crude furniture and other attempts they had made to make them habitable. Each bunker was below ground, so it was cooler than outside, and once my eyes became accustomed to the lack of light, it was almost pleasant down there. In one particularly large bunker that may have served as a command post, I looked out one of the gun ports, slots six to eight inches wide and two feet long. The VC would fire through them at advancing GIs. From the outside, it would have been nearly impossible to hit any VC firing through that gun port. I was very glad that the VC had *didi mau*'d.

Standing in the coolness of the bunker, I envisioned the destruction that we would have endured had the VC chosen to fight. Somewhere in the middle of my daydreaming, I noticed several wires coming in through the gun port. The wires looked exactly like the kind that we used to blow claymore mines. "Now how would gooks get a hold of U.S. claymore wires?" I said to myself aloud. I was still too new to realize how much United States equipment the VC used against us. I continued to ponder the question until the next one entered my mind. It was too complex a problem to keep in my head, so I verbally questioned, "If this is the ignition end of a command-detonated mine, what is at the other end?" And in the same breath, "Hell—I'll bet I know. Let's go find out!"

In a moment of inspiration, I crawled out of the bunker and crossed over the top of it to the gun port. I selected one of the wires and began to coil the wire as I followed it through the jungle. I had no fear of anything blowing up because I held the business end of the wire. In addition, a firing device would have to be attached and then squeezed to produce an electric spark to fire anything that was on the other end. I was safe from harm as far as this wire was concerned.

Forty feet from the bunker, the wire led to an earthen mound about as high as a kitchen table. The wire disappeared into the dirt about halfway up the outside of the mound. I stood there for a moment and studied the situation. Although trained as a history teacher, I had absorbed enough biology to know that wires don't naturally grow from an old anthill in the jungle. Something was under the dirt. Again using the utmost caution, I began excavating the mound. Sure enough, there, about six inches under the earth, was a claymore mine and an RPG round set to fire.

I didn't totally dig out the find. Instead I went back to the ell-tee and Karate to make another report. I loved the look of amazement in their eyes when I told them that I had found some more stuff. In a rush they bolted to the far end of the complex. Immediately, Karate and several other veterans started to complete unearthing the mine. I cringed as I watched them hack away with entrenching tools. I had been very cautious, and their actions looked dangerous. They were so caught up in their exuberance that they didn't notice me slip away again.

I went directly back to the bunker that contained the wires. I now believed that I knew the VC's system of defense. I was certain that each of the other five wires would lead to a similar earthen mound and similar hidden explosives. I was correct. Each time I followed a wire, I found something, then I would have Karate and his gang of miners unearth it.

The last wire did produce a new wrinkle. The last mine had a U.S. hand grenade under it. If someone had just picked up the claymore, the spoon on the grenade would have gone off and a terrible explosion would have taken place. Karate caught on to that one and felt under the claymore before picking it up, and then felt the grenade. Carefully he dug around it and took the grenade out first. He put a pin from a smoke grenade in it and the booby trap was neutralized. Karate was smart, and brave, too. I had to admire him for that.

As for me, I was feeling pretty good about my finds. I hadn't told anyone about the command bunkers and its wires. With each new find, people were starting to acknowledge that I was doing something beneficial. It felt good to be considered a functional part of the platoon. But all my claymore wires had been used up, and I now had to develop a new lead if I wanted to find anything else. It was getting late, and I was tired from the excitement and repeated adrenaline rushes. I had done my part. I realized that I had been uncommonly lucky.

I started to meander back to Jimmy and the machine gun. Why push my luck? In an effort to get a feel for the dimensions of the bunker complex, I walked around the outside of the perimeter from bunker to bunker. Since I wasn't using the interior trails, I had to break jungle. Walking through the thick vegetation was difficult and, at times, made for clumsy movement. Thorns pulled my clothes. Wait-a-minute vines and exposed roots grasped at my ankles and feet. Some areas were more open than others. Thick areas demanded more effort and determination.

In one particularly dense section of jungle, an overly aggressive vine snared my foot and sent me sprawling flat on my chest. I lifted myself off the ground to a kneeling position and mumbled an oath. In the middle of "You son of a," I quit. Out of the corner of my eye, I saw an exposed RPG in the crook of a tree five feet to my right. All the other RPGs and mines I had found had been hidden in some way or the other. But that one was exposed. "Booby trap!" The electric shock of fear zipped through my body.

I knew that somewhere in my immediate vicinity was the wire that would trigger it. Where? Where was it? My mind was alert to the danger, but I simply couldn't figure out what to do. I was full of panic. I didn't move and couldn't move. The thought crossed my mind that I really didn't have to move. I could wait out the war in this spot. I wouldn't need to eat or perform bodily functions. After the truce, the U.S. Army could come back with a bomb disposal team and get me. I would be waiting here for them. There seemed to be no reason to twitch a muscle. If the mosquitoes and red ants came, I would volunteer for supper. I had been fearless with the command-detonated mines. I understood how they worked. I had held the business end in my own hands. They couldn't have gone off. But this was different. Anything could set off this RPG round. I needed help.

"Jimmy!" I called in a low whisper. Jimmy and the machine gun should be somewhere ahead of me. I got no answer. "Hey, Jimmy!" I called again in a voice not quite a yell. Still no answer. I was now prepared to break all the rules I had learned about talking quietly while on operations and scream for assistance when I heard a reply from someone directly behind me.

"Professor, is that you?" It was Larry, the company's designated sniper. Still on my hands and knees, I looked back over my shoulder. Larry, in the meantime, walked toward me, using the same path that I'd broken through the thick undergrowth. Soon he was standing right beside me. While looking down at me, he asked. "Something the matter?"

"There's an RPG over there," I said and pointed to the base of the tree off to my right.

Larry turned his head to follow my finger to its target. "I'll get it!" he said with exuberance, and walked over to it.

"Wait!" I pleaded. "You might trip something, and we'll both go up in . . ."

But my warning went unheeded. Larry was already bending over the RPG. My heart was in my throat the entire time.

"Sure enough." He bent over to examine it more closely. "Wow! Look here!"

I found my feet, and despite their being a bit wobbly, I made my way over to the tree. I watched as he examined the RPG. Under it was an American hand grenade. The pin was still in the grenade. Attached to the pin was a dried old vine that led to the path through the bush that I had made.

The far end of the vine was attached to a tree about ten feet away. Suddenly, the realization of what had just happened crashed down upon me. I had stumbled over the vine. Instead of the vine pulling the pin of the hand grenade and creating a deadly explosion, the vine had broken. The break in the vine was about ten inches from where it was attached to the grenade pin. If the vine hadn't been old and dried, I would have been a goner.

Larry didn't comprehend what had taken place and how close I had come to the ultimate big bang. "Tricky little devils, no?" he commented and picked up the grenade and the RPG. "Say, Professor, how do you find this stuff? When I came up you looked like you were smelling the ground for it," he said with a laugh. In a more serious tone he questioned, "Want me to take this stuff to the ell-tee?" His question was more of a plea.

"Yeah, go ahead. I'm finished for today. I've used up all my luck," I said, and with that, I tiptoed to the nearest well-used path and gingerly made my way back to the M-60 position.

We spent another two hours in that base camp. First Squad piled all the munitions we had discovered in a bunker and put C-4 around them. Karate inserted a blasting cap into the C-4 and ran a claymore wire back a good distance from the bunker. He attached a clacker to his end of the wire. Yelling "Fire in the hole!" he blew the whole mess. The enemy would never use that matériel against us or anyone else.

Karate must have been a little too close to the bunker when it blew. He rejoined us looking a little disheveled and acted a bit punch-drunk. The explosion had scrambled his brains. We waited until he had his wits about him, and then looked for a thick piece of the jungle in which to hide. We'd messed with the enemy and were afraid that they might trail us and seek revenge. We posted double guards that night, and no one complained.

CHAPTER 5

Blooded

My apprenticeship was over. Although I hadn't been mistreated or shunned, the veteran grunts in the platoon had been reserved and patronizing in the way they had treated me. I'd been watched over, protected, and pampered. I felt as if I were being constantly observed like a person on trial. After I found the VC cache, their attitudes toward me had changed. I was now a working member of the unit. The jury had found me "not guilty" of being a doofus.

Being one of the gang gave me a nice warm feeling. Just as when I had become a member of the Key Club in high school and later, in college, a brother in Sigma Chi, I was now an initiated and accepted member of Mike Platoon. My fellow 11Bravo20s had decided that I had my shit together.

The night after I'd found the cache, Mike Platoon hid in thick jungle. We didn't want any multicultural interaction with the VC. We lounged under the trees and, in hushed tones, talked about our adventures during the day. Each person told and retold something that he had seen or done or felt or thought. I, or course, went over my role several times to various audiences. I now had earned a war story to tell. Eventually, we tired of talking about that day's action, and old war stories of other encounters with the VC and NVA resurfaced. Once again, we heard how Sergeant Karate and the grunts of 1st Squad had killed a North Vietnamese soldier and would have gotten another one if the machine gun hadn't jammed. But to me, their stories were now antiquated and tiring.

Later that night, wrapped head to toe in a poncho liner, I listened to B-52 mosquitoes buzz as they sought exposed portions of my skin for their dinner. I pondered the day's events. In the secrecy of my mind, I marveled at myself. I had done something fairly important when I found the cache and the hidden munitions.

In real life, back in the World, I'd never made a winning touchdown or a game-winning base hit. In Nam, one of my greatest fears had been that I would get injured or killed before I ever did anything even semi-important. In the back of my mind, I reserved the thought that I might endure a whole year and have nothing to show for my efforts. People back home would ask, "And what did you do in Nam?"

My reply would be a sad and forlorn, "Nothing."

Now, at least, I would have one war story to tell my kids and grandchildren. Perhaps I had been somewhat brave. Perhaps I had made a little contribution to the war effort. Maybe my actions had helped defeat the enemy in some small way and had helped to make the world safer for democracy. The VC would never be able to use the matériel I found against us or any other GI or South Vietnamese unit.

On the other hand, maybe I had been a little too eager. Maybe I had done the macho thing a little too much. I had pushed my luck a little too far. I thought of the RPG and how close I had come to blowing myself up. It was chilling and thrilling. I made a mental note that in the future, no matter how much I thought I knew, someone else—in this case, one of our little yellow brothers—could be just as smart, or even smarter. "Do what you have to do and no more," I coached myself. "Make this near miss a lesson for next time." The teacher in me taught, and the student in me listened.

Still, I understood that I hadn't faced the real test yet. The real test would be when I experienced my first firefight. How would I react when someone was shooting at me? Would I run? Panic? Freeze? Could I shoot another human being? Humans are not the rabbits and squirrels I hunted in my native Missouri woods. Could I join the ranks of John Wayne, or Vic Morrow, or Audie Murphy? A big question mark still remained in my mind.

Luck had been with me, so far. But the reality of my situation kept coming back to me. Sooner or later, somewhere, somehow, the first firefight would come. Would I be able to conduct myself appropriately? Would my next trial end in honor, or disgrace?

I don't believe that I was unique in these thoughts. Every man, young and old, carries fantasies inside his head. Fantasies of situations when he is brave, when he defeats some foe or enemy. Sometimes, there is a woman involved. Sometimes not. If a female is included, she rewards her defender and champion for his efforts on her behalf with sexual pleasure. Such dreaming often leads to male fantasies of another sort. These thoughts and their outcome are said to cause blindness, insanity, and red hair on the palm of one's hand.

The devil's side of these dreams is when the hero doesn't overcome his opponent. Then it is incumbent upon him to die bravely and quietly. I hadn't ever seen anyone die in real life, so my best comparison would be a movie death. I realized that movie deaths were very shallow. But should I catch an AK-47 round in the gut, I wanted to have some great words of wisdom to impart to the grunts around me.

All the original dying words seemed to have been used up, and anything I thought up seemed to be trite. Besides, I couldn't be sure that any of the guys in our platoon would have a pencil and paper ready to record them. Even if they did, would they know how to get my dying words to the attention of the world press? Most of my new buddies were semiliterate. They considered *Playboy* and the *National Enquirer* great literature, so I assumed that if I was killed in a firefight, immortality would escape me. No, the best I could do was pray that if and when the time came I would at least slip into death stoically without screaming.

Such were the hidden thoughts that crawled around the recesses of my mind. Maybe they were extraordinary, but

I doubt it. I think that people in and out of the army in everyday life harbor similar thoughts. Wartime and its imminent danger allow only repressed ideas and fantasies to surface.

Two evenings later, we were airlifted to a new AO farther west of Ben Cat. The lift was late in arriving. By the time we flew to the new landing zone, it was getting dark. We humped off the LZ as fast as possible and headed into the deep jungle. Mike Platoon was the lead element. November Platoon, the captain, and his CP were about five hundred meters behind us to the east. Our mission was to assist Echo Company in trying to break into a VC base camp similar to the one in which I'd found the cache. Unlike our earlier experience, this VC bunker complex held hard-core VC and NVA soldiers who didn't wish to budge. Echo Company was located somewhere west of our location. With our late start, it would be impossible for us to hook up with them before dark.

Mike Platoon would try to get close to Echo Company. Then, instead of stumbling around in confusion—and danger—in the dark, we would set up a hasty ambush on any available trail and wait until morning to join forces. Echo Company had been in contact most of the day and had suffered several wounded and one killed. The KIA had been killed as an indirect result of friendly fire. The shock waves from artillery shells had caused a termite-weakened tree limb to fall, landing on him and crushing him to death.

None of us were really anxious to hook up with Echo Company. The thought of forming an assault line to charge the bunker complex was ominous. Nevertheless, Mike Platoon made a semivaliant effort to reach Echo Company. When we failed, we set up an ambush on an unused VC trail. We stayed in platoon size and formed a circle with each man an arm's length from the next. Had the circle been the face of a clock, the claymores were set along the trail at five and eight. The two machine guns were placed at three and nine. Not having been in a firefight, I was still considered a partial FNG, and I was positioned away from the kill zone at the other side of the ambush circle. I was told to face forward, or directly away from the trail.

In the dark, we ate cold C rations. We had the whole night to worry about what we would have to do the next day. During the whispered evening conversations, the more experienced grunts in the platoon decided that our chances of getting into contact were slim. It was their contention that the VC would slip away during the night.

Jimmy and I had first guard. We sat very close, and talked in hushed tones. We grumbled about the hasty setup, the cold Cs, the uselessness of the army, and the stupidity of the war. In short, we had a general, everyday Vietnam conversation. I took Jimmy's word that the VC would have *didi mau*'d the area by morning. We were relieved by Chris and Rod.

Later that night Jimmy moved his poncho farther away from mine. Ants or termites were tormenting him while he tried to sleep. Mulling over the next day's mission, I anticipated a restless night, but within moments of reclining, I performed an excellent imitation of a rock.

Kabooom! The first explosion ripped me awake. *Kabooom!* The second spun me around, and I faced the inner part of the circle. The gook trail was on the far side of our perimeter. *Kabooom!* The third explosion blinded me and took away my senses. Machine-gun and small-arms fire raged. I was living a facsimile of hell. I'd never heard such a torrent of gunfire in my life.

"My God!" I screamed. "We're being attacked!" Although disoriented, I soon discovered that most of the firing was coming from the section of the circle near the trail. In the early-morning haze, guns roared and muzzles flashed. I couldn't focus my eyes quickly enough either to see or comprehend what was taking place. I spun and grabbed my glasses from their storage area inside one of my boots. I jammed them onto my face and again tried to distinguish what was taking place along the trail. It certainly was an attack of some sort. My next impulse was to grab my M-16, which was lying next to me on my right side, between a grunt named Jersey and me.

Jersey had also been jarred awake. He, too, felt the immediate need of a rifle. A brief but vicious tug-of-war took place for the possession of my weapon.

"This is mine! Damn it! Mine!" I yelled over the din of the firing. "Yours is on your other side!" These directions triggered some recognition in Jersey's mind. He looked at me and then at his own M-16 with an expression of realization. Then he pivoted on his butt and grabbed his rifle.

I plunged my feet into my boots. I had broken a cardinal rule when I had taken off my boots to sleep. Now I had my boots on, untied, but on. Jersey was a more experienced grunt, and he rolled back next to me.

"You're facing the wrong way, Professor! Face out! Watch for gooks coming at us from our side of the perimeter. Forget about that stuff back there. They'll handle it. We have to watch our kill zone, not theirs. Get ready!" With that, Jersey spun around to face the jungle directly in front of us.

I followed suit. All was quiet in our direction. There was definitely no VC on our side of the circle. Not a bang came from in front of us. The turmoil was behind us. Bullets coming from the enemy behind us whizzed and popped over our heads. Because Jersey and I were on a slope higher up the hill, it seemed that at any instant bullets would rip into us. I just *knew* that I would be shot in the back. I imagined a direct hit on my asshole. My buttocks tightened to repel the invading projectile when it came. A bullet in the butt would be comical to many people back in the World, but not to me.

I felt as if my spine had a big, red target painted on it. I would be shot in the spine, I was sure. I would never walk again. How could I explain a bullet in my back to my friends and neighbors back home? Sure, they would be understanding as they pushed me around in a wheelchair, but what would they say behind my back? "Coward"? As I waited for the inevitable bullet, I pleaded with Jersey for enlightenment. "What's happening? Are we being attacked?"

"No, we are blowing a 'bush on the gooks! We are at-
tacking them!" he screamed over the noise. "The VC must
have tried to sneak out of their base camp before it got too
light. They must have thought that this old trial was okay
to use. Why didn't you wake me up?"

World War II raged on behind us. The guys behind me
were throwing a wall of lead at the enemy. "Good Lord! At
least allow me to see it." I peeked back over my shoulder
every few seconds. "Jimmy didn't wake me up either. I
guess it all happened too fast. I . . ."

"Did you see something move out in front of us? Fire!
Fire so they don't try and get around us!" With that, Jersey
opened up with his M-16 and sprayed the jungle in front of
us. With my M-16 already off safe, I followed suit. I fired
one shot at a time from my gun, blasting the jungle before
me. I did not spray back and forth as much as Jersey did.
Six times bark flew from a tree five feet in front of me. I
was killing the hell out of a hardwood and causing no pain
to the gooks. I adjusted my fire. Thirteen trigger pulls later
the magazine ran out. The standard M-16 magazine held
twenty rounds, but I had been told to load only nineteen,
to prevent putting too much pressure on the spring that
feeds the bullets up into the weapon, which would cause it
to weaken. Just then, nineteen bullets didn't seem to be
nearly enough. I reloaded.

During the five seconds it took me to change magazines,
I felt naked and exposed. But I was afraid our firing into the
jungle had started something. Surely now that I was in the
process of changing magazines, any VC who had been
creeping up on us would charge, AK-47s blazing on full
automatic. None did. Our part of the circle remained quiet.
There wasn't any incoming fire in our sector.

Jimmy on the machine gun yelled, "Professor! Fire this
way! Cover me! Cover me!" Jimmy had been firing M-60
ammo as fast as he could, and several hundred rounds had
gone out in the last few moments. Jimmy hadn't been
firing in six-to-eight-round bursts as we had been taught in
training. Instead he had been sweeping the area in front of
his position with the gun on full automatic. The army

called this establishing suppressive firepower. Of course, once he was low on ammunition, Jimmy and the machine gun would be the target of any VC who had noticed from what position the red tracers had been originating.

I turned to my right and emptied a magazine into the jungle in the general direction Jimmy indicated. Once again, I reloaded and continued to fire another magazine in the same direction.

As I was popping in my fifth magazine, a great silence enveloped us. We didn't fire. The VC did not fire. No one fired, and everyone listened intently for any sound, and watched for any movement.

From the first explosion to the last shot, maybe ten minutes had elapsed. Probably, it was even less. There is a distinct difference between minutes in combat time, and minutes in real time. At first, while lying there waiting to be shot in the back, it seemed as if eons had elapsed. But while firing the magazines, it had seemed like only seconds had passed. Now everything in the jungle was silent. No animal dared to move or peep or chatter or squeak. The enemy was either dead silent or dead gone or just plain dead. Everyone in the platoon listened and looked. Then listened and looked again. After a full five minutes, Jimmy rose to his knees and peered out into the solitude. Slowly Karate, the ell-tee, and others joined him in a kneeling position. The jungle was hazy from early-morning fog and gunfire. No one could discern a target or any movement. Cautiously, life returned to the platoon.

"Rod's hit! Rod's hit in the the neck! Medic! Medic!" the lieutenant's RTO screamed as he looked down on Rod, who was lying about ten feet to my right and on the other side of Jimmy and the machine gun. Horror and curiosity made me look at Rod. I had never seen a casualty, so I steeled myself for a grotesque sight. I expected to see blood spurting out of Rod's neck and to see him struggle for breath. A neck wound should be fatal, and Rod would be dying. It would not be a pretty sight. Still, like a voyeur at an accident scene, I looked.

The medic, called by most of the grunts "Niner-one

Quack," a combination of his army MOS and his profession, grabbed his rucksack and duckwalked over to us. Rod was facedown in the dirt. Another grunt turned him over. Rod had been hit in the helmet by a small-caliber bullet. The bullet had pierced the steel pot. The carom had sent it around the inside of the helmet and down the back part. The bullet had broken skin on the back of Rod's neck when it exited the helmet. Rod was semicomatose and bleeding. He had a very bad cut, but the wound didn't seem to be life threatening.

Rod slowly gained consciousness. When he heard he had been shot in the neck, he panicked. He felt the back of his neck. Despite the efforts of Doc to stop him, he felt the abrasion, and pulled his hand back, full of blood. He assumed the worst. The medic, Ell-tee James, and Jimmy all took turns calming him down, reassuring him that he was not badly wounded.

Rod begged for the real truth. I knew what was troubling him. I remembered hearing Rod tell a story about how when he first joined the platoon eight months before, one of the grunts had been severely wounded by a booby trap. To calm him down, Rod and Jimmy had told the guy that he wasn't badly hurt, but the guy really was messed up bad and died. Now he thought that others were telling him the same-same thing.

Slowly, Rod began to move his head. He had to be convinced that he wasn't dying. There was blood on the dressing, but not really that much. The repeated and earnest reassurances of the ell-tee and Niner-one Quack helped to persuade him that he'd had a very close call, but not a fatal one.

Rod's thoughts quickly took another tack. This wound might not be bad enough for a ticket home! It might not be bad enough to get him out of the field for his remaining four months. It might not be bad enough to get him a coveted REMF job. Those thoughts mingled with thoughts of how the erratic bullet had almost zapped him, and he began to curse his bad luck. Jersey, who wasn't known for his tactfulness, finally told him to shut up and be thankful that the bullet wasn't inside his head. Rod regained his composure and paraded around, showing off his wound and the dressing.

Further inventory of the men in the platoon showed that no one else was wounded or hurt. Now we had to move the ambush circle down into the kill zone to search for bodies and weapons. It was a tense time. The grunts who had popped the 'bush were already high-strung from the fire-fight and fearful of the move. At the ell-tee's urging, they had adjusted the circle down the hill, and we covered the ambush area. Special care was taken to be sure that the VC had not left any booby-trapped gear.

Mike Platoon came back with a good haul. We were starting to congratulate ourselves, when all hell broke loose from November Platoon's position. November was about three hundred meters to our east. We had blown the 'bush on the rear end of a thirty-five-man VC contingent. The front end had taken flight and had just run into No-vember Platoon's ambush site. Stray bullets snapped and cracked through the air over our heads. We hit the dirt and took cover. After five minutes, the firing stopped. Once again the jungle was quiet. Lieutenant James called No-vember and the CP unit that accompanied them to ask for a situation report. "What's going on over there? You get some gooks, too? Break."

"Not even! But we have all the damn bacon you want!" the captain replied half in mirth and half in disgust. "Your ambush stirred up the wildlife and my guys' nerves at the same time. A wild boar ran into our position ahead of the gooks, and my guys crocked it! Some gooks must have been just behind it, because they opened fire, too. We got the oinker from both sides. The VC dropped a whole mess of clothing and ran across the stream to our south. We fired at them but didn't hit anyone. They're halfway to Hanoi by now. Finish a search of your area and come on over for bacon and pork chops. Break."

Lieutenant James gloated on the radio to November's ell-tee, "We've found some AK-47 ammo and assorted personal items from ten rucksacks. We must have hit their medic, because one of the sacks has all kinds of medicine and stuff in it—both U.S. and NVA issue. We smoked some kind of NVA officer. We have a map of some sort. Looks like we made a good haul. The major wants the papers we've got, so we are going to look for a break in the canopy. Do you have any break in the overhead cover down your way? Over."

November's ell-tee responded in the affirmative. "We got a hole over the creek you can use. Come on down. Over."

By then, we had gathered up our stuff and distributed souvenirs. Those who had taken the most active part in the action got first choice of VC and NVA paraphernalia. I received a plastic bag of Vietnamese rice, a fake silver spoon, and some black VC pajamas. We destroyed anything we couldn't carry or didn't want.

It was only 0800 hours. We still had several important tasks ahead of us. We had to clear the area as soon as possible. The VC might have marked us and could hit us with mortars from some far-off hill. We had to find the clearing and give the captured documents to the brass, get a new supply of ammunition, and get Rod airlifted to a hospital. We were down to three hundred rounds for both the machine guns. It was the first time that I wished I had carried more M-60 ammo.

Air cover arrived. The gunships had gotten there too late to be of any use during the brief firefight. Since VC and NVA seemed to be in our area, they made us the project for the day. The action had been too brief to use artillery. So we had pulled this ambush off by ourselves.

All we had to do now was join November. This might seem an easy task. Although we were a short distance from November, we didn't take our task lightly. The VC and their cohorts, the NVA, had been beaten badly. They might be bitter. If they hadn't totally freaked out, they would have had ample time to prepare booby traps and set up snipers. They could have left a dying comrade along the trail with a hand grenade and orders to take one or two GIs with him when he went to Red Heaven. Or they could be regrouping and setting up a hasty ambush for us. The enemy could be ornery and unpredictable when irritated.

It was times such as those that my heart went out to the point man of the platoon. It was his job to lead us to November's position, where our combined numbers would provide a margin of safety. The point man would probably be the first person to feel the sting of any reprisal the enemy had in mind. Each tree or stump or banana leaf could hold an ominous and deadly secret.

We had ambushed the middle and the end of the VC column. Would the VC do the same to us? Gingerly, we moved toward November's position in single file. Our gun team was in the rear, and I was walking rear security, second from the last. The thought crossed my mind that I was in the same position in our line of march as the VC medic had been in his column. I had used or given away 75 percent of my ammo to other members of the platoon and wasn't carrying any M-60 cans. Our ambush had been successful. Karate had made an inventory of our ammo and had even seen fit to pay me a compliment. "Good work, Professor. You kept your area clear. How many magazines did you shoot?"

I replied, "Five, I think."

"That's good, too. Keep five and give me the rest you have."

In all the time I had spent on operations in Nam, this was the lightest I had traveled. If we walked into trouble, we were awfully low on ammo. Warily, Denny and I kept close eye on our rear.

We followed the VC's path to November's platoon position. Twice, we stopped to examine blood trails and remnants of clothing soaked with blood. We found seven or eight spent cartridges from a 9mm pistol. Probably that was the position from which Rod had been hit.

I also fancied that the position must have been somewhat in line with where I had been firing when Jimmy had requested cover. I am sure that I hadn't greased a dink, but maybe I had enticed a couple of them to move smartly out of our area.

In the meantime, the command-and-control guys were getting impatient for the map. They tried to hurry us to the clearing. The ell-tee refused to be rushed. In addition, he demanded ammunition in exchange for the map. When the brass realized that he wouldn't give up the map unless we got ammo, they acceded to the ell-tee's request to meet us at the break in the overhead cover. M-16 and M-60 ammo were lowered in a duffel bag hanging from a rope suspended from their helicopter. We sent the map and captured documents up the same way. Rod was medevacked using a jungle penetrator.

With mixed emotions, we watched as Rod was strapped to the yellow steel seat that was lowered from the Dustoff. The jungle penetrator was heavy enough to break through the overhead canopy so that casualties could be attached and lifted out.

Our mixed emotions included relief that Rod was not wounded badly and envy that he had a really "good" wound. At the very least, he could nurse his wound for a month or two of REMF duty. At most he could get a medical profile and not have to hump for the rest of his tour. Rod was an 11Bravo20, turning REMF right before our eyes.

We arrived at November's position amid beaucoup excitement. Everyone was on a personal high. We had done harm to the enemy but had suffered very little of consequence. We took turns looking at the boar, which was gathering a considerable collection of flies. Of course, we didn't butcher it. It would have been dangerous to make a cooking fire, and besides, the old porker looked to be as tough as leather. The boar was adequate only for ragging on November Platoon's ambush skills. More souvenir clothing was there for the taking. I got some NVA stuff and humped it back to the fire support base.

About two in the afternoon, resupply choppers hovered overhead and dropped us food, water, ammunition, and mail. Word came back via the radio that Rod was okay but that the wound had damaged some muscles in his neck. It was unlikely that he could wear a steel pot again. This gave Rod a beautiful, military medical profile. It was the perfect excuse never to hump the boonies again. Rod would become a REMF. No one blamed him; everyone envied him. It seemed only right that anyone who had come so close to death had paid his dues and should be awarded dispensation for the remainder of his tour of duty in Vietnam.

That night as we hid with November in the jungle, more information made its way back to us via the ell-tee's PRC-25 radio. The map and papers we had liberated were plans for a full-scale attack on an Australian firebase, showing details of bunker positions and gun emplacments. The map showed how the NVA planned to breach the defenses.

In 1970 in the Central Highlands, the enemy wasn't strong enough to pull off a full-scale attack. They could take ground but could not hold it. The maps seemed to be the hopes and dreams of some NVA big shot who had blown too much grass; they could not have been successfully executed. Still, we were pleased to have secured them. It made us feel good to think that we were thwarting their plans.

I crawled into my poncho liner that night to ponder the day. It was at such times that I analyzed what had happened during the day. I had been in my first firefight. I had not run. I had not panicked, wet my pants, or fainted from fright. I had not gone crazy. I had broken a rule when I had taken off my boots to sleep, but I had gotten away with it. I had seen a casualty, if only a slight one. I had kept my head and used my military training properly. I had not played a major role in the firefight, but that was okay, too. I had not been shot in the back, I was not crippled or maimed. I had a second war story to tell. I even had some enemy souvenirs to show the kids back at school.

Most importantly, I was now entitled to the Combat Infantryman Badge (CIB). I could wear the long silver rifle on its blue background on my uniform to show others that "yes, I had done something in Vietnam." I had engaged the enemy, at least once. I was now a full-fledged 11Bravo20, a blooded infantry grunt.

CHAPTER 6

A Night on the Town

Delta Company got a lot of praise for its achievement. By standards set earlier in the war, say 1965 through 1968, our contact would have been considered very, very minor. In comparison to contacts made later, in the spring of 1970 during the Cambodian incursion, our cache would have been a drop in the bucket. In contrast to contacts made in other areas, such as up north, our accomplishments would have seemed insignificant. But considering the lack of recent action in our area, the Central Highlands, we had found a good-size enemy force where there shouldn't have been one, and had soundly defeated it. The U.S. Army and the people of Vietnam hadn't forgotten the 1968 Tet offensive.

If President Nixon was to withdraw U.S. troops as he had announced, then the supposedly pacified areas such as the one we worked had to remain clear of enemy troop concentrations. The thirty or so VC and NVA we had encountered didn't represent a sizable force by any means. In areas up north, the 101st Airborne or the Marines would have laughed at us. But the Big Red One wanted to keep its area of operation clear of any possible intruders. Nixon and Kissinger hoped that the Central Highlands could be used as an example of the success of the United States war effort and a justification for U.S. troop withdrawal. It wouldn't look good to have enemy units of any major size suddenly start popping up in what the United

States and South Vietnamese governments designated as a liberated area.

Several days after our firefight, our sister company, Bravo, found seven fresh VC graves several thousand meters north of the area in which we had blown the ambush. They dug them up and said that the bodies had been zapped by claymores and small-arms fire. No other major contact had been made in that area for several weeks, so Delta Company got the credit for the kills. Along with the recognition came a reward. Our company was notified that we were to be extracted from the field and given three days of R & R in Lai Khe. We would still have to pull night perimeter guard, but that would be the extent of our duties.

Choppers extracted us from the same clearing in which we had been inserted and ferried us to Lai Khe. Immediately after arriving at our base camp, we received the supplies that we would need for our next mission. Mail from home was distributed, and we headed for Rocket City's mess hall. Passes to the town were to be issued at 1300 hours. The men of Delta Company now having shit, showered, and shaved felt that it was time to get laid. So following the time-honored tradition of fighting men in foreign lands, we divided up into groups of ruffians and headed for the sex-and-sin part of Lai Khe, a place innocently known as the Plaza.

Likewise, the Vietnamese, following the time-honored tradition of a conquered people, had turned out their daughters to provide for the needs of the conquering army. United States money in the form of scrip, military payment certificates (MPC), would serve as the medium of exchange and discourse, if not intercourse. That the MPC temporarily resided in the pockets of the recently paid troops of Delta Company was only a minor detail.

During the next few hours, GIs would trade their money for the pleasures of the Orient. For the rest of their lives, Vietnam vets would sit around bars and campfires back in the States relating, reliving, and embellishing their sexual experiences and exploits. If the Vietnamese thought they were rooking the GIs out of money, they were sadly mistaken. For the GIs who didn't catch the clap or some other sexually transmitted disease, the experiences that seemed to be an extravagant waste of money at the time would be well worth the cost years later as sexual fact gave way to sexual fiction.

My first view of Lai Khe Plaza rattled my orientation for a moment. Stretching out before me, lining the red, dusty street, were bars and bathhouses strongly reminiscent of an Old West town in a Hollywood movie. Was I in Nam or a western cow town in Kansas or Colorado in the 1870s? Maybe it was the wooden facades. Names such as Hank's Grill, Fantastic Baths, Showers and Massages, and Kitty's Laundry also helped to give the town the flavor of Dodge City or Tombstone. The streets were crowded with hucksters selling food, clothes, and souvenirs. Black-market jungle boots and fatigues could be purchased at prices that rivaled those of the PX. Why not? The material had been stolen from the army distribution system at some point between the port and the local PX or army unit. The Vietnamese were only too happy to sell these articles to the GIs or other Vietnamese. Knives, pistols, rifles, machine guns, and even tanks could be purchased, although some of the items were more or less kept under the counter.

Need some grass, GI? Twenty bucks would get you a moderately well-filled garbage bag. Hell, if you held out, the dealer would throw in his twelve-year-old sister for an additional ten bucks.

The street activity seemed to have a terminus at a place called the Golden Nugget. There the Oriental East met the American Old West. It was to that bar that the more experienced in our group headed. After all, we were ass-kicking infantry and self-proclaimed heroes. We owed ourselves a good time.

Personally, I had already decided what I wanted in the way of a good time. I hadn't really seen any authentic Vietnamese life or culture except from the flatbed of deuce-and-a-half trucks as we sped through Vietnamese towns. I hadn't really met and talked to a Vietnamese national other than the PX workers. That level of conversation had been centered around how many sodas or beers I wanted to purchase. In short, I hadn't actually met, up close and personal, any of the people of Vietnam whom we were there to liberate and defend. My trip into Lai Khe would now afford me the opportunity to do just that.

I hoped that I could make a long-lasting friendship with a gook that would transcend the boundaries of race, religion, and cultural heritage. Maybe a Vietnamese would thank me for my efforts and sacrifices. We could discuss philosophy and our different views on the meaning of life. We would exchange addresses and correspond when I got back to the real world. I would become some poor Vietnamese's benefactor, and he or she my grateful dependent. Maybe I could make such a contact at the Golden Nugget. I anxiously awaited my debut into Vietnamese society.

Red, our point man, misinterpreted my enthusiasm. "Professor," he quipped, "you've never been to a dink bar, so watch yourself. Stay by me. I'll show you around in there. Watch out for those girls. They'll skin you alive. Just stay by me. I'll see that they don't get too much of that money in your wallet. Also remember those VD films you saw at in-processing."

"Oh, I'm married to—" was all I got out of my mouth as we stepped through the swinging doors of the Golden Nugget. Immediately we were engulfed by a bevy of Oriental beauties. Any hope for the men of Delta Company, 2d of the 16th Infantry, making a stand dissolved. We were obviously a newly paid unit in from the field, and the girls knew that they had a limited amount of time before curfew to fleece us.

Red, our steadfast point man in the jungle, was the first to fall. In the bush he could be counted on to guide us safely past hidden mines and booby traps; but in the Golden Nugget, he succumbed immediately to only partially concealed boobies openly displayed by the Vietnamese bar girls. My would-be guardian went down in the first wave of girls, the victim of a slender raven-haired beauty. Using feminine allure, she took control of him and guided him to a table.

Two miniskirted girls, trying their best to display their Americanized breasts via the help of a French push-up bra, replaced the vacuum left by Red's girl and began to compete for my attention.

"Hey, Joe!" one sang out. "You come sit with me!"

"No, GI, me number one," cooed the second coed. She looked deeply and directly into my eyes. "Come sit with me!"

"Oh, you got beaucoup muscles!" squealed the first girl in a high nasal voice as she grabbed my right arm and began to rub her breast against it. "Where in States you from?" she sincerely wanted to know.

The second girl, not to be outdone, was at work grinding her pelvis against my left leg and pulled on my left arm. "My name Suzie. How rong you been in Nam? Come sit by me? Please?" Her cooing was in direct contrast to the shrill singsong voice of the girl on my right. I kind of liked this.

"Joe, I make you velly happy. You see," sang the first.

"But, Joe, you-me we make velly good short-time. No sweat. I clean. You rook wonderful! Please! Come with me!"

Stupefied, I stood there. I had never had two women so enthralled with me. They both showed all the signs of being deeply in love with me. I could tell! Had someone asked me about my moral convictions or, say, my wife's name, I am afraid that I could have answered only with a blank stare. Never one to make snap decisions, I stood there looking left and right as if I were about to cross a dangerous intersection.

"Now ladies . . . ," I began to stammer, but "now ladies" was not enough. The girls redoubled their efforts to win my attention. Either they didn't understand the word "ladies," or they weren't aware that I was referring to them.

Abruptly, a rude and vicious shove from behind brought me back to my senses. At the same time I heard someone growl, "Let him go!" From behind me, Larry, the company sniper, reached past me and broke the grip of the girl who held me by my left arm.

"Yeah!" I agreed and tore away from the girl who had cemented her breasts to my right arm. With Larry's hand implanted in the small of my back, we forced our way into the room, brushing off girls as we brushed off clinging red ants in the bush. We made it to the quiet end of the bar.

"Thanks," I said, "I—"

"That's okay," he mumbled, and we exchanged a fleeting glance. Larry and I had just recently started to become friends after the incident with the cache. He had been on R & R to Hawaii during most of my neophyte period. My questioning him about how to get R & Rs and what Hawaii was like had caused us to pull the same guard duty and to start to gravitate together in various situations.

Larry would talk for hours about his wife. They had gone to the same university and had only been married about a month before he had come to Nam. Karen and I at least had six months together before I had shipped out. I suspect there were a lot of quick marriages due to the war. A man wanted to have something or someone to come back to. A wife served as an anchor. That is, an anchor in the nicest sense of the word, of course.

Seeing me in the door of the Nugget, Larry must have concluded that I was a good kid about to go wrong, and he had nudged me figuratively, as well as physically, back onto the right track. Our glance had assured me that I need not say more, and he also accepted it as a quiet thank-you.

"You drink?" he asked as he leaned his elbows back on the bar and surveyed the room.

"There it is," I had learned to say in GI talk. "I'll buy the first round."

"Good, I'll have a rum and Coke."

"Okay . . . Hey, bartender."

I continued to try to get the attention of the barkeep, but he was working as fast as he could to provide drinks for the grunts with girls. A heavyset mamma-san supervised both drinks and girls. She was perched like a vulture on a high stool behind the bar, and nothing escaped her notice. She saw we wanted to buy drinks, but since we did not have girls she mentally placed us in the proper descending order. During a lull in the action, the bartender made his way to our end of the bar.

"Two rum and Cokes," I ordered, and to clarify my order I held up two fingers and motioned back and forth to both Larry and me. The gesture made the order too complex, and a few minutes later he brought back four drinks, two apiece. As I handed him twenty dollars MPC, Larry and I laughed and assured each other that the mistake would work to our favor since it would save us time on the next order. I wasn't sure how much the drinks should cost. It took about ten minutes and eighty glares to get change from the bartender. It came in the form of Vietnamese piasters, and since I wasn't versed in exchange rates, I never did know how much I had paid for the refreshments. I assume that I got bilked. I let it be. Leaning back against the bar, I sipped my rum and Coke. I joined Larry in a general reconnaissance of the barroom.

"You understand what's happening, Professor?"

"Well, yes, I guess . . . Naw, not really."

"Well, first a girl gets a guy to select her. You saw how that works as we came in."

"Yep. How do we get out?"

"Never mind. I'll show you. Then she takes the guy to a table. See over there. She sits down with him and orders a tea, a Saigon tea. The grunt orders booze. See those boys, those little Vietnamese kids? They bring the girls the drinks. Two shot glasses of tea for five bucks. The girl then talks to the guy for a while and plays with his leg. Gets him to buy some more booze. Maybe she will sit on his lap. When she thinks she can get away with it, she will give a secret signal, and the kid will bring another tea to her. At five bucks a shot, she'll do that every time she can. If she gets the dope drunk enough, she can have all his money in no time. She doesn't even have to put out. Mamma-san up there keeps track of everything. The girls have to keep hustling. If a GI stops buying, the girl moves on."

Two girls approached us.

"You ready, Joe?" one lovingly enticed.

"No, no thanks," I responded. She turned and melted into the scenery.

"Wasn't that one of the girls who attacked you at the door?" Larry inquired.

"I think so, but I'm not sure. I never looked at her face. The tits did look the same." We laughed. This was chauvinist pig talk. We liked it.

"I guess she didn't score with you, and now she's kinda screwed. All the girls have guys. Mamma-san over there won't be pleased; she won't get a cut of anything."

"Yeah! I'm sorry. Maybe I could give her a few bucks for a nice try. She probably needs the money."

"I don't think you should. It would fuck up their system and could cause you and her trouble. Mamma-san wouldn't understand and might even think that she's doing some independent contracting after work. Sometimes girls are just Saigon Tea girls, not short-time girls. There's a subtle difference between a tea girl and a whore. It's a status thing. Some girls do short-time when they are not young and pretty enough to do the tea thing. Some girls do both."

Jersey came over to show off his prize. "She's half French!" he gloated.

Sure enough, she was the most beautiful woman in the bar.

She was slightly taller and better built than most of the other girls. Her features were Oriental, but softer. Her carriage and demeanor were more polished. Her eyes penetrated mine and caused me to glance away.

Putting his hand beside his mouth to shield his words from the beauty, he continued, "She thinks I'm drunk. Sure I had a few. No big deal. She's expensive. I've spent forty bucks on tea and another ten having a guy with a Polaroid take our picture together. I gave her fifty bucks on the sly. She's going to short-time for me tonight. I'll give her another thirty then. Smart? Am I smart? Wait until the guys on the block see this picture of me and this chick. Wow!"

With that he turned to the girl and said, "Come on, baby, let's go say 'Hi' to the sarge," and Jersey steered her off. The French half-breed and Jersey caused jealousy and envy at every table they visited. GIs who had been perfectly satisfied with the girl they had hastily chosen at the door were reevaluating their choices and finding their companions to be substandard in comparison to the French knockout. The tea girls realized this and sat closer to their marks. They talked even more ardently and when all else failed, they rubbed their soldier's leg higher and more aggressively. After a few more beers or whiskeys, most of the girls began to reclaim their position in the grunts' hearts and wallets. Loneliness, whiskey, and availability can make a woman, Oriental or not, look much more appealing as time passes.

Larry and I moved away from the bar and made the rounds of the booths and tables. We talked with our friends and their girls. Because of staunch moral convictions, lack of money, or fear of Brand X venereal disease, some members of our platoon hadn't selected girls. Some of the married men had. We had a gentlemen's-club agreement. We all respected each other's definition of moral character. Periodically, during the next few hours, we were approached by stray girls and asked if we wanted to talk. And, of course, newcomers to the bar were swarmed over at the door. Twice more "my girl" came over. Each time, I respectfully declined. The entire scene was a great sociological as well as a psychological study. I enjoyed watching more than participating. As curfew hour approached, the girls got even more flirtatious and ordered tea at a faster pace. If a "Joe" resisted paying for the tea, he suddenly became a "Cheap Charlie." Cheap Charlies were either out of money or demanding sexual favors for their tea purchases that afternoon.

Curfew was approaching, so Larry and I prepared to leave. I was never a heavy drinker, and the rum and Cokes had made me slightly light-headed. It had been fun playing the part of voyeur. The Vietnamese and the Americans had used each other for their own purposes. I considered it a draw. Larry and I headed for the door. My tea girl glided across the floor and joined us. "One more try," I thought and glands took control of my brain as I imagined what sex with her might be like. My fantasy ended. I was with Larry and had already committed myself to the role of good guy. I decided to walk the straight and narrow.

"You leave?" she inquired and pressed up against me. "Now you-me go . . ."

"I'm sorry," I started to say. I was truly feeling bad for her. I would have loved to have slipped her a few bucks just for effort. She had been faithful and persistent. Maybe there were baby-sans at home in need of food. The few bucks that I could give her would be a charitable contribution, sort of direct foreign aid from the United States. Besides, maybe she really did like me. No girl had pursued Larry the way she had badgered me.

Leaning very close to me and pulling me down so as to communicate directly into my ear, she whispered in a sultry voice, "Joe, I have something special for you!"

My manhood reacted in anticipation. "Oh, yeah?" I said, and was about to turn to Larry with some sort of humorous male chauvinistic remark when my sweetie suddenly reached down and pulled the waistband of my jungle fatigues away from my waist. The pants yielded enough room for her to shove in her hand. This could have been the start of a very romantic encounter, as I was now a seasoned grunt and, following the standard GI fashion custom, I wasn't wearing any underwear. Unfortunately, she had concealed something in her hand. Ice cubes! In astonishment, I began a jerk-and-jiggle routine which could have been part of a floor show in any bar in the Orient or America. I maneuvered the cubes past the more sensitive parts of my anatomy only to find that they didn't exit through the cuff. Jungle fatigues have drawstrings in the cuff to prevent bugs and spiders from crawling up. Just then they were keeping ice cubes from sliding out. I bent over to untie the drawstring and relieve myself of this form of Oriental torture.

I straightened up and saw immediately that I was the

center of attention. My tea girl cupped her hands in front of her mouth, gave a quick, high-pitched laugh, and fled into the recesses of the bar. The guys in the booths started to hoot and jeer. Some wiseass bellowed that he would "like to see that dance again, Professor."

I turned to Larry, who was doing a poor job of hiding his mirth, and with a look of bafflement, asked, "What the . . . ?"

"I think you've just been same-same as insulted," he said, grinning.

"Why, the bitch! I'll—" and I swung around. "If I get my hands on her, I'll . . ."

"Come on, Professor. It's not nice to strike a lady. Especially one smaller than you. Come on; let's go. She's got her evens."

I withdrew with one last glare in the direction of the inner sanctum of the bar. The girl had vanished, and I wouldn't have been able to find her or to do anything if I did. I could only continue to be the center of undeserved derision and embarrassment. Larry and I left.

"Want to try another bar?" Larry mocked.

"No. No, thanks. Why did she do that?"

"I guess you didn't take up with her, and she couldn't connect with anyone else, so she had to blame a bad afternoon on someone. I think she was teasing you. You've heard of hot pants. Well, I guess she thought you had cold pants. Don't let it bother you."

The street scene was changing. Here and there were hints that the commerce for the day was over. People were closing up their shops and boarding up their stalls. Larry and I made our way back to the American part of Lai Khe. Slowly, others of our platoon joined us, and we milled around the company rear area, drinking beer and soda. Jersey was one of the last ones to arrive. He was euphoric. "I'm going to get some prime short-time off that girl I met in the Nugget tonight!" he bragged. "I'm taking first guard, and at midnight I'll meet her at a hole in the fence between the gook area and our base. I'm goin' to get fucked tonight."

We all felt envious. Some of the guys eased their jealousy by describing in detail their exploits from the afternoon. Red, the point man, had spent eighty bucks and had gotten laid twice, a different girl each time. I reminded him that he had volunteered to be my guardian. He laughed and apologized for being such a poor example. Several good-natured comments were offered about my dancing ability. In retrospect, I, too, could laugh at my misfortune.

"But if I ever get my hands on that . . ." slipped through my lips several times. The guys knew that I was sincere. "If I ever do get my hands on that bitch, I'll turn her over my knee and, with great pleasure, spank her soundly."

The sun turned amber and grew in size as it set in the west. We took our M-16s and equipment and reported to the bunker line for perimeter guard duty. Jersey was with us. He demanded and got first guard. And true to his word, he left immediately afterward. No one missed him until the morning.

When the sun returned to us from the east, we noticed that Jersey wasn't among us. At first, we were too concerned about unraveling the knots from our backs after another night of sleeping on the ground to care about our wayward comrade. Eventually, we missed Jersey, and we initiated a search of the bunkers. He definitely wasn't among our rumpled and unshaven cohorts. Everyone began to conjecture why he hadn't returned to the bunker line.

"He got lost in the dark," Red said, "and couldn't find his way back." We disagreed.

"He got drunk and stoned," Larry offered. We thought that a strong possibility.

"He got mugged and skinned by some gook!" was also proposed. "If he is alive, he is in a hospital somewhere, or lying dead by the fence," Jimmy ventured. That gruesome suggestion was discarded at first, but after some debate, it began to receive more support. Soon, we were all convinced that it was a strong possibility.

The captain of the guard relieved us and accepted without hesitation our explanation that our missing member was in the crapper. We headed for the mess hall, but detoured to the hole in the compound fence just to be sure that the last guess as to Jersey's absence didn't hold some value. We didn't find a body. Nor were there any blood trails. We were almost disappointed.

Someone advanced the bizarre notion that Jersey had been kidnapped by the VC in the village. Like mothers of a returning runaway child, we were both happy and angry when we entered the mess tent and saw Jersey eating breakfast. Jersey almost deserved to be kidnapped by the VC or at least cut up a little. Yes, a nice stab wound would have been appropriate, was the consensus.

After receiving our SOS* and other scrumptious breakfast fare from the polite, courteous, and caring mess hall cooks, we gathered around Jersey at his table for a full accounting.

Jersey leaned back on his folding chair, placed his hands behind his head, and, in his thick Hoboken accent, started his yarn. "Youse guys know I met Sherri, or that's what she said her name was, at the Nugget. I slipped her fifty bucks on the sly, see, so she would stay with me. I bought her forty bucks' worth of tea. Then I got this Polaroid picture of us to show the guys on the block. That costed me another ten bills. Anyway, as we leave, she tells me she'll fuck for another thirty dollars more. I just got paid. I don't care. I gave her the money, and she promised to meet me at the hole in the barbed wire at eleven o'clock.

"Last night after guard I go to the fence and no Sherri. So I wait. No Sherri. I wait until about one-thirty. No Sherri. About two, I figure that she isn't coming, so I cross into the gook compound. The place is a maze of shacks and streets and alleys, but there are people walking around. So I grab a kid, light my cigarette lighter, and I show him the picture, the Polaroid one, and tell him I want to find the girl. He says he can take me to her for ten bucks.

---

*Shit on a shingle, i.e., "creamed chipped beef on toast," as army menus frequently had it.

So I figure that I'm into this thing for a hundred and forty bucks, so what's ten more. The kid then takes me on a tour. We walk up streets, down streets, up alleys, and down alleys. We crawl up ladders and over trash heaps. We knock on doors and look in windows. No Sherri. Pretty soon the kid stops and says, 'No can find.'

"So I grab him and tell him I'm going to beat the shit out of him, so he says he knows someone who can find her. He goes to a house and knocks on the door. Another kid comes out. They yap for a while and the second kid looks at the picture. He says he can find the girl for fifteen dollars. Well, what's fifteen more bucks?

"This kid takes me on a tour, too. Finally he knocks on a door, yells something in Vietnamese, and runs off. Just as I turn to chase him, the door opens and there's Sherri!

"Well, she is half asleep, but when she sees me she snaps awake and tries to slam the door. Well, by that time I'm pissed. So I kick at the door. I knock it open, and she falls back on her ass. 'You bitch!' I yell, and start to cuss her out. Well, I wake up the whole damn house. I wake up papa-san, mamma-san, and half a dozen baby-sans. She starts crying, and they start jabbering. She grabs me and says that she is so solly that she forgot. She pulls me outside and keeps saying that she is so solly. After a while, things calm down inside, and she agrees to come across. We went back into the hootch, and I screw her all night. You know how these gook short-time girls are. They just lay there. Sherri even fucks back. No one bothers us. In the morning I got up, checked my wallet to make sure all my loot was still there. I left another twenty on the table and head on back. I walked around that place forever until I met an ARVN MP. I gave him five bucks, and he showed me the way to the hole in the fence. Now I'm here!"

Jersey's story added such flavor to the army chow that several people went back for more. Meanwhile, critics began a barrage of questions, and Jersey fielded them nicely. It gave him a new excuse to describe in more detail exactly each of the 947 positions he used to screw his date. In awe, several of our troop reacted with, "Aw! I wouldn't do that with a gook," or "What else did she do?" Or "I don't believe that!" As we broke up and left the mess hall, we debated the truthfulness of Jersey's story. We each tried to find a weakness in it.

Finally, two sets of opinions emerged. One side staunchly believed Jersey's story. They cited as evidence that Jersey wasn't smart enough to compose such a yarn. The other group, while giving him credit for lack of common sense, contended that Jersey hadn't met the girl at the fence but had slipped into some REMF's bunk and slept the night away while we were on guard. Only Jersey and, of course, Sherri, ever knew the real truth.

CHAPTER 7

It's Our Turn

The choppers put us down in a nondescript clearing located, heaven-knows-where, southwest of Saigon. Our instructions were to seek and engage VC, but the area was reported to be fairly clear. In 1970, the Big Red One kept a tight rein on its AO. Upon hitting the ground, we scrambled off the landing zone and headed for the bush. Once in the jungle, our platoon broke down into squads. At squad level, we set about our business.

We were ordered to search and destroy. We did a lot of searching but no destroying. Each day, one of the squads would conduct a sweep while the other squad waited in a blocking position. Like a Kansas pheasant hunting trip, the squad doing the sweep was supposed to flush the game so the blocking squad could blow them away. Unlike a pheasant hunt, there were no daily bag limits, and both VC cocks and VC hens were legal to shoot.

We found little adventure. Nothing developed. Supposedly, we did chase some VC around a knoll about a mile long and a half mile wide. Actually, we were so burdened with equipment and the jungle was so thick that we just lumbered after them. To be completely candid, we were not overly enthusiastic about catching up with Mr. Charles. To be downright brutally honest, we were not sure we were chasing anyone anyway. We saw no individuals, nor did we find fresh signs of recent activity.

However, the circumstances didn't prevent us from putting on a good show. We called in phony reports and made up stories about what we were doing. We lied about what we were finding.

One particularly sultry afternoon, Karate led us on a full-scale phony sweep of the entire knoll. He called in co-ordinates to the ell-tee while he described our mission. Karate gave a glowing account over the PRC-25 of what we were doing and seeing. Any lifer brass who might have been listening to our radio transmissions would have applauded our squad's gung-ho efforts. In reality, we stayed about twenty yards from the ell-tee and his CP. Most of the guys were lounging around, playing cards, sleeping, or reading.

Karate ended our escapade with the transmission, "Ell-tee, we are approaching your position from the November [north]. Don't fire us up. We should be in sight contact soon. Can you see us now?"

Upon asking the question, Karate and four grunts dropped their pants and mooned ell-tee James.

"We have you in view." Ell-tee chuckled. "Your little hike has improved your looks, but your breath still stinks. Please, take up a position downwind."

"That's a roger," Karate retorted and pulled up his pants. It was rough, crude humor, but we all broke noise discipline to howl with laughter.

The next day the "demand and control" part of the army surmised we were fishing a dry hole. We had found a few old bunkers and a little sign of activity, but nothing of any great military importance. We found no caches of ammunition. We made no contact with live VC. We had been on a U.S. Army–sponsored camping trip. They knew we were just roasting marshmallows.

Our camp-out terminated when we were abruptly ordered off the knoll and told to hump to a pickup zone near its base. Somewhere in our AO, a platoon from Charlie Company found an area with active VC. They had participated in a few minor skirmishes and were licking their wounds. Because the Old Man had decided Delta Company was ass-kickers and that we hadn't been doing much to merit our earlier three-day stand-down in Lai Khe, he ordered us in to replace Charlie Company.

We were not briefed as to the nature of the operation. The choppers came and transferred us to the new location. Maybe the ell-tee or the captain was privy to more information, but to us 11Bravo20 infantry grunts the order was to load up the choppers, unload the choppers, climb another hill, inspect some bunkers.

It was just another day in Nam, but we were a bit perturbed because it was getting late in the afternoon. Just as the wise traveler on vacation in the States likes to pick his accommodations for the night early, so did we. By choosing early, we could avoid the evening rush for the best ambush sites.

The choppers swooped into the LZ and dropped us off. Our two squads formed into two lines, sixty meters apart. We went up the hill in single file; Red, our point man, was at the head of our squad. This hill didn't seem to be as high as our last knoll, but it was a bit steeper. We were hiking straight up the hill rather than around it.

Red was determined to get us to the top and check out the bunkers before dark. Old Southern Grits liked walking point. Despite his Confederate heritage and his cracker daddy's warnings, he took pride in leading this small part of the Yankee Army through the bush.

Red was two-thirds up the hill when our column was suddenly and fiercely raked with AK-47 fire. Green tracers, as well as invisible bullets, tore through our rank.

I hit the dirt. Because there was an extensive root system covering the ground beneath me, I couldn't get down as low as I wanted. The roots held me suspended six to eight inches above the ground. I felt as if I were fully exposed six to eight feet above the ground. As the second pass of bullets hit the ground in front of me, pain shot through the left side of my face. My left eye stung, and my cheek lost feeling. I couldn't see from the left eye; I knew that I had been hit!

"Oh God! Not in the face!" I wailed. "Not in the face!" I

put my hand to my face to feel the damage to the torn flesh and to stop the bleeding.

How bad? How bad could it be? I brought my hand down from my cheek. It contained no blood. I wasn't bleeding yet. Again and again, I felt my numb face. How disfigured would I be? My left eye burned in its socket, and I couldn't open it. I had to rely on my right eye for sight.

"How could I be shot in the face and there not be any blood?" I didn't understand what was happening.

Then I theorized that I had been hit, not by bullets, but by the rocks kicked up by the bullets when they hit the ground near my head. The theory proved to be reality, because when the VC hit us with the next spray of bullets, the same thing happened. Bullets struck the ground in front of me and slightly to my left, splattering me with more rocks and debris.

Again I was hit in the face with rocks. In disbelief, I kept feeling my face with my hand. I couldn't persuade my mind that my cheek and eye were still intact.

Using my good right eye, I surveyed our predicament. It was obvious that no one in the column could return fire without shooting the squad member ahead of him in the back. We were pinned down and helpless. More fire raked us. Then I noticed that Jimmy wasn't down on the ground. He hadn't hit the dirt! Lucky for him, too. Where Jimmy would have taken cover, the bullets seemed to kick up the most dirt.

Jimmy, standing upright, was inventorying the situation. "They's only firecrackers!" He directed an offhanded observation to me in the causal manner of a lesson to be learned. He showed a white-toothed grin. "They's only firecrackers, Professor!" he repeated.

"How can that be?" I thought. I had faith in Jimmy's combat experience, so I looked up into the trees to see if I could spot the VC who was lighting and throwing down firecrackers. But why would he be throwing firecrackers and not hand grenades? In either case, I was set to blow him out of the jungle canopy.

"How can they be firecrackers?" I pleaded out loud to no one in particular.

"They ain't!" Jimmy confirmed in sudden realization of the truth, and hit the ground. "They's real, Professor! They's real bullets!"

Almost in the same instant, the VC who had been shooting at us started yelling something in Vietnamese. What that gook said, I have no idea, but it must have been an insult, because he ended his tirade in English: "Fuck you, GI! Fuck you, GI!" He must have relieved his emotional problem, for he once again buzzed us with a magazine of AK-47 fire. Then he quit shooting. All was dead still.

A hundred heartbeats later, the silence was broken by someone up front. "Red's hit! Medic! Medic! Get the medic up here!"

Larry had been hit, too. Larry was walking behind me when he caught an AK-47 bullet in his left arm from the barrage that had splattered rocks into my face.

Niner-one Quack started to bandage Larry's arm. He looked up the hill in fear and dismay.

"I'll be up in a minute!" He shouted without a hint of resolution in his voice. "I've got wounded back here, too."

Up front, someone else screamed, "Get up here now! Red's hit bad, and he's gonna die!"

"I'll get there when I can!" our medic snarled, again without conviction.

I could sense from the painstaking care with which he was wrapping Larry's arm, and his general lack of urgency, that Niner-one Quack was not anxious to make a house call to the front of the column.

Eventually, with the ell-tee's urging, even Doc had to admit that Larry's dressing was a medical work of art and that he should go forward. He started a slow, low crawl forward. At his rate of speed, it could have taken him thirty minutes to reach Red.

I was getting desperate to help Red, my well-intentioned guardian in the Golden Nugget bar in Lai Khe. I had always felt a special bond with him. Now I felt helpless.

The gook had not fired at us for the last few minutes, and I realized what had just taken place. The VC was gone! Just like a bully on a playground, the gook had yelled an insult, then run back to Uncle Ho. Just when he could have cleaned our clocks but good, he had turned tail and run. I knew he was gone. I just knew it! I knew it by intuition, and because I had worked with enough smart-assed juvenile delinquents to recognize the signs of a fucking bully.

The ell-tee was in the process of calling in arty and a Dustoff. I interrupted his transmission. "Lieutenant, let me go get Red!" I asked. My confidence was up. "Let me get Red!" I demanded. The ell-tee looked at me as if I was crazy; and Doc, who had crawled a full body length in front of me, looked back in astonishment.

"No!" the ell-tee commanded.

"Let him go!" Niner-one urged with passion.

"No! We'll bring Red back!" he ordered. In a louder voice he yelled, "Bring Red back! Drag him back!"

In a few minutes, the jungle parted and three or four figures emerged. Sergeant Jefferies carried Red's rucksack and weapon. He was breaking the jungle for the others. One guy wrapped Red's left arm around his neck and was supporting Red's weight. Another grunt held Red's bloody, damaged right arm and shoulder. Every step caused Red to cringe in pain.

Red was covered with mud, blood, and bandages, and his face was ashen. "We've been hit, Professor!" he moaned as our eyes met. "We've been hit bad!" And with that, Red passed out of my life forever.

Red's escorts assisted him as he passed me on his trip down the hill. Those were the last words of communication between Red and me. Red didn't die, although he had been shot three times in his right arm and shoulder.

A medevac chopper was already on the way. One thing about the medical service in Nam, if the situation would allow it, the medevacs were there pronto, and medical treatment was started immediately. The army boasted that a GI wounded in Nam got better medical treatment faster than he would get if he were in a car accident in the States.

Red and Larry were already in the pipeline bound for home. After the Golden Nugget in Lai Khe, Larry and I had grown close. We did not have a chance to say a final good-bye when he was wounded. He just looked up at me and nodded. I nodded back. Larry had only fifty-seven days left in the field, and he knew that he would be going home for sure. Larry would even have a souvenir wound to show off.

With the wounded out of the way, we still had a situation on our hands. We were sure that the VC had gone, but we still had to check out the bunker complex. Our squad wasn't equal to the task. We had been too shaken by the past moments to move any closer to the top of the hill.

Luckily, Sergeant Penny's squad was moving in from the west. Penny threw hand grenades into bunkers as his squad entered the complex. He just found empty bunkers, and a pile of spent AK-47 shell casings. At the top of that particular hill in Vietnam, there was nothing worth having for us and nothing worth defending for them. Whether at the top or at the bottom, there was nothing of importance there. It was just another piece of real estate over which human beings from different cultural and political backgrounds could try to kill one another.

We scooted back down the hill to find a thick place in the jungle to hide. That night, we posted double guard. No one objected. Jimmy and I were on guard duty together, and we had a chance to talk. In muffled tones, we discussed the two wounded and their chances of permanent injury.

Finally, I brought up the subject of the firecrackers. I hadn't said anything earlier because we had been too busy. Jimmy had been avoiding me. I felt I was about to tread upon a touchy subject, but I just had to know what Jimmy had thought was taking place on the hill.

"Jimmy, what was all that firecracker stuff about?" I inquired in a low voice.

"Professor, I thinks I was crazy. I thinks that I was

crazy. I saw them green tracers, and I thought they was firecrackers. I don't know. You think I's goin' nuts? Be honest. You think I'm crazy?"

"Well . . . no, Jimmy, I don't. But I was so convinced that I started looking up in the trees to see the guys who were throwing them down on us. I guess if you're crazy, so am I. You know, I got this eye, and my cheek, all bruised from the rocks that hit me. That's how close the bullets were coming."

"Yeah, I know."

"Well, if you would have hit the dirt, I judge that you would have been just about directly in the line of fire. It would have been really bad for you. We must have been just out of reach on either side of the gook's gun port."

"That was close. You think the Lord had something to do with that? You think He put them firecrackers in my head?"

"Maybe; I don't know."

We both turned inside of ourselves for a while. I guess Jimmy prayed, and I know I did.

"You tell anybody about what I said?" Jimmy asked.

"No."

"Don't! I mean it!"

"Okay."

We turned our attention to the radio and listened for sitreps. In silence, Jimmy and I monitored the radio.

The next morning was a good news–bad news situation. The report was that Larry and Red were okay. "Okay" meant that they weren't dead or in a life-threatening condition. "Okay" also meant that they both were headed home. Larry's wound was less substantial than Red's. He would even get some money from the VA. All his life, Larry would remember that with fifty-seven days left in country he had almost been killed.

Red, on the other hand, was seriously wounded. He would lose some function of his right arm. He would have something special to remember about the Nam. His VA check would be quite a bit larger than Larry's. Red, too, would remember how close he had come to the ultimate.

I'll bet his daddy and Gen. Robert E. Lee were both very proud of him. Larry and Red had million-dollar wounds, and every member of the platoon envied them.

Shot up as badly as he was, we considered Red to be lucky. At least Red knew for sure that he would be going back to the World alive. Not one of us could make that same claim.

So much for the good news. The bad news was that we had to go back up the hill again.

"That's right, folks!" Lieutenant James whispered to the platoon. "The major wants us to check out the bunker complex more thoroughly. He wasn't happy with the brief look that Penny got yesterday."

The entire platoon protested. Karate stated the obvious. "Not even! If we go back there again today, the gooks could do the same-same to us today. They could put us in a beaucoup world of hurt. This is bullshit!"

"That's right!" the ell-tee confirmed. We could tell that he was displeased about putting the platoon in the position of going back into the bunker complex again. Ell-tee did not want to go up the hill any more than we did. "The major wants us back up. And we are going to go. But maybe we'll try something different this time." This comment contained the barest bit of a smirk. We surmised that he had an idea we could live with.

We saddled up to retrace our steps from the day before. Jersey led the way. We reached the base of the hill and started to climb. Halfway up, we found numerous signs of our retreat. The brush was broken and chopped up. Bandage wrappers littered the ground. We saw where vegetation had been cut by the AK-47 bullets. We prepared ourselves for the assault.

As we started to reclaim the hill, the ell-tee directed us off to the right about forty degrees, east of the position we had faced the day before. As we climbed, we moved farther and farther to the east. Soon we were over the hill and past the area of previous contact. We had avoided a direct assault on the same area.

We found a few bunkers that had clothing and several

spools of thread in them, but that was all. Penny's squad made a side journey more directly into the complex but found nothing.

We called it a day. Then we found a place in bamboo to conceal ourselves. Though our mission had taken about an hour, we were exhausted physically and mentally. Ell-tee James was praised by all for his discretion. We had achieved our objective in an indirect way and had not suffered a replay of the preceding day's folly.

We set out an automatic ambush with claymores. I counted my blessings. January was winding down. As I looked back, I saw that I had two whole months behind me and only ten months in front of me. I seriously began to think of R & R in May or June, the earliest possible dates that I could have it. But at least I had a goal. I had a serious target date on which to focus.

I wrote Karen about R & R. We started to dream about what we would do when we met in Hawaii. Some of the letters may have burned the hands of Karen's postman. We were very descriptive. R & R was my major emotional focus. I might not leave Nam alive, but I wanted to make it, at least, to Hawaii. R & R represented Karen, the real world, and real life. Nam was a fantasy life of gunfire, blood, heat, and superhuman toil. Even though I lived it every day, it was just not real.

February was an ominous month. The Oriental New Year, known as Tet, was about to start. In 1968, the VC and NVA had staged massive attacks on U.S. installations and major South Vietnamese population centers. In the end, these attacks had proven to be extremely costly for them, but the media coverage in the United States had made it seem as if the NVA and VC had achieved some sort of major victory. In truth the VC practically ceased to exist as a fighting force after Tet '68. The United States and the grunts in the field in 1970 weren't going to let another '68 Tet happen again.

Our platoon remained in the field on operations. We licked our wounds for a few days, then we were choppered to a new area. We sat down in an open field not too far from a Vietnamese village. I never knew the name of the village, and I doubt that anyone else in our platoon did either. It was just "the ville." We never got much closer than half a mile to it anyway.

The new area was more open. Often, we humped through elephant grass that was at least six feet tall, well over my head. One night, we walked through the grass to make a trail that was easy to follow. We then doubled back on the trail to set up an ambush. If VC had been trying to track us, we would have ambushed them. But nothing happened. After the earlier incident on the hill, we were in need of calm.

Walking open fields in the sun was hot and miserable. It was harder in some respects than cutting and crawling through the shade of the jungle. Because we were in the open as we walked, we maintained a distance of ten to fifteen feet between each man to make it harder for the enemy to shoot up the entire squad at one time. But it also made staying in formation difficult. At times, the column was in disarray because someone would lose sight of the person in front of him. Then he would take himself and the portion of the platoon behind him on an unscheduled and misguided tour. The integrity of the column would fall apart, and we would have to find each other in the high grass.

One afternoon, in an unusually thick stand of razor-sharp elephant grass, I lost sight of Jimmy ahead of me. Our rear security man, Denny, had lost visual contact with me, as well. I realized that I was becoming separated from the rest of the platoon, and I froze in my tracks. I listened for any sound that would direct me to the main body of our platoon. I could hear none. I swallowed back panic. I was completely alone and abandoned. I froze in place. I thought it best not to wander around aimlessly looking for the others.

After about five minutes I heard the distinct banging of two army helmets together. The sound guided Denny, me, and rest of the Lost Boys, as the ell-tee called us, back to the rest of the platoon. I never admitted that I'd been lost, but I could have kissed the ell-tee on the lips for getting me back into the fold.

Two days into this mission, I was, as usual, following Jimmy, who was carrying the machine gun. I was still the ammo carrier and sweating under the twenty-six pounds of deadweight. My status hadn't changed and neither had my assignment. If a firefight broke out, my job was to get the ammunition to Jimmy, no matter what, and help him if needed. I still hadn't learned to enjoy the erratic behavior of the cans. Thoughts of how I was next in line to give up the cans, and next in rotation to walk point, bounced back and forth between the pleasure and dread parts of my brain.

After midmorning break, we took our positions in line. I was second from last. Denny was behind me on rear security. Jimmy was third from last, directly in front of me. Enshrouded in the high grass, the rest of the column extended in front of us.

We had been humping for half an hour when Denny caught my attention from behind with a loud whisper. "Professor!" I turned to see what he wanted.

Denny was an even six-footer, and he was obviously disturbed by something happening in the tall grass to his right. Denny became more animated in his efforts to pierce the grass with his eyesight. Something was amiss.

I turned to Jimmy, who was now almost out of sight in the tall grass, and gave him a loud, "*Psssssssssss!* Jimmy!" But Jimmy didn't hear me. He'd continued walking. I thought about throwing a rock at him to get his attention, but I didn't see any handy at my feet.

Apparently Denny was hot on the trail of something. I turned back to let Denny know that the rest of the column was out of our reach. His eyes met mine. Denny's eyes had expanded to the size of hubcaps as he mouthed the word *gooks*. He pointed to the tall grass to our right. In desperation, I, too, tried to see through or over the grass. I simply wasn't tall enough.

Once again, I turned to where Jimmy should be. He was completely out of sight. Before I could even think about my next course of action, a shot barked. I hit the ground and twisted to face the same direction Denny was indicating that he was seeing gooks.

Denny was still standing. Following his single shot, he flipped his selector switch to rake and emptied his M-16 into the grass in front of him. Immediately, there was return small-arms fire. Denny hit the ground and started to reload.

By now I had my rifle off safe, ready to fire, but there were no apparent targets—only thick elephant grass. Then I heard feet running horizontally to my position in front of me. The sound had to be the enemy trying to scamper away. I opened up as the sound of one set of footsteps crossed my field of fire.

Silence.

Then another set passed, and I fired another burst, trying to gauge just where the target was and how far to lead it. I fired at sound, not sight. I reloaded again. Once again, I heard the sound of running through the grass. I raked the area with more M-16 bullets.

By now, Denny was spraying the area. I locked in another magazine and followed suit. Again, there was silence.

The rest of the platoon ahead of us had hit the dirt when they heard us fire and were squeezing off a few stray shots. They had no targets, and their reaction was halfhearted and bewildered. They were just trying to support us with noise.

The front of the column was at a loss as to what Denny and I were up against. We had no radio, and no way to contact the rest of the platoon. Jimmy crawled back through the grass and asked, "What is it?"

"I shot a gook!" Denny yelled to us.

"Where?" asked Jimmy.

"That way," and he indicated the area to our south and in front of us. "In the grass! Out there!" Denny was shaking.

"They ran in front of me, too! I don't know if I got any, though," I interjected.

Karate arrived on the scene. "What the hell is going on?" he demanded.

"We had gooks in front of us, and I got one!" Denny answered.

Karate relayed the information to Lieutenant James via the PRC-25 that arrived on the back of Thomas, the RTO for our squad. The ell-tee in turn called the battalion CP. We must have been the only contact in the area at that time, because he got the full attention of the command-and-control group. By then Lieutenant James had joined us and we heard ell-tee report. "We have one possible dead gook. And maybe some others. We aren't sure!"

Some command-and-control guy, mindful of the My Lai crisis where GIs in the Americal Division had fired up Vietnamese villagers, came on the net. He advised, "Don't shoot the individual if he is wounded! You can be court-martialed if you shoot a prisoner!"

Lieutenant James replied, "But, sir, he is in the elephant grass, and we can't tell exactly where he is or if he has a weapon. He could be playing possum out there. When we walk up on him, he could blow us away with a grenade! Break."

The higher-up, whoever he was, replied in his command voice, "Repeat. Do not shoot the individual unless he threatens you! Now sweep the area! Over."

By now, we had been joined by several other members of our squad. A debate broke out as to who, if anyone, should go see if the VC was dead or alive. "Hell, I don't know what to do," the ell-tee said. "I don't want to send you guys out there unless we recon by fire first."

"I think we have them on the run. Let's get on line and go get them!" I said. Everyone looked at me in astonishment. I was amazed myself at what I had just said. I had never dared to think that I would want to charge the enemy. Now I was eager to do so. I really wanted to kill some more gooks. For the life of me, I think that I had been overcome with some type of blood lust or temporary chemical imbalance. "Let's get them!" I urged again.

Calmer heads prevailed. Lieutenant James pushed the

button on the hand mike and yelled into it, "There! There they are! Fire! Shoot! That one's got a weapon! Shoot!"

We looked at him in puzzlement. Off the mike, he said in a less frantic voice, "Now recon the area with fire. Use the M-60 and the grenade launcher. If the Old Man says anything, we all saw something move."

We understood. We fired up the area to our south. As luck would have it, one of our M-79 grenades went off too close. Denny caught a piece of it in his shoulder. Since we received no return fire, we assumed that it was now safe to sweep the area.

Ell-tee James had shown courage, wisdom, and good judgment. We formed a line and headed out. First we covered the high grass where Denny had fired up the VC. There, stretched out on the ground, clad in traditional black PJs, was a body. Part of his skull was missing, but that was the only wound on his body. We turned to the right and swept through more grass, looking for bodies and blood trails.

During part of the sweep an earthen mound, remnants of an extinct red-ant hill, loomed up in front of me. I knew that I should fire as I walked over the top, but I was too embarrassed to pull the trigger. The others hadn't fired their weapons on the sweep, so neither did I. Basically, the lemming condition had hit again. I would recon by fire the next time, I promised myself. No need to take chances, and bullets are cheap.

We found nothing more. Attention turned to the dead VC and away from the area that I had fired up originally. I didn't really want to know if I had shot a gook. If I had, fine; if I hadn't, fine, too. I wasn't about to send a dead Viet Cong soldier home to have him stuffed and mounted.

A medevac was on the way for Denny. Karate and the ell-tee were making a search of the VC's pockets and pack. They started the touchy task of dividing up souvenirs. Denny had first choice. The VC had about three hundred dollars in MPC on him. The money could be claimed by Denny if he wished. He declined.

In a stroke of insight and charity, Denny proposed that

the money be given to a former Vietnamese Kit Carson scout who had been with the unit before I had joined the platoon. A Kit Carson scout was a reformed VC, or turn-coat NVA, who had converted to capitalism. They worked for Americans as scouts and informers. Papa-san John, as he was called, had been with the platoon when it had walked into the same booby-trapped bunker complex where Red had received his first wounds. Papa-san John had been crippled by the booby traps and he couldn't walk very well, so he bought a motorbike for transportation. The trophy MPC could help him pay it off.

Everyone applauded Denny's action. We wished him well when the medevac came to extract him. Denny wasn't badly wounded. He would rejoin us after he was stitched up.

The rest of us haggled over trinkets. I was presented with a plastic bag of some kind of tea. I did not recognize it as Lipton. Some of the guys said that it might be pot. I carried it for a few days, and then threw it away. I neither drank it nor smoked it.

Military intelligence claimed the Viet Cong's letters and wallet. Denny took them in with him aboard the medevac. I did get a look at the gook's wallet. Inside, he carried a picture of his wife and son. This was the last time I ever looked at personal material from an enemy body. It was not a good thing to do. Looking through personal effects humanized the individual too much. For survival reasons, I felt that it was better to keep the war on an impersonal level.

The reason that the VC was walking around with such a wad of money in his pocket was that he was a local tax collector for the Viet Cong. Records on his body indicated that this guy had been going from village to village collecting money, rice, and South Vietnamese sons of fighting age. In real life, he was probably not a very nice person. Why he had been walking at the front of his unit was a mystery. Another mystery had been how the other VC had been able to grab his weapon and get away with it, while Denny and I had been firing at them.

We moved off into the jungle after Karate booby-trapped the corpse with a hand grenade. If the VC's friends came back to retrieve the body without checking under it, they too would go up in smoke. We set up a night defensive position about seventy-five meters away from the body, in light jungle. All night we waited for the big bang. It never came. The next morning, we had to move; the stench from the body was horrid when the wind blew our way.

We moved farther into the jungle and set a night ambush. At two in the morning, we were put on alert. Sergeant Jefferies, one of the NCOs in second squad, whispered that he heard sounds outside our perimeter. We grabbed our weapons and awaited the enemy onslaught. A night firefight would have been wild, but nothing happened. We asked him what he had heard. The eight-month veteran described how he was certain that he had seen the silhouette of men walking down the trail. They were carrying radios. The radios had been playing the song "Sherry Baby."

Everyone questioned the tale, but it was a tribute to his past experience, expertise, and leadership that we stayed up the rest of the night. Such a story from any less an authority on military survival would have been immediately dismissed as a hallucination.

Once started, the delusions spread. One of our troopers convinced himself that he saw a gook sitting behind a tree smoking a cigarette. He was the only one in the platoon who could see the VC.

It was a weird night, one of those minor experiences that made sleeping in the jungle less than relaxing. We were all more than tired the next day, but not too exhausted to make Sergeant Jefferies the butt of beaucoup jokes.

So far our good fortune had continued, but Tet was still two days away.

CHAPTER 8

It Don't Mean Nothing

It was close to Tet, and all the VC and their buddies the NVA were coming into the villages to celebrate. As usual, we were in a free-fire zone, so any individual we saw was considered to be an enemy soldier, and we could fire him up. Friendly South Vietnamese were restricted from ranging out too far from their villages. Despite weariness from our all-night vigil with Sarge and the VC who were listening to "Sherry Baby," we moved closer to the scattered assortment of shacks. Our squad placed command-detonated claymores on the main trail leading into the village. Command-detonated claymores must be fired by a human; there are no trip wires, and they are not automatic. A grayish-blue detonation device called a "clacker" is the firing mechanism. These were the U.S. Army's version of the enemy antipersonnel mines I found in December in the VC cache.

The lieutenant put one man on the west and one on the east side of the footpath. Each man would be looking directly down the gook trail as it intersected our position. The rest of us formed a semicircle on the north and south sides of the path facing outward. This type of ambush, intersecting the trail, was different from the usual ambush set up alongside the trail. In the normal type of ambush, we just hid in the bush parallel to the kill zone and waited for an enemy soldier to walk down the path and trip a wire connected to our automatic claymore. That type of ambush was a no-brainer. But with the trail cutting directly through our ambush site, we had to be far more alert. The enemy could be on top of our position before we would notice him. On that particular morning, the grunts of Mike Platoon were not especially happy campers. There would be no card playing or writing letters home that afternoon. We had to stay alert or, at least, semiconscious.

A guy nicknamed Yellow Dog because of his big ears and blond hair (some code names were not really very kind) lay down behind a log on the side of the circle facing away from the village. On the other side of the perimeter, I hunched down behind a big tree. Jimmy, Jersey, and I were not too far away from each other. It seemed that every time I got too far away from Jimmy and the M-60, shit happened. That had been true on the morning of my first firefight and when Denny and I had jumped the gooks in the open field. Now I had become a wart on Jimmy's rear end. Where Jimmy and the M-60 went, I was not far behind.

We had claymores strung out down the trail in front of us, and I had the clackers laid out in order on the ground by me. We took turns alternating between being fully alert and watching the trail and being semicomatose. Boredom soon took hold.

Kaboom! A claymore from Yellow Dog's position shattered the air, our tranquil scene, and our nerves. *Kaboom!* A second claymore spoke.

Yellow Dog was in the process of blowing an ambush on his end of the trail. Since it wasn't my turn to watch the trail, I had been dozing. Once again, I was at the wrong end of things. All I could do was face forward and look away from the explosions. I had to watch my sector, the one that faced the village. Jimmy and Jersey turned the machine gun around, but that was of little use since they couldn't fire at the opposite side of the circle without hitting one of our own guys. We sat tight and waited. I sometimes wish that an objective observer could take a stopwatch and time periods such as we experienced. I never knew if they were only seconds long or if they were minutes. They always felt as if several hours had passed. A few M-16s cracked off several rounds, but there was no intensity in the firing. It was probably for show and to relieve anxiety. No one at the other end of the circle seemed to have a definite target. More silence followed. Lieutenant James quietly ordered the circle shifted toward the action. There was a general concern for Yellow Dog, who had fired the claymores from his position.

Everyone was relieved when Yellow Dog's blond hair and big ears appeared over the log he had been using for cover. He flashed us a sheepish grin. "I think I got one!" he yelled to those around him. "He's down the trail about twenty meters."

Part of the second squad formed up and swept the area he indicated. Sure enough, there was a dead VC. His AK-47 was beside him, and a small sack of food was half under him. He was dressed in black shorts, a light blue, short-sleeve shirt, and Ho Chi Minh sandals. He had been standing directly in front of the claymore closest to Yellow Dog. The claymore had literally made garbage out of the gook. The left side of the VC's body was bloody clothing, exposed organs, or gone. Most of his legs were missing. Pieces of flesh could be found, if one searched for them, everywhere down the trail for about twenty meters. Death had been instantaneous and gruesome. To that point, my experience with dead bodies had mostly been confined to pristine viewings at funeral parlors. Even the dead VC in the elephant grass had been almost whole. I'd never seen a human body look so distorted or grotesque.

The gook was dead, but our nerves were a mess. We needed a calming down period. Jersey wrestled the VC's bag out from under the disgusting body and searched it for military information as well as money and souvenirs. To our amazement, we found items in it that we had discarded at our ambush the night before. He had been following us and policing up our area. As prizes, he had collected two cans of Cs. Powdered-egg C rations were considered Number Fucking 10,000, and no one wanted them. From other discarded Cs he had gleaned small packets of coffee, cream, sugar, and hot chocolate. He had little packs of GI cigarettes that people like me who did not smoke just tossed away. All in all, he had a fairly good collection of our trash. It had been his personal treasure. The items would likely have been gifts to his family and friends at Tet.

The fact that he had cleaned up after us caused us to speculate that he was not one of the more prosperous members of the guerrilla movement. That conclusion was supported by the fact that he looked to be about fifteen or sixteen years old.

"I blew the wrong claymore," Yellow Dog said. "When I saw him coming down the trail, I got so excited that I grabbed the wrong clacker. I had them draped across the log. The furtherest one on the left and the closest one on the right. I forgot which was which. It didn't matter much. When I blew the first one, he was well past it. It went bang. He jumped around and looked down the trail to see what the fuck had happened. That's when I grabbed the other clacker and blew the one closest to me. Sure made a fucking mess out of him."

We all agreed. Souvenirs were few and far between, and no one was anxious to touch the body, so we did not booby-trap the remains. Instead, we put a Big Red One shoulder patch on the corpse as a macho reminder to the VC who would eventually find him that we had made the kill. Before leaving the grisly sight, I took a quick picture. It wasn't a "step on" kind. Sometimes a guy would have his picture taken with his foot on a dead gook. These were kind of a "Been there, done that" photo op.

We looked for a place to hide in the jungle. We now had accounted for two VC step-ons and seven dead-and-buried enemy soldiers. There were a lot of phony body counts in Nam, but of these stats, I am sure!

We spent the next day hiding. Then the command-and-control guys extracted us, and we were taken into a fire support base. The first night, I called Karen on the MARS radio. This connection worked through cooperation with shortwave radio hams (licensed amateur radio operators) around the world. We had to say "over" each time we stopped our portion of the communication, because messages could only go one way at a time. Karen had trouble getting the hang of it. Finally, I ended our conversation with the daring comment "I love you all. Over." I thought that I was being clever. The five-minute phone call made us both sad.

I had the chance to talk to Karen because we had been taken to a Thai base. Thailand had bought into the Vietnamese War, but the Thais thought it better to fight the Communists in Vietnam than in their own backyard. The American REMFs and Thai soldiers on that base had it great. Short-time houses were legal! Thai soldiers used the girls to boost their morale and income.

On the second night, we were told that the REMFs would show porno flicks, the silent 8mm kind, to anyone who would pay two bucks. Beer was also served at double the PX price. There was an overflow crowd. For the next three hours, we watched a makeshift bedsheet projection screen while tattooed guys in sunglasses and wearing one sock did some pretty sordid things to raunchy-looking, round-eyed women. I attended the film feature purely as another study in sociology. I wanted to note the reactions of my fellow grunts, of course.

When the last "actor" had shot his rocks and the show was over, I could not help but notice that only two people and a dog were left. I was one of the people, and the other guy had gotten so drunk that he passed out and threw up. The rest of our unit had either left for the Thai whorehouse or were in hootches writing letters home to their mothers, girlfriends, wives, former girlfriends, former wives, etc. I wrote Karen.

On February 9, we were trucked out to Firebase Dakota. We were supposed to resume operations in the field. Driving through the villages, we chucked C rations and candy to the kids who made the V-for-victory sign with their little fingers. During the entire time in the village, only one purple smoke grenade accidentally ended up in a Vietnamese shop. We grunts weren't really bad guys at heart.

As the day slipped by, it began to look as if the army had

screwed up. The choppers failed to show up, and we began
to believe that it was almost too late for them to come. Unfortunately, they arrived at twilight, and we had enough
time to load and fly to a landing zone in Indian territory.
We didn't have time to move very far from the drop area,
and that caused us concern because the VC would have
heard the choppers and would know pretty well where we
were. In addition, while in the rear area, some of our
number had overindulged on beer and weren't functioning
at their usual peak levels of performance. We moved as far
as possible off the LZ and split up into squads. Each squad
found a trail and set up a very hasty ambush.

Bravo Company had encountered heavy contact in
the area. We were all a little edgy, but the next day, we
settled into the routine of standing guard, reading, writing,
and sleeping. Some of the hard-core cardplayers revived
the poker game. At approximately 1300 hours, 1st Squad
popped an ambush. They were not too far from us, and
their spent rounds cracked over our heads. We all hit the
ground and hid behind two giant red-ant hills the size of
an office desk. The popping and cracking continued off
and on for about five minutes. We whispered jokes about
getting hit by our own fire. In an attempt at levity, I stuck
my hand over the mud protector and said, "Here give
me the million-dollar big one!" With that I stuck up my
middle finger and yelled, "And this is for you, Sergeant
Karate." More spent ammo zinged our way, and I jerked
my hand down.

"You don't seem to be real sincere about that wound,
Professor," Jimmy quipped.

Sergeant Penny was on the radio. He was getting a play-
by-play. He relayed what had happened to us. "Karate
says they popped a 'bush on a VC."

Penny continued, "They thought that they had him
dead, but he jumped behind a log. No one could get a good
shot at him, so they kept firing-and-moving on him until
Karate got close enough to grab him. Karate pulled him
out from behind the log and drug him out of the kill zone
and into the ambush site. They didn't see any other VC at

the time, but we should be alert. They may have chased some others our way. The gook was wounded in the leg and either was skinned in the head by a bullet or hit his head when he jumped for cover."

We all gathered around the PRC-25 as the higher-ups came on the net and talked with first squad. First Squad recovered the gook's AK from behind the log, and the medic treated the prisoner's wounds. Eventually, Cousin Charles revived and sat up. Immediately, he was covered with every weapon in the squad. He quietly slipped off his Ho Chi Minh sandals and offered them as a peace offering. A medevac helicopter had been called, and it arrived. The prisoner was bound and tied to a jungle penetrator to be lifted up to the helicopter. The poor guy nearly died from fright, because rumors had long circulated among the VC and NVA that one of the ways the U.S. and South Vietnamese intelligence officers loosened the tongues of enemy soldiers was to push one of their colleagues—or fake push him—out of a chopper. No wonder the guy was frightened.

The Viet Cong soldier was taken to a MASH unit where he got better treatment from Delta Company and the U.S. Medical Corps than he and his crew would have given to any one of us.

Just as it was getting dark, we received some bad news over the radio. S-2 had interrogated the VC. He indicated that he had been walking point for a contingent of seventy-five to eighty VC. They had been walking fast. He hadn't noticed the surroundings. That's why he got caught. Both our squads became alarmed. Since we were in squad-size ambushes, there were only twelve of us in each group. We couldn't join up with each other that day because of the failing light. I wasn't sure I wanted to join the men of the other squad anyway; they hadn't moved since the ambush, and their position had been compromised, not only by the ambush but by the ensuing Dustoff. It would have been better for them to join us, but they didn't know exactly where we were, and finding us could be difficult in the daylight we had left. So the ell-tee decided that each group would hold tight. The thought of eighty VC charging down on us at night made us all very jumpy.

During the day, we had talked endlessly about the rumored pullout of the 1st Infantry Division. After we found out what our POW had to say, we dropped that subject and began to dwell on the fact that we could be attacked that night. I really let the topic get to me. I was more frightened than I had ever been in Nam up to that point. My mind played and replayed every piece of information we had heard. The captured VC had said that there was a VC base camp not three klicks from us. It was protected by a stream and a wooden bridge. It was inhabited by hard-core VC and NVA. The more I digested those facts, the less I digested my dinner. I was becoming completely paranoid. I was convinced that every VC in that camp had to be coming our way!

Kaboom! At about 0200 hours the automatic claymore outside our perimeter exploded. The claymore was situated to our front and out about thirty meters. We all jumped up. As usual, it had been my turn to sleep, so once again, as with my first firefight and the ambush outside the village, I was rudely awakened. Grabbing our weapons, we peered into the darkness. We listened. Nothing. Then double nothing. The creatures of the night listened with us. Back in the States, I had never heard a classroom that quiet, even during a test. I almost hoped for a sound. But there was triple nothing.

After a long and intense period of silence, the creatures of the forest assumed that everything was okay. The mosquitoes returned to their buzzing, and the other creatures commenced their nightly choruses. A fuck-you lizard seemed to lead the way. A fuck-you was an amphibian whose nocturnal cry sounded exactly as if it were saying "Fuck you" to the world. Most of our squad began to calm down. I didn't; I was really hyper. We whispered among ourselves that no one had heard any movement before the explosion. After the explosion, no one had heard any cries or moans from a wounded animal or man.

It was too early for my turn on guard duty, so I went to

sleep. Well, I went back to lie down. Sleep was impossible. Every sound was magnified. Soon I even began to think that the fuck-you lizard was Charlie taunting us. I tried to remember if I had heard it before the claymore went off or if it had started afterward. This screwed up my mind to the max. When my guard duty came, I was an emotional wreck. I just knew that seventy-nine of the eighty VC were out there sneaking around waiting to overrun us. I spent my guard duty thinking about Karen and praying. Both helped only a little.

After I was relieved at the radio, I went back to my poncho liner. It was about 0400.

I was exhausted from my deliberations. In desperation, I dug down into my pack and found some Bufferin. I swallowed three of them. I knew the Bufferin would help me sleep. In a sense, I was almost sure that I was committing suicide. I felt a little ashamed that I was not staying up and worrying us through the rest of the night. But I thought, Hell, they might as well kill me in my sleep. As it is, I won't be worth anything tomorrow anyway. Maybe I won't feel the pain of dying if I'm zonked. Those thoughts were really stupid, especially when coupled with trying to remember if the fuck-you lizard had been calling from the tree before the automatic ambush had gone off. Sleep came and, almost instantly, so did the dawn.

Our camp stirred, and I snapped alert. I noted that I was not dead. A whispered argument was taking place. One fire team proclaimed that they had set up the automatic ambush and that it was the other fire team's responsibility to see what had tripped it. I joined the argument and reflected that our fire team didn't know exactly where to look. It was a lame attempt. The claymore had been set up just outside our position. One would have had to be deaf not to be able to mark the spot. Our argument about placement was also weak because it would be found where the jungle was blown away, an obvious landmark. Nevertheless, we seemed to be more persuasive, and the fire team that had placed the claymores capitulated.

We formed up. I took rear security. I didn't envy the

point man. Out he stepped. Denny was on point. As each man joined the train, it became obvious that the line of men would stretch from the ambush site all the way to my bedroll. The claymore had been so close that we could get a column of twelve men, two or three apart, to span the distance between the ambush and our sleeping positions. I had not realized that the claymore had been so close. Now I was really gorking down bile in my throat.

The report came back up the line. No dead VC. No dead animal. A limb had fallen from a tree and had hit the trip wire. In essence, I had spent the night worrying about an act of Mother Nature.

That excursion was the highlight of the day, and I hadn't even left the area of my poncho. I had stood on it and watched the column snake its way down the hill. I was exhausted. So was everyone else; no one had slept well. We spent the rest of the day in more peaceful pursuits. The readers read. The cardplayers played cards and quietly argued. The sleepers slept. The eighty VC stayed away.

About noon, the captain called on the radio and told us that the interpreter who had interrogated the captured VC had made a mistake. There had been three VC, and they had been walking seventy to eighty meters apart. That was a big difference from eighty VC walking three meters apart. The captain seemed almost jovial in his apology for the screwup.

I celebrated with a C-ration pound cake. For icing, I mixed peanut butter and grape jelly. The purple goop tasted great. I marveled at life and more than once thought, And fuck you back, lizard!

Our mission lasted six more days. As always, the U.S. Army provided us with an itinerary for our daily tour of Vietnam. Each day, we had a day's worth of jungle to cut through. A day's worth of wait-a-minute vines to trip over. A day's worth of trails to follow. A day's worth of heat. A day's worth of SOS, same old shit. In short, a day's worth of constant aggravation and frustration. But there was no contact, so we chalked up each day as a "good" day. It was during that time a unique occurrence took place.

On the fourth night, we moved into the nightly perimeter late. With all the jungle we had trampled, we should have been able to find a better place, but we were not picky. We had been humping through patches of thick bamboo. Everyone sported sores from obnoxious bamboo thorns. All we wanted was a safe place close enough to an enemy trail to look as if we were on some sort of ambush. It was getting dark when we selected our final perimeter area. We quietly moved into a small clearing and began to set up the perimeter defense, put out the claymores, and send out three-man groups on observation or listening posts. All that took just a few minutes. We were experts, and we were hungry. Sometimes, even a meal of C rations can be a motivator. During that time, we began to notice that the area that we had chosen and where, barring extreme difficulties, we would stay the night was infested with daddy longlegs spiders.

I've never really considered daddy longlegs to be part of the spider kingdom. They had always seemed one of God's more gentle and awkward insects. They were non-threatening. Not like praying mantises or walking sticks, harmless creatures that look vicious. Not like the black cockroaches in my childhood home that cracked and squished under my feet when I got out of bed in the middle of the night. Daddy longlegs spiders had always been fun to play with. Of course, I remembered hearing somewhere that they are the most poisonous of all spiders but that their mouths are so small that they can't bite a human. But the ambush area was *covered* with daddy longlegs. By covered, I mean there were literally thousands. It was the mother of all daddy longlegs nests. Every daddy longlegs in the jungle had come to that convention spot to meet and, I guess, to hold a mating orgy.

At first they seemed just an irritation. They crawled all over the rucksacks, but it was fun swatting them and flipping them at other people. Not a few went up in smoke, the victims of cigarette lighters. We enjoyed watching them walk up our arms or legs. But some of the more sensitive members of our platoon felt the same way toward daddy

longlegs as I did toward cockroaches, and they began to
freak out. They voiced strong objections to our ambush
site. Unfortunately, we were too deep into the evening and
the night's preparations to reestablish our situation, so we
just had to gut it out until morning.

Eventually the novelty of the situation wore off, and
even the most ardent supporters of the not-move opinion
were beginning to change their minds. Maybe daddy longlegs are nocturnal creatures. I don't know. I do know that
their numbers increased in direct proportion to the amount
of movement exhibited in their area. Soon they covered
everything and everyone. No one had less than three or
four spiders on him at any one time. No amount of swatting, flipping, or cussing could keep them off.

They crawled in slow lumbering strides into the middle
of the can of C rations that you were eating. They walked
on your toothbrush if you left it on your rucksack for a moment to find some toothpaste. Daddy longlegs got into
personal places when one answered nature's call outside
the perimeter. Now, some people might find the dainty
footsteps of a daddy longlegs crawling on one's buttocks
alluring, but most of us just did not.

"Don't let them crawl into your ears," I admonished
those around me. My mom had often talked about how
cockroaches crawled into the ears of boys who fell asleep
on the floor and did not go to bed when they were told.
Some of us stuffed our ears with toilet paper. Not a good
idea during an ambush in the jungle when you could not
see anything and depended solely on your hearing, but it
did keep the damned spiders out of our ears.

The worst, the very worst was guard duty. During the
two hours that it was my turn to stay awake, I usually
fought off only sleep, mosquitoes, loneliness, and boredom. But the invasion of the daddy longlegs added a new
dimension to sitreps that night. The little devils were all
over me. When I detected the movement of tiny feet and
the breath of movement on an exposed portion of skin, immediately I would swipe the spider off. A few minutes
later, another one would take its place. After a while, I

began to feel for spiders, and none would be there. But I felt them anyway. I just *knew* my clothes were covered with spiders that I couldn't detect. Revulsion set in.

Sleep was a little better. Wrapped up in our ponchos and poncho liners, we felt that we were safe. Yet the buggers often breached our defenses. If they can crawl in ears, would they not crawl up your nose? I fretted.

Disgusting! It was a fitful night, and by morning, we were more than ready to move out. As early as we could, we saddled up and got started on the next leg of the mission. We started, that is, after emptying every can of bug spray we had on the daddy longlegs enclave. Each grunt took one part of the clearing and on command commenced to take his revenge. Several cans were emptied, and those who did not have cans of bug spray squirted mosquito repellent from plastic bottles. It gave us joy to watch the turmoil and confusion. We didn't even mind that some of them ran up our legs. We were getting our evens.

I don't know if any humans have passed by or stayed in that particular small glade in Nam since that evening, but if they did or if they do, I'm sure the descendants of those daddy longlegs will seek revenge. When Nam fell to the North Vietnamese a few years later, I felt many shades of disappointment about not stopping the spread of Communism. Yet, on the other hand, the VC and NVA could keep a country that was so filled with rats, daddy longlegs spiders, maggots, termites, mosquitoes, snakes, and other miscellaneous creatures. The gooks may have won the war, but what they won wasn't worth it. If they had been smart, they would have let us win. I'll bet after the war, when they took a good inventory of their gains, they realized that there was really nothing worth having.

Three days later, we took resupply, which included an above-average amount of bug spray. I received life-renewing letters from home. More and more rumors circulated that the 1st Infantry Division was going home. The rumors had it that one or two GIs who had a month or two left in country would take the division colors home. The rest of us would not go home, since it would cost too much to send us home and then replace us. We would just be transferred to another combat unit already in Nam to complete our tour of duty. During that three-day period, there was little to do, so we gossiped about reassignment. We read the *Stars and Stripes* and tried to guess which division would claim us.

No one wanted to go to the 101st Airborne, the Screaming Eagles. "They are up north and you don't even *want* to go there. They fight the hard-core NVA," Jimmy said. No one wanted to go south and work the Delta either. "Walk in mud up to your waist every day. Beaucoup leeches. Jungle rot your feet. Stay out of the south," Jimmy instructed. No one liked the prospect of going to the Americal Division. "They got problems over there." Again Jimmy was the source. The 1st Cavalry Division was only "okay" in his book. "Too many helicopters. They get to the trouble too fast," was Jimmy's sage advice. Other divisions and other areas of Nam evoked other learned opinions.

I had come down with a cold. Maybe it was from the nights of seventy degrees that were chilly compared to days that registered one hundred plus. The cold wasn't in itself a big thing, but piled onto all the misery, it was the last straw.

I spent a lot of time writing Karen and my parents. I always used letter writing to keep my sanity. After reading letters sent from home, I burned them. I usually kept the pictures of Karen in my wallet, but that would only work until they started to stick together and had to be destroyed. A valentine from home was a special treat. I had thought myself clever to have gotten one in Lai Khe and to have sent it to Karen with instructions not to open until February 14. Karen was a college graduate, and I think she knew it was a valentine.

February was slipping away. Occasionally, we heard another platoon or company in our area blow a 'bush on some of the enemy. A couple of times, we were guided to blocking positions in the hope that the VC would run into us. It never happened; sometimes they would scare up a wild animal or two.

One time, we were working with a Kit Carson scout, a former VC who had converted to the good guys' side. We just called him Papa-san due to his age and the fact that none of us could pronounce his real name. One day he was walking second in line and pointed to the ground beside the trail. There was the spoor of a cat. We assumed that he meant a house cat, which in itself would have been rare because we had been told that the Vietnamese ate cats, but we realized that he meant a leopard. The spoor did not seem especially fresh. Still, we all got a little more nervous.

Another time, we were walking along a VC trail looking for signs of life when he started laughing loudly. Since none of us spoke above a whisper, we immediately shushed him. He continued his boisterous laugh.

"What's going on?" Sergeant Penny demanded.

"VC too scared to shoot!" he stated in broken English.

"What are you talking about?" we all gathered around and asked.

"We just walk through VC ambush!" he stated with triumph in his voice. "VC way back there now. They *didi mau*'d!" And he made a wide gesture with his hand.

We all looked at one another in disbelief. None of us had seen a thing. Papa-san told that story several times to others. We never did know if it was true. But if it was . . .

It seemed that during the latter part of February and the last few days that the Big Red One remained in Nam, we stayed in the field longer and longer. Maybe it just felt that way because we were all so anxious to get to the rear and try for a REMF job when we changed units. Everyone had some scheme up his sleeve. Some guys swore that if they were reassigned to a division up north they would re-up (re-enlist) for a door-gunner position on a chopper. Others were going to plead sick, lame, or crazy. Some were too short of time to ever see the boonies again.

I kept saying that I could type. Also, I thought I would have my teeth checked. That ought to take a day or so.

Then there was my ankle. It was actually stronger than it had been at any time in the past six months, but I still needed to have it X-rayed to be sure. I could miss assigned transportation. Maybe I could lose my paperwork or 201 personnel file. Anything to get good time in the rear was fair game. At the very least, in the new unit I would refuse to carry the M-60's damned ammo cans.

"I'm too short for this shit!" Jimmy yelled over the sound of the helicopter blades. We had just been picked up in a clearing and were on the way to act as a blocking force for a platoon from Alpha Company that had gooks on the run again. It always seemed that Alpha would find trouble and then get us involved. At the Bob Hope show, they had been the company that received all the honors for chasing away the VC who had been trying to set up a rocket attack on Lai Khe. We had been unceremoniously stuck in the mud, so to speak. That day, we were out to help them once more.

Jimmy was especially concerned. He calculated that with the change in divisions and a little slack time, he might not see the field again in his life. All he needed to hear was that we were in hot pursuit of some VC. Jimmy's feelings paralleled those of the rest of us.

To make matters worse, the door gunner told us that we were going into a hot LZ. "It's under fire!" he had informed us as he locked and loaded the M-60 machine gun mounted in front of him on the chopper. He would lay down suppressing fire for us as we jumped from the chopper and headed for the bush. Everyone in the chopper was dead silent. We watched the door gunner for information and instructions. His downward gesture indicated that we were going into the clearing. Sitting on the deck of the helicopter, I would be the first one out.

I leaned out of the chopper to get a better view of the clearing and an orientation of where the enemy might be hiding. November Platoon was on the ground ahead of us. They had already off-loaded in the clearing and were in the jungle cover beside it. If they were under fire, we had to—just had to—go in after them. I saw the clearing ahead. To my astonishment, the clearing was not *under* fire, but *on* fire! Red flames covered 50 percent of the grassy area. In the minute it took for the helicopter to reach the ground, I had my camera out and snapped a picture. I needed to record this one for my personal history.

The helicopter hovered, and the door gunner shouted, "Get out!" I hit the ground running, or at least lumbering fast under my load of sixty-plus pounds. I was carrying M-60 ammo, M-16 ammo, claymore mines, hand grenades, C-4 explosives, and a variety of other semiflammable, inflamable, or just plain explosive materials. I didn't need to be urged to get out of the flaming elephant grass.

Immediately, I headed for the tree line by the route that contained the lesser amount of flame and heat. I was sure I would explode or be engulfed in flames. I don't think I ever ran with such agility in my life as I wove in and out of lanes of grass and fire. Each step of the run required an instant calculation of flame location versus ability to get around it or through it.

I made the tree line and collapsed. At that point, I may have taken my first breath since I had unassed the chopper. November Platoon had set up a perimeter and was protecting us. Mike Platoon was a disorganized mess. It took us a good hour to assemble ourselves. No one had been burned, although several of us had been toasted a little. After a period of recovery, November took point, and we followed.

Further inquiry produced two accounts of why the LZ had been on fire. November ell-tee said that the VC had set it on fire to trap them in and us out. Our lieutenant thought that when someone in November Platoon had thrown out smoke grenades to mark the landing zone the grenade mechanism had set the dry grass on fire. Either way, we were glad to be out of the clearing. Despite a valiant effort to catch any VC in the area, none materialized, and we continued to count down days until reassignment.

Word came that Delta Company would help tear down a firebase that the Big Red One was about to abandon. This had the sound of "good time" to me. We hadn't seen much in the way of action, other than the confrontation with the daddy longlegs, and we were getting a bit careless. When the order came, we were about three hundred meters from a medium-size clearing that would serve as the pickup point. A very short walk for a change. The choppers were scheduled for 0900 hours, but that fell through. Then 1300 hours was set, but that, too, came and went. Finally, we were all beginning to worry that we would have to spend another night in the field. We had been dumped on more than once in the last few days, what with the attempt to barbecue us on the LZ and late supplies, so when we were told 1600 hours, we were not entirely sold.

We were ordered to "be ready." Needless to say, we had been ready all day. Now we really had time to kill. Since the clearing for the pickup was so close, we didn't want to move that way until the last moment. All we had to do was walk down a Viet Cong trail that we had used twice before. It would be a piece of cake.

"Come on, Professor, play some cards," a group of poker players coaxed. "Come on. We're going in soon anyway. Maybe you can win some money."

I knew I wouldn't win a dime and could in the flick of an eyelash lose all the cash I had with me. I rarely carried much money in the field. There was no need. The U.S. Army graciously gave me everything I required to maintain body and soul. I had played cards only once before with those guys, to be friendly. It had been a game where the pot grew and grew until someone had a great hand and won big bucks. It wasn't my luck to win that time. Those guys were professional cardplayers, and I knew it. I kept myself and my money out of their league. It seemed that the Kit Carson scouts could beat the GIs in Vietnamese poker, a three-card game, but then the scouts would lose the grunts' money to South Vietnamese soldiers on the fire support bases. Some of the GIs thought the only reason that Papa-san and Duo, his Montagnard sidekick, came out on a mission was to fleece them at cards. My money had never been and never would be part of that Southeast Asian economic cycle.

"You too, Jimmy," they said. Jimmy saved a lot of his pay to send home and didn't play cards, either. I think he may have either been very smart or a Baptist.

We both respectfully declined the offer.

The ambush site went really stale. We had read all the paperbacks we'd brought along. Letters to loved ones at home had been written. Nothing seemed to hold anyone's interest. For all practical purposes, the mission was over, and we were tired of ambushing that piece of jungle real estate. The cardplayers broke the dullness with a proposition. "Let's play a game of hearts. Professor, do you know how to play hearts?"

"Well, yes, I do. In fact, at the frat house, I was considered quite good."

"Okay, Sigma-whatever, let's play hearts, okay?"

I agreed. Denny, who had lost a good deal of money to Papa-san, plugged an earphone from a transistor radio into his ear, sat down, and leaned against a tree. He opened a romance novel to a well-read sexually explicit section and declared that he would watch the trail and the ambush kill zone. I sat down on some sandbags we had filled and camouflaged and began to play hearts with the boys. "Not for money!" I declared, and they didn't seem to balk. It was fun, and as we got more and more into the game, even the most disgruntled gamblers began to enjoy themselves. I was beginning to have visions of a Delta Company hearts tournament and eventually a bridge club. "Next time," I mentioned, "we might play old maid." I made the suggestion in jest, but several of the gamblers nodded in serious agreement.

We must have played at least ten hands when Denny rasped in a hard, urgent tone, "Jimmy! Jimmy!" We all looked at him and then, in unison, at the ambush area. There in the middle of our kill zone was a Viet Cong soldier. He was walking from our right to our left, or roughly east to west. As one, we all hit the dirt. Denny flipped the selector switch on his M-16 to rock and roll. He sprayed the kill zone. Because he was still sitting with his back to the tree, he was in an awkward shooting position. The radio jack in his ear and the wire connecting it to a transistor radio tangled him up, too. That particular stance wasn't one of the standard firing positions for the M-16 taught in basic training.

He did scatter nineteen bullets in the general direction of the VC. Jimmy couldn't get to the machine gun in time. I had no idea where my M-16 was. When I had seen the gook, my first reflex had been to dive behind the sandbag barrier we had erected to conceal us from the trail. I landed on top of the radio and the claymore wires that we had tied to it for safekeeping. The VC had hit the dirt and was returning fire. I looked down and realized that I could blow the VC from here to kingdom come by firing the right claymore wire. But I was lying on a tangled mess of wire and clackers.

I frantically searched through the maze of wires for the one that should fire the claymore directly in front of us, where I had last seen the VC walking before I'd hit the dirt. The wires were a bird's nest, and I realized that I couldn't find the right one.

The captain and the CP group were closer to the clearing than we were, and when they had heard the firing, they came on the PRC-25 and demanded to know what was happening.

It seemed rude to have the captain urgently firing questions into my chest, so I picked up the handset, pushed the talk button, and stated in my best controlled military voice, "This is code name Professor. We have sighted a gook and are firing him up!" With that I found what I thought might be the correct claymore wire and clacker. I flipped off the safety and fired the thing. It wasn't the right one. Dirt, rock, wood, and jungle debris went up in smoke to our right. The gook took off to our left. Frantically, I searched for another claymore to blow. By now, the VC had disappeared into the jungle to our west. I blew another claymore in the fleeting hope that it would at least pepper his behind.

"What's going on?" the captain demanded again. "I blew a claymore on the Charlie, but he is in the jungle breaking bush and headed in your direction." It took every ounce of control that I had in my body to sound matter-of-fact about the transmission. I wasn't accustomed to talking on the radio and certainly not versed in giving a play-by-play of a firefight over one. I always forgot to say "over" when I talked on the horn, and there was a long period of silence. "Over," I interjected.

"Good, Professor," the captain replied. "Sweep the area and keep me informed. We'll watch for the dink on this end. Be careful! Break." And he was gone.

We formed up and swept the kill zone. As always on a sweep, our hearts were in our mouths. We found nothing. Denny swore he would have had him if he had not been reading and listening to the radio. I swore I would have blown him to Hanoi if I hadn't been playing a damned game of cards. Short-timers in the squad swore that they were "too short for this kind of shit." And I'll bet there was a young Viet Cong soldier hotfooting it through the jungle swearing that GIs were "number-fucking-ten thousand-capitalist pigs." Jimmy did not sweep the kill zone with us but had stayed in the ambush site with the M-60 to fire over our heads if we needed it. Upon our return, Jimmy pointed to the sandbags that had protected our position. There were gaping holes where AK-47 bullets had entered. The VC had fired at least a magazine at us. The sandbags had protected me while I had been talking to the captain and trying to find the right claymore to blow. Had they not been there, I would have been shot in the head.

We all felt dejected that Cousin Chuck had gotten away unharmed. We had been careless and knew it. I reaffirmed my stand on card playing. I would never play a game of cards while in Nam again. Neither would I forget the fleeting glance I had of that Viet Cong soldier as he walked the trail with his gun at the ready.

Too soon, we had to saddle up and walk down the same-same trail the VC had used to the pickup point in the clearing. We were not anxious to go the same way the VC had gone. Thoughts that he might be waiting in ambush for us filled everyone's mind, and the conversation turned that way. The fact that the captain and his entourage weren't happy that we didn't have a step-on didn't help much either.

Jersey took point, and in his damn-the-torpedoes-and-full-speed-ahead fashion, we made it to the pickup point in very good time. It was a matter of debate, especially after the earlier incident with the Saigon Tea girl in Lai Khe, whether Jersey was very brave or very stupid. He certainly didn't recognize a dangerous situation when it presented itself. In this case, no one objected to his taking point.

The lift arrived and took us back to Firebase Rhode Island. The fire support base was alive with excitement; the 1st Infantry Division was really going home, and the REMFs were as busy as ants. They had a million and one chores to do as they prepared to transfer men and matériel to other divisions.

Each of the 11Bravo20 grunts hoped to be part of the packing process and thus stay in the rear area for as long as he could. Maybe, we reasoned, we could even snooker a rear job with a new unit. At best, we each hoped that we could get lost somewhere in the confusion of the transfer. Many grunts demanded to see a doctor, dentist, or chaplain. Some demanded to see not only those but everyone or anyone they thought might help them secure a safer position in the rear. Every grunt in our company wanted out of the field. I kept telling anyone who would listen that I could type.

We pulled perimeter on Firebase Rhode Island for two days and then hit the bush again. Our instructions were to make one more big push for the good ol' Red One. Send the colors home in glory with more enemy kills. Bullshit! We hid most of the time and contemplated our impending separation from the Big Red One. I was surprised. Everyone seemed to detach from one another. We turned inside ourselves and pursued individual thoughts and dreams of the future.

When we did move, we moved slowly and cautiously. One would have thought that the war was about to end and that no one wanted to be the last casualty. That was pretty much true. We didn't want to take any chances that could end up in disaster before we had a chance to rotate to a new unit and maybe secure a REMF assignment.

During that time, we worked the rubber. That is, we walked through rubber-tree plantations. The rubber was always neat. It was really quiet and really orderly. The trees were in perfect lines, no matter what direction one looked. Unfortunately, undergrowth had sprung up in many places, and our view was sometimes obstructed. There were no VC in the area, so we entertained ourselves in various ways. I took to cutting red ants in half with my Swiss Army knife as they walked up the rubber trees. I hated the red devils, and anytime I could do them some harm, I was up to the task. Their relatives had bitten me and other members of the platoon so many times that it was impossible to count. They might be on leaves or hiding in the grass. Their bite was like fire, and anyone who has been bitten by one knows that they truly deserve to be called fire ants.

Jersey and Denny alternated walking point. I preferred Denny on rear security; Jersey was too unpredictable. One day we were on an excursion through tire-making country, and Jersey was walking rear security when he started playing with the pin in a hand grenade. "Psst, Professor!" I turned around and there he was, pin in one hand and grenade in the other. The pin was so badly crimped that it did not fit back into the proper place in the top of the grenade. "Help me get this back in," he pleaded. In disgust, I turned to Jimmy and caught his attention. Jimmy stopped the rest of the platoon and walked back to see what was the problem.

Words couldn't describe the look on his face when he saw what Jersey had done. He was really angry. "You go over there and put that pin back in," he demanded. "Professor, you come with me. Let this fool kill hisself!" Together we walked away. The safety wire that helped to hold the hand grenade handle down was still in place, but he couldn't straighten the cotter pin and insert it back into the grenade. Jimmy continued to swear and cuss. He wasn't about to help Jersey, who had gotten himself into a touchy situation through sheer lack of gray matter. Finally, the ell-tee and Sergeant Penny came back and decided that they would take a pin out of a smoke grenade and use it in the hand grenade. If the smoke grenade went off, it would not be as much of a problem. Sometimes, Jersey did really goofy things.

Finally, the word came. We were going in for good. We would hump to an airstrip by an obscure village named Duc Than. From there, we were to fly by fixed wing to Lai Khe and then on to Di An. From Di An, we would be reassigned to our new units.

I looked at the pocket calendar I carried. I had cut the months of December and January out and sent them home to Karen as a present. Now I cut out February and enclosed it in an envelope. It was February 28, and February was done. I looked at March and decided to enclose it in another envelope. I was sure most of March would be wasted in transit to my next unit.

I now had three months in the country and was a seasoned veteran. I had earned the Combat Infantryman Badge and had been recommended for a Bronze Star. I had experienced several close calls, and I had learned a whole lot about jungle fighting and the VC. I felt confident that I could walk point if need be and that there was little that any new unit could ask of me that I could not produce. After finding the enemy cache, I was pleased with my small contributions to the United States war effort. After all, I hadn't signed on to win the war by myself. I hadn't cracked under pressure, and even though at times I'd been very frightened, in most cases I had acquitted myself modestly well. If I had not been as aggressive as I might have been in certain situations, I chalked it up to being prudent.

I had been praised by others. I had my own personal war stories to tell to the members of my next unit.

Our final order was to hump to the airfield, our last mission as part of the legendary 1st Infantry Division. We spruced ourselves up and almost marched out of the jungle. We covered about seven klicks and moved from rubber trees to grasslands and onto a dirt road. We were not in a free-fire zone anymore and could not shoot unless fired upon. We walked a dirt road for another klick and became covered with red dirt and dust. Sweat poured from every pore, and we looked a mess when we made the airstrip. There to our delight were clean clothes and a hot meal. And if that were not enough, some REMFs had set up canvas shower bags on three-legged poles. We formed a perimeter and took turns drawing water from a mobile tank we called a water buffalo that had been airlifted out to us. This was REMF first-class service. The tank had been in the sun all day, so the water was warm and wonderful.

The local inhabitants had turned out to greet us. They weren't a happy, cheering, liberated people who appreciated us as freedom-fighting allies. We were money and meat on the hoof to them. Little kid-sans tried to sell us semicool sodas and hot sisters. Short-time went for five bucks a pop; we were under orders not to fraternize, and no one did. Modesty gave way to cleanliness, and we showered in the open. Since the local villagers did not have any 8mm porno films to watch, we provided the local females with a good look at real US of A manhood. Some of the guys had tattoos and may have taken showers in the sun wearing their sunglasses, but I am sure everyone removed their socks.

The plane arrived, and we struggled aboard. We had given away our C rations, water, and other items to the villagers. Our hearts were as light as our rucksacks as we looked forward to the reassignment period. The future was still only a day away.

CHAPTER 9

I Join the Cavalry

We were flown to Di An, the rear area for the 1st Infantry Division. My stay with Delta Company, 2d of the 16th Infantry, 1st Infantry Division, was about to be terminated. Our company settled into wooden barracks and real bunks with real mattresses. We were given steaks, beer, and letters from home. The REMFs even arranged to show us three-year-old movies at a makeshift outdoor theater. Seeing Hollywood films reminded us of home and the round-eye women we were doing our tour in Nam to protect. We were issued clean clothes and had to pay a mamma-san to sew on our names and ranks so we would look good and military for the REMF brass who inhabited the rear regions. We had turned in our weapons, and therefore, we didn't have to stand night perimeter guard. Short-time girls made appointments with our guys in the showers. The girls swore that they didn't have VD and that their husbands had been killed by the Viet Cong. I'll bet they could have sold Delta swampland to the Disney Corporation for future real estate development.

I started to spend a lot of time waiting to use the MARS line to call home to Karen. I spent hours waiting in line. For some reason, the connection could be best made at night on our side of the world, so I lost hours of nighttime Zs. I usually made them up during the day. It was a topsy-turvy life, but I enjoyed the change. When I did contact Karen, it was heaven to hear her voice. We could only talk for five fleeting minutes, and since there was someone on the circuit flipping switches every time we said "Over," there was little privacy. Over the phone, I boldly told Karen to start taking birth-control pills and to prepare to meet me for R & R in Hawaii in May. I was getting optimistic as well as horny, and the month of May didn't seem that far away. I was very anxious to be with Karen, and every time one of the guys returned from the showers with a tale of Oriental delight, I became more anxious for Karen's body. Exercising great moral restraint, I used the showers only for hygienic purposes and to dream of May and Hawaii.

I noticed that once we hit the rear area, our close-knit platoon broke up into factions. The blacks all formed soul-brother groups, and the heavy boozers started to buddy up. A few potheads emerged, and they sought out REMF dopers and soon were zonked. I can truly say that until that time, I hadn't seen any of our guys do any dope in the field or on a fire support base.

I was kind of the odd man out. I didn't short-time, get drunk, blow smoke, or take part in any other form of self-abusive recreation. For that reason, I was one of the suckers who was lying on a bunk reading a paperback when a REMF captain came to our barracks and recruited volunteers to be in the ceremony retiring the 1st Infantry Division colors. We reluctant volunteers were given starched uniforms and rifles without ammunition. In an effort to get us to look really military, the captain and an E-7 sergeant rehearsed us in drill exercises. Most of us had forgotten how to march in any kind of order, and we were halfhearted participants who didn't really want to reacquire past proficiencies we'd just as well forget. Finally, the captain did get us lined up in front of a reviewing stand containing some VIPs, brass, and media. Some generals or such began to give speeches, and the media covered them on film. The ceremony took place in the heat of the day and soon grunts began to faint. One guy passed out and, on his way to the ground, managed to ram up his nose the blade sight on the M-16 of the person standing next to him. It tore a big gash in the poor guy's nostril, and several

GIs had to carry him off the field. He may have been the last casualty the Big Red One suffered in Nam.

Then other people fainted, some from the heat; some faked it. The generals and VIPs wisely cut their posturing short and ended the ceremony. We all went back to the barracks and cold sodas. I felt a little ashamed that I hadn't played a bigger part in the exploits of the 1st Infantry Division in Vietnam. I had listened halfheartedly to what was being said, and it did make me proud to have been part of the tradition the 1st Infantry Division had stood for over the years. The Big Red One had kicked some Viet Cong and NVA butt. It seemed to have been a good unit. At that time, I didn't have anything to compare it to. I just looked forward to reassignment to my new unit, whatever it would be, and eventually to the Freedom Bird that would take me home to the real world.

My new orders arrived too soon. I had never seen the army more efficient. We had been in Di An for only three days, and already I had been reassigned. I was to join the Sky Troopers! I was going to the 1st Air Cavalry Division! Now I asked to see the doctor to have my right ankle checked out. Permission denied. I asked to see the dentist. Permission denied. "Take care of these matters when you reach your new unit," I was told. That sounded okay to me, so I didn't push it. There would be time when I reached the 1st Cav.

When it came time for the jeep to take me to the Chinook pad, no one was around to say good-bye. Jimmy was with the blacks listening to soul music, Karate was at the PX, and others were scattered all over the compound. Some of the guys were getting their tubes cleaned in the showers again. As I left the barracks, I waved farewell to a few remote acquaintances and just left. No Hollywood parting took place. I hoped that someone would miss me sooner or later.

I arrived in the Cav's rear area and was rushed through in-processing. The REMF clerks must have been told that either we hit the field or they did. In two days, I was out of there. Permission to see doctors and dentist denied. "You should have taken care of that at your last assignment," I was told. I sensed that the army had just pulled one over on me . . . again.

My chopper landed in Song Be, a small village in Phuoc Long Province in the Central Highlands. It wasn't far from the Cambodian border, and north of Nui Ba Ra, one of the Black Virgin mountains. Nui Ba Den, its sister mountain, was farther to the south. It was a tribute to how well things were going for the United States in Vietnam in 1970 that we were able to pull out a major infantry unit and still feel confident enough to extend the war to the frontier area in the western part of the country where the major Viet Cong and North Vietnamese regulars held forth. All that after the 1968 Tet offensive when we supposedly had been kicked. I think that we were on the brink of victory, and with less negative media hype and less of Jane Fonda's support for the enemy, we could have "won" the war then and there. It was obvious from the large finds of enemy weapons and supplies that we were cutting deep into the VC and NVA heartland.

Of course, all that relates to the "big picture." I was more interested in a personal snapshot of the big picture. My original assignment was to the 5th of the 7th Cavalry, but that was changed in the Cav's rear area. I was reassigned to Headquarters Company of the 1st of the 8th Cavalry. I was euphoric! A headquarters company was a REMF unit. They do paperwork and get supplies, anything to support the grunts in the field. At last my true talents had been recognized. I would be good in a safe and secure support role.

Along with several other grunts, I caught a chopper out to Song Be as soon as possible. I didn't delay for fear that they would give my REMF job to someone else. I found the 1st of the 8th's rear area and reported in. Words cannot explain my disappointment when the eagle-beaked headquarters clerk informed our group of replacements, "We assign everyone to headquarters. Then we reassign them in line companies once they get here." With that, he handed us our new unit assignments. I was to be a grunt again.

I walked across the red dusty company street and poked my head into the Bravo Company tent. The sun was bright, and when I first stuck my head through the tent's open door flap, I couldn't see into the darkness. My nostrils detected a whiff of pot. Someone was smoking shit in the back. Three of the other new recruits who had also been assigned to Bravo Company pushed into the darkness behind me. A voice from the back of the tent questioned, "Who are you guys?"

"New guys," I replied. "This is Bravo, isn't it?" New guys was an inappropriate term to use.

"Oh, no, FNGs!" came the reply.

My eyes had become accustomed to the darkness, and I could make out four GIs sitting in the back of the tent around a makeshift table. They had been playing cards. I was pissed, really angry, at their reply. I was angry about not being in a headquarters company. I was angry about humping again. I was pissed about smelling dope. We'd had very little of that stuff in my old platoon. I was just generally in a bad mood when I shot back, "Not fucking even! We are from the Red One come to help you ladies kill some dinks!" I no more had the words out of my mouth when I started to regret my brashness. But a general murmur from the other replacements bolstered my confidence. Two of the three guys behind me were true cherries, but I was sure as hell not an FNG. I was a fucking combat soldier, and they were probably REMFs. So stick that. What could they do to me? Put me in the infantry? Send me to Nam? Make me walk point?

One of the group left the table and came forward to have a look. None of the men had on shirts, and sweat ran down his chest and stomach. The heat in the tent was oppressive.

"All right, let's see what we've got. Show me your papers." Since he was not wearing a shirt, I didn't know if he was an officer or not. I handed him my papers, and so did the others.

"Get them on the guard duty roster," came a jeer from the table.

"I'm Michaels, the company clerk, and I'm getting short. I'm so short I need a ladder to climb into my boots in the morning. Welcome to Bravo Company. We'll get you some gear and show you around. You will be on guard duty on the berm tonight, and tomorrow, I'll get you some transportation to the company. They're in the field."

We spent the next few hours learning the lay of the company area. The 1st Cavalry mess halls held the same culinary appeal as did those in the Big Red One, so that seemed an even trade. We were assigned M-16s and field gear. The equipment was similar to that used by the Red One except that they didn't have the two-quart canteens that doubled as both water container and pillow. No provision was made to zero in our rifles. They were just handed to us. That was really bad; the rifles we were assigned could have shot anywhere. The sights might not have been true. In a way, it didn't matter. I hadn't ever had to worry about accurate shooting, because up until that point I had used the rifle only to spray. Pinpoint shooting in the jungle was rare. Still, I would have liked to have had time to zero in my M-16.

After we had our gear squared away, we sat down to talk with the company REMFs. They were mostly people who had been in the bush and because of merit or lack of time left in country had been rotated into Song Be to help with the war effort from a rear-end position. In most cases, they had paid their dues and were a source of real information. We new guys wanted to hear about the company—how it worked, where it worked, what kinds of missions it performed, what the guys were like, what the captain was like, and on and on.

Each of us tried to glean some scrap of information that would give us an edge. Was one platoon better than another? Did they work jungle or was the AO open? Did they go into villages a lot? Was the company due for a stand-down soon? One of the true FNGs had already told Michaels that he wanted to re-up for a rear job. He wanted to spend one more year in the army and be reassigned to some kind of cook's job. During our brief relationship, I had found him to be obnoxious. Remembering my first guard duty with Commo Guy, I suggested he reenlist to be a field wireman.

The information we received wasn't heartwarming. Bravo Company worked out of several firebases around Song Be. The village of Song Be was located on the Song Be River in Phuoc Long Province. The firebase protecting it was called Firebase Buttons. Song Be and Buttons were about forty miles from the Cambodian border. The surrounding firebases were even closer to Cambodia. The 1st Cav bases were positioned to protect the Central Highlands and stop the infiltration of Communists down the central corridor of the country and into South Vietnam's capital, Saigon. Cambodia was a major resupply and sanctuary for the Viet Cong and North Vietnamese Army. They would hit across the border and scurry back to the staging areas in Cambodia. A system of trails called the Ho Chi Minh trail ran roughly north and south close to the area to our west. One firebase was within BB gun range of the border.

The bad news continued. We would be fighting hardcore Viet Cong, and more important, we would be up against North Vietnamese regular troops. They were tough. They would "fight you all day and come back again the next day," we were told. "Bring your lunch when you hit those bastards." That was really scary news. I was more accustomed to the skittish VC around Lai Khe and Long Binh. Contacts had been short and quick. Even though we had taken some casualties, I felt that we had kicked their butts a lot more than they had kicked ours. But the NVA sounded bad!

The good news was really good. My new company and the whole battalion put the cherries on point. This meant that the guys with the least amount of experience in country would walk first in the column. On the surface this was really poor. The standard philosophy was that a new guy's life was considered less valuable than the life of someone who had put in his time. Even a little time in country made that person short or shorter than someone else. Quickly, we new guys compared our time of entry into country. I was senior over one other guy by two weeks. We were both senior over the two other recruits. They were true cherries just off the plane from the World. The news that they would walk point didn't comfort them. I felt sorry for them, but not enough to volunteer to take their place. That is, unless I was going to be handed some of those damned M-60 ammo cans to carry.

The Bravo REMFs and I spent about two hours telling tales. I got all my Big Red One war stories in, and so did the other veteran. The FNGs sat quietly and listened.

That night on guard, the new guys and I talked some more. The cherries hadn't pulled a perimeter guard, so we sat up into the wee hours of the night and talked about stuff. They anticipated the horror of the next day's flight to the field. I guess I calmed myself down as I tried to soothe their fears. I know that I silently thanked the Big Red One for not putting FNGs on point. Even though I had carried the M-60 cans, the Red One experience had been good for me. I had become acclimated to the jungle, and had learned most of the techniques of jungle warfare.

I had learned about myself as well. I made myself a promise, one of these promises that is so sincere that it is etched into your soul. I wasn't going to carry the M-60 ammo cans again. I would carry the machine gun, or the M-79 grenade launcher, or even walk point, but I had made up my mind that I would not take on that weight again. I was quits with the fucking M-60 ammo cans.

The sun came up on March 11 as it had on most Vietnam mornings; it was a red ball through a hazy horizon. It held the promise of a superheated day. Everywhere in Nam, Americans yawned, scratched, and marked one more day off their short-timer calendars. Our guard detachment was relieved and wandered back to the Bravo Company area. We cleaned up and went to the mess hall for a hot meal. Cav cooks didn't do SOS for breakfast any better than Big Red One cooks. They had the same

training and used the same recipes. Creativity wasn't a
strong point with army cooks.

All morning, we lounged around in the back of the company tent. We didn't go into the tents behind the office
tent; they served as living quarters of the REMFs. I
watched the company clerk, the company mail clerk, and
the company supply sergeant go about their daily business. Each had a set routine that he had to perform. The
work didn't seem to be very hard, and the danger was relatively minimal. I envied them their positions. I did mention several times to the company clerk that I could type,
and that I would be happy to help him with his office work
if he needed anything done. He declined the offer. I guess
he didn't want any competition for his job.

We would join the company as it received resupply in
the field, so the supply sergeant was in a state of panic to
get all the necessary equipment, ammunition, food, and
assorted indispensable items assembled. We were part of
the consignment. Around noon we were taken to the Song
Be chopper pad, and when an available log bird (general-
duty helicopter) came in we were taken to the battalion
firebase.

This firebase was located somewhere to the northwest
of Song Be and closer to the Cambodian border. When we
disembarked, we were greeted by some kind of command-
and-control freak, an E-7, who assigned us a bunker to
guard. We sat on the bunker all day and all night. It was
"good time," since there was no action or harassment. On
12 March, we were again escorted to the firebase chopper
pad and placed on a resupply lift that was going out to the
company. Despite my apprehension about going out to
the field, I did enjoy the flight. There is something special
about a helicopter flight into combat and the unknown.

The pilot located the hole that the company had literally
carved out of the triple-canopy jungle. There were no nice
open fields or paddies there. The helicopter hovered at
about two hundred feet, then started its descent straight
down into the opening. I'd never been on a helicopter
going straight down a chimney before. As usual, I was sit-

ting on the floor on the port side of the chopper. I had let
my feet hang out over the side so that I could watch the
countryside glide beneath my boots. At about fifty feet, I
reached up with my right hand and grabbed onto the door
frame of the chopper. I stepped out onto the chopper's
ground skid. I rode the slick down that way—gun in one
hand and one hand holding on to the handhold. I gave a
good John Wayne impression.

As the chopper hit the ground, so did I. Ducking under
the whirling blades, I headed for a group of grunts protecting their faces from the dust and dirt blown up by the
chopper's blades. When I reached them, they pointed me
in the direction of the captain's CP. I followed their directions and arrived at Captain Roy's position on the edge of
the clearing. He had watched my gung-ho descent and
must have thought me some kind of eager beaver or West
Point graduate.

"Spec. Four Schneider reporting for duty, sir," I yelled
above the noise of the chopper.

"Go get those other people and spread them out over by
those trees. We'll get to you guys after we secure this resupply," he said, and almost as an afterthought, "What's
your name?"

"Schneider, sir, Schneider!" I turned around and headed
back to the drop point. The slick had been off-loaded and
was cranking up to take off. The wind from its downdraft
kept me from making much progress. When it was sufficiently airborne, I went over to the new guys and told them
to follow me. We squatted down behind some cover, and I
positioned each of them so that he was facing out. Several
members of Bravo were in front of us, and we had little to
protect. We just sat there on alert, ready in the event that
something happened when the next resupply bird arrived.

The cherries followed my direction without hesitation.
They were frightened. The other transferee from the Red
One looked at me like "Who the hell appointed you God?"
but he followed my directions.

The captain, lieutenants, and 5-Mikes (resupply coordi-
nators for each platoon) were busy distributing matériel,

so we were placed on the back burner. I accepted that as standard procedure, and having been in the field, I understood priorities. I also knew that sooner or later some lieutenant or sergeant would come over and claim each of us as his prize.

Another bird came in, and more men and matériel were off-loaded. The men ended up by me, and I dispersed them. Some of them were back from R & R and various other functions in the rear, and they reported directly back to their former platoons. Curiosity forced one of the sergeants from the platoon directly in front of us to wander over to get a preview of the pickings. Between log birds, he sat down by us, and we commenced to talk.

"I'm short! I'm so short that last night as I was sleeping an ant pissed on my head," he said. "I've got six-one days and a wake-up. I've got seven days' leave in Bangkok between now and then, and I'll stretch that until it's time for me to do my last thirty days in the rear. Once I get my leave, I'll never see the field again. All I've got to do is stay alive until R and R. I've got a wife and a job at home. Which one of you guys is my replacement?" He looked inquisitively at our group. No one said anything. I was the oldest person crouched in the group, so he directed his next question to me: "You an E-5?"

"Not even," I replied. "I'm a schoolteacher turned grunt for nine more months, and I'm out of here!"

The look he gave me was one of astonishment. I was used to people finding it humorous that I was a former schoolteacher, so I was immediately on the defensive. I already knew that he was going to say, "With your education, what are you doing here?" I had heard that line all too many times, and I was still not short enough for even a giraffe to piss on my head.

His reply caught me off guard. "I was a teacher, too!"

We stared at each other in amazement and almost hugged. "What are you doing here?" I asked before I could stop myself. It was the first time I had had the chance to use that line, and it kind of slipped out.

What followed for the next half hour was one of those

get-acquainted conversations. "How did you get here? Where are you from in the States? What subject and grade level did you teach?" and on and on. We exchanged information about ourselves. His name was Chris, and he had been drafted when his rural Iowa school district had merged with another school district. As the social-studies teacher with the least seniority, he had been bumped from the job and into the army. He had married before coming to Nam and had attended NCO school to upgrade his rank to reduce his time in Nam. The reduction hadn't worked, but he would DEROS Vietnam and ETS the army at the same time. He had been promised a position in the new consolidated school district when he returned.

Our talk wound down, and he ambled over to a meeting of the NCOs, ell-tees, and the CP group. The horse-trading session had begun. After about twenty minutes, the captain came over and assigned us to platoons. "Schneider, you look like you're strong; you go with Chris and his heavy-weapons platoon."

My heart sank. I was very pleased to be assigned to Chris's platoon, but the term "heavy weapons" sounded ominous. What the heck did the U.S. Army consider a "heavy weapon"? I almost asked, "How heavy, sir?" but I had the good sense to bite my tongue.

The other new arrivals were divided up among the other platoons. Since it was getting late, we gathered up our resupply, destroyed any excess, and headed for a hiding place in the thick jungle. We moved out in three lines or columns. One platoon on point, and my new platoon, designated 4-6, walked second. Two other platoons followed. I'd never worked with such a large group of soldiers. The biggest unit I had been in with Delta Company in the Red One had been when Mike Platoon had Delta's captain and his CP group join us for an operation. At that time, we had numbered approximately thirty people. Now I was walking with a contingent of about 100 to 120 men. I loved the companionship. Going from platoon and fire-team size to company size was very different.

First of all, we seemed to be noisy. A large group of

people tends to make much more noise than a smaller group. But the Cav group seemed to be clumsy in the bush. Second of all, most of these Cav guys slept on air mattresses. They were surprised that I used only a poncho and a poncho liner. My old platoon had never used air mattresses because they made too much noise at night. In addition, air mattresses constantly leaked air. I considered them hardly worth the effort to carry.

The "heavy" part of the heavy-weapons platoon was that they carried a 90mm recoilless rifle. It looked like a five-foot hollow metal tube and was as bulky as the M-60 ammo cans had ever been. It wasn't a pleasant weapon to cart around the jungle. Basically, it was to be used to fire HE (high explosive) rounds at tanks or bunkers. In the Red One, we had used LAWs (light antitank weapons) for that. The 90mm recoiless rifle—affectionately called a "piss tube"—could fire beehive rounds, shells that contained about two thousand small darts, or flechettes. They would fire at any advancing enemy and could put out a world of hurt. Unfortunately, the 90mm recoilless rifle had a back-blast area of about forty meters and could kill anything or anyone to its rear. Since we usually set up in a circle, the backblast aspect made it almost useless. The captain and the CP were directly behind us. I didn't know if I liked the new CO yet, so I kept the backblast option in mind. Accidents do happen. In any case, we didn't ever use the recoilless rifle and later replaced it with a small 60mm NVA mortar. Standard procedure was that the person carrying the tube also carried a .45-caliber pistol. This made me feel a little more like John Wayne. In truth, the .45 would be useless in most cases. It just felt good on the hip. Besides, I always thought that I looked macho wearing it.

I was also told that 4-6 would never walk point. Our duty was to pull security for the captain, to take ammunition forward when it was needed by the point element, and to bring back wounded or dead as necessary. All in all, this didn't seem like such a bad situation. Immediately I wrote Karen and informed her of what could be considered "good" news.

A ten-cent military payment certificate (MPC) of the kind used in Vietnam to hinder black-marketing. For obvious reasons, the small bills were frequently referred to as Monopoly money.

Chieu hoi leaflets were dropped in areas where VC and NVA were thought to be. A soldier displaying a *chieu hoi* leaflet was not to be shot or otherwise harmed. Displayed above is the front side of one such leaflet. The verso has a long text in Vietnamese explaining the rules of surrender.

Members of 4/6 Platoon on patrol in the waterfall area east of the Cambodian border.

The author checking out the entry to an NVA bunker in the Central Highlands.

An NVA tunnel leading to a storage area.

Interior of a very well constructed NVA bunker in which we found an arms cache.

Arms cache: AK-47s (top), a 60mm mortar round, a couple of B-40 rounds, and other equipment.

Members of 4/6 Platoon receive supplies dropped in white water balloons: C-ration cases and, most important, mail from home. The author is in the background with a letter in his hand.

What the grunt took to the office on a typical day: "the tube" (90mm recoilless rifle), personal M-16 rifle and ammo, plus assorted items in the rucksack.

The author popping smoke (goofy grape) to mark a landing zone for helicopters.

Sitting on the floor of a helicopter and dangling your feet as it flew above the jungle was great sport.

The rubber plantation in the Big One area of operation.

Exterior view of a bunker on the berm at Song Be.

Bunkers at Fire Support Base Judy after a monsoon rain in the Central Highlands. The bunker at right, in the berm, was the killing ground for rats.

The author, as the Bravo Company clerk, posing with a sniper rifle.

Max and the author in the Bravo Company area.

Crossbow and the author—when they were still friends.

I spent the next few days in the field learning how to work in company-size operations and developing friendships. I swapped stories of the exploits of the Big Red One. I even kept them semitrue.

Late one afternoon, as I was setting out claymores for the evening defense perimeter, I had the opportunity to find another cache. After setting three claymores so that the printing, THIS SIDE TOWARD ENEMY, pointed away from our position, I looked around one more time to be sure that I would recognize where they were the next day when we came to collect them. I also made a mental note of the fire zone in front of our position. I thought I discerned a small bunker or low hut another twenty-five yards farther out in the jungle undergrowth. I told Schacker, one of the guys in my new platoon, to cover me, and off I went to explore. Inching my way from tree to tree, I began to make out a small hut covered with bamboo, and I could see cans of gook ammo strewn around. My heart jumped to think that I'd found another cache. Not this time. The cans were all empty. I did take one of them back to the perimeter and showed it to Chris, who took it to the captain. I am not sure that I got credit for the find. In any case, the ammo dump didn't appear to have been used recently. After a few fruitless days in the bush, we went into a fire support base to guard the artillery.

Bravo Company celebrated March 17, St. Patrick's Day, wearing green. Everyone in the area had on green, except the VC, who wore black and lacked a sense of Irish tradition and humor.

On 19 March, we went out on operations again. This mission didn't get off to a very good start. We'd been told we would be lifted out at 0900 hours. The lift didn't appear. Then we were told we would be picked up at noon. That lift didn't appear either. By 1400 hours our company was well cooked by the tropic sun, hot, tired, and pissed.

Some high-echelon lifer type used his personal chopper to pay us a visit as we assembled on the helicopter pad. He had come out to cheer on "his boys." We didn't feel much like anybody's boys. He started off wrong. "Well, it sure looks like a good day to kill us some dinks! I'm proud of you boys, and we're going to kick some ass on this mission! Huh?"

No one seemed to want to confirm his enthusiasm. We'd been told that there had been a lot of contact in the area where we were headed and that Alpha Company had sustained a KIA and six guys had been wounded. We grunts knew that any gook ass-kicking would be done by us while he flew around in a command-and-control chopper calling for support and assistance. I knew that choppers did get shot down, but I would have changed places with him in a moment.

He tried again. "Well, is there anything that you guys want or need?" was his next attempt to boost our sagging morale. A chorus of "A trip home! To get out of this place! A round-eye woman," and a thousand other grunt quips followed.

One smart-ass Sky Trooper piped up. "No thanks, Colonel. We got everything we need. We even have a machine gun that won't fire. We can throw the damn thing at the zipper heads." This remark was on target. Third Platoon did have a machine gun with a weak firing spring. It jammed quite often. They couldn't seem to get a replacement part. The theory of humping it into the field was that they would get resupply after three days and that the spring might show up and then could be inserted into the gun at that time.

Well, that remark set him off. The colonel cursed and swore. He got on the horn and turned red. Off went his personal helicopter. Soon it was sighted flying toward us over the trees in the distance. It came to a screeching halt on the pad. Out jumped some REMF in starched fatigues. He threw a big salute to the head man and handed him an M-60 spring. The big guy took the spring and gave it to the 3d Platoon machine-gun team.

We perked up. Hey, this guy was getting things done for us. "Now, you guys need anything else?" Well, we could have gone through the round-eye-white-woman-and-a-trip-home routine, but now we got serious. It was silent while everyone desperately sought something in their minds to request. Some quick wit or alcoholic offered, "Sir, we haven't had our rations of beer and soda while we have been on this here firebase."

This was true as well. The army supposedly rationed two beers and two sodas per trooper per day. We hadn't gotten any and this, too, had added to our general state of dissatisfaction. The colonel picked up the PRC-25 and called heaven or whomever he knew. His helicopter took off again. A little while later, it was inbound at top speed. We got to our feet and started screaming and yelling. The bird landed, and there was a load of beer, soda, and ice blocks.

In Nam, ice was a rare and precious commodity. Ice was transported in great big long sheets four feet long and a foot thick. The beer and sodas could be iced down by placing the cans on the ice and spinning them. Some kind of heat or cold transfer would take place. Whatever the scientific principle is, it worked. The beer or soda cooled down after being spun.

The same REMF jumped off the pile of cases of beer and soda and started to help unload. He was sweating bullets, and his starched fatigues were now soaking wet and limp. I bet he put himself in for an Air Medal after all that action. The company mobbed the REMF, the beer, and the ice. It does take a few moments to spin a beer until it is cold enough to drink, and there was a limited amount of space to use for the maneuver, so many of the guys just broke out church keys and commenced to chug. Many bragged that warm or cold, they could outdrink anyone in the company.

I rolled a beer or two and drank along with everyone else. I couldn't do the warm beer bit in spite of the fact that we Germans are alleged to be warm-beer drinkers (actually, we're cool—not cold—beer drinkers!); it isn't a genetic trait I inherited from *das Vaterland*. I took a couple of sodas and put them in my rucksack. I didn't really want to hump them, but I figured I could carry them for the rest of the day and drink them that night. I might even be able to save one for the next evening's treat. It didn't take much to make me happy at that point in my life. I knew that if I kept the sodas wrapped up in my poncho liner they wouldn't get hot. They wouldn't be cold, but I had learned to drink warm soda. It wasn't nearly as yucky as warm beer.

As a washed-out astronaut who had turned to studying and teaching history and English because I lacked brains enough to do mathematics, I was seeing a good lesson in inverse proportions in front of me. Our company was experiencing one of those algebraic equations that is difficult to solve from a textbook, but easy to understand in real life. The more beer that went down, the higher our morale went up. We were actually transforming into ass-kicking Sky Troopers right there on the tarmac. Now we were looking forward to kicking some gook butt. The Old Man had done us good. Word came that the eight-chopper lift was inbound. That news created a surge in drinking, and the chugging suddenly took on serious proportions. Two-handed drinkers emerged. When the choppers arrived, there were enough to carry 1st Platoon and our 4-6 group. We were to be the first element inserted into the LZ.

In the air, things began to disintegrate. Schacker turned green. Gomer barfed in his helmet. I teased him that he might have to wear it if the LZ was hot. Other guys didn't look or feel too good. The motion of the chopper and the booze took their toll. The helicopters landed in line, and the heavy-weapons platoon fell out. I realized then that Chris and I may have been the only sober people in our unit. First Platoon was in worse shape. They staggered to the tree line and set up security for the next platoon to come in. We tried to follow.

Schacker never made it that far. He was a lean six-footer, but he was so sauced that he just got off the chopper and stood there until it cleared the field. He took one end of the 90mm rifle tube and put it against his forehead. The top of his forehead fit into the tube's opening. Using the tube as a support, he upchucked beer. "Go on without me—" he almost got out before the next wave of nausea hit him. I picked up his pack and someone else got some of the other equipment scattered around, and slowly, one person helping the other, we limped to the tree line.

The line platoon was there, and some were in good shape. Not everyone was drunk. But enough people were that we could have held a substantial alcohol-abuse clinic. The platoons that followed were in much the same condition if not worse, since they had been able to drink more while the choppers had been in the air inserting us. The mission had been for Bravo Company to hump off the LZ and go kill some VC. Now Bravo Company couldn't move. We labored to get a little distance between the LZ and our final night position, but it wasn't very much. We stayed about two hundred meters from the clearing.

That night, I realized the seriousness of our state. Sure it was funny to laugh at those who were vomiting up their insides; that is just good sport anytime, anywhere. The problem was that we were supposed to be quiet and pull off ambushes, but there was just no way that could have happened. I guess we were lucky that someone didn't shoot himself or someone else. Booze and guns, hand grenades, claymore mines, and plastic explosives make for a hazardous situation. Niner-one Quack—the term given to almost any medic, I discovered—distributed what antacid tablets he had.

I volunteered for LP, or listening post, that night. This meant that I would be about twenty-five meters outside of the company perimeter. Two other guys and I were to listen for the enemy. We were the early warning system for the company. A new guy, named Candy Sergeant, and Scooter were with me. All night long, we heard the company moaning, groaning, and barfing. It was really scary and really funny. The next morning was also a rip.

As the sun came up, our company was sleeping off the ill effects of the night before. We were one sad bunch of grunts. Those of us who were useful talked about how delicious our C-ration powdered eggs tasted. The campsite, for it would be stretching it to call it an ambush site, was a mess. It smelled like vomit. Yet no one seemed anxious to leave. Eventually, the company got body and soul together, and we started off through the jungle toward some military objective.

Again, I wasn't privy to the grand plan for the operation. It didn't matter much since I was just a tagalong anyway. We didn't move far, then we stopped. We sent out a patrol, and nothing happened. Then we moved on. We took a break about noon. By then, most of the guys had the hair off their tongues. An hour later, Bravo began to move again.

We crossed a small stream and were generally headed up a slight incline of thick jungle when we got hit by PRGs, automatic-weapons fire, and AK-47 fire. The company went down. The firing came from the left front and the left side of our column. That was where I was walking. I hit the ground and returned fire. I didn't even think. I'll bet my weapon was off safe and firing on the way down. The intensity of the enemy fire was the greatest I had yet experienced, and it all seemed to be coming at me or at least into the area around me.

Three grunts who had been walking directly in front of me took cover behind a big tree. Heedless of everything around me, I continued to pour fire back at the enemy. I had a brief thought that I could stop the insanity if I could just shoot enough bullets back at the bastards. But then, I needed to change magazines, and the naked factor struck. Once a new magazine was locked and loaded, I felt as if my pants were back on. I must have gone through four magazines before the rest of the company opened up. I hadn't realized that I was doing a one-man show on my part of the perimeter while they scurried for prime cover.

I was accustomed to hit-and-run VC fighting. Previous contacts had only *seemed* to last a long time. But that fight was, in fact, *actually* lasting a long time. These VC and NVA weren't running, they were ready to hold a rumble that would last all day. When the company opened up, it was a marvel to behold. I had thought a platoon could put out tremendous firepower, but that was nothing compared to a company of one-hundred-plus men pulling triggers in anger. A solid curtain of lead flew out at the enemy. How anything, human or otherwise, could have survived that horror I don't know. But the gooks did, and they gave it back to us. An RPG feathered through the bamboo. It exploded not far from the big tree, and the three people behind the tree ducked and cringed. Hot pieces of lead flew up into the air, and some landed harmlessly around me.

Basically, I didn't have any cover, not even bamboo to obscure my silhouette. There were several trees about an inch or two in diameter in front of me, but no real protection. I was down in a little depression, but it offered little protection. After the company started returning fire, I looked around for some way to improve my situation. Nothing presented itself. I really wanted to join the group at the tree, but a quick evaluation showed it was a three-man, not a four-man, tree. A fourth person would have been dangling outside its range of protective cover. Because of their fire and the fact that the RPG had struck so close to them, I considered that they were marked, so I stayed where I was. A gook machine gun seemed to fire from off to the left of my position, so I buzzed a magazine over that way. I saw nothing and just fired at the sound of the incoming gunfire.

After a little while, the firing from both sides quit. It was as if both sets of adversaries needed to rest and to listen. I could hear the captain and the field artillery observer (FO) calling in artillery, Cobra gunships, and resupply. What I didn't know then was that they were also calling in a medevac. The captain's RTO had been shot in the head. The bullet had gone right through his helmet, and he'd never known what hit him. People said that Teddy was a good guy, and although I didn't know him, I hated to see any American hurt or killed. Teddy was the first KIA I had ever seen. Looking back over my shoulder, I watched the medic try to wrap his head. It was a gruesome sight.

The artillery arrived with a marking round first. The FO adjusted the range, and the redlegs (artillery) got down to some serious blowing the crap out of the jungle. Once again, I don't know how the gooks could survive under such heavy explosions. The ground shook. I do know that some of the enemy stayed and buzzed us with bullets every once in a while.

Then the Cobra gunships came on station and worked out. The snakes may not have had any specific targets, but they sure could lay down fire. They hit the dinks with rockets, miniguns, and grenade launchers. It was reassuring to have that kind of help.

A resupply helicopter showed up and was just about to dump out some ammo when the gooks opened up on it. We fired back, and the helicopter gave us a hasty drop. We were almost out of M-79 grenades, and we greatly appreciated the M-60 machine-gun ammo. I still was astonished that there were any gooks left to fight. Yet there were. The NVA had brought sack lunches and intended to make a day of it. When the medevac came in, the enemy still hadn't had enough and shot it up. Each time we tried to medevac out the KIA, two slightly wounded, and another guy who had hurt his back when he fell, the gooks opened up on it. That was poor sportsmanship in my book. Each new crescendo of AK-47 and automatic machine-gun fire sent new dread and foreboding into my heart. "Why didn't these guys just go away and leave us alone?"

The fixed-wing aircraft came on station, and now they began to blow more hell out of the jungle in front of me. Pieces of metal hit the trees all around, and small hot particles landed on my back. I remained in my position. The Kit Carson Scout next to me on the left had crawled up and begged for more magazines of M-16 ammo. I gave him three and saved the last four for myself. The ammo resupply hadn't yet reached our part of the perimeter; others were replenishing their personal supplies first.

During one of the lulls, I examined the immediate area. One of the small trees in front of me had been hit by a bullet that blasted a path through the bark. So I could trace where the bullet had come from. By the angle I knew that some of the gooks had been shooting down on us from the trees. I reasoned that if I put the muzzle of my M-16 on the tree and slanted it in the same angle as the incoming bullet, I might be able to get a gook sharpshooter. That is if, after all that time, he hadn't been blown out of the tree by the artillery, the gunships, or the fixed-wing aircraft. Maybe he had been wise and *didi mau*'d back to Uncle Ho; he had no future in that tree. In any case, the gunfire had been quiet for some time, and I didn't want to stir up anything.

The medics and others finally moved the RTO's body to the rear of the area and it was airlifted out. The captain told someone to pick up the RTO's gear and hump it. He appointed another person to be his radio operator. There wasn't a rush for that position. The company broke off contact and moved off to the east of our original line of march. All the RTOs bent their antennas down and tried to blend into the environment. Bravo Company moved off to find some thick jungle where it could lick its wounds.

CHAPTER 10

Mortars, Maggots, and Maybes

The Bravo Company felt it had been through hell. We had sustained one KIA and, if you counted the guy who wrenched his back, three wounded. A rumor circulated that one of the grunts had experienced a ridiculously close call because two bullets had ricocheted off the sides of his steel pot. Even though he hadn't been physically hurt, he was in a state of shock.

We moved off into the jungle. I didn't envy the point men in the lead platoon. Walking in company file meant that we were walking three abreast and had three point men. The enemy could have slipped in and set up booby traps anywhere on our perimeter. The point men would be the first to feel the sting of a vengeful adversary. We moved along gingerly.

The firefight had lasted seven hours, and we were all exhausted. I had even dozed off during one of the lulls in the firing. It seems impossible to understand, but sometimes at the end of a very dangerous situation, people would fall asleep or disconnect from life for a while. Although not a recommended action, it happened.

When we reached a section of the jungle that seemed safe and defensible, we set up for the night. No one needed to be encouraged to dig a deep foxhole. The ground was hard, so we took turns digging and resting. That night, we huddled around the hole and ate cold Cs. The other members of the heavy-weapons platoon teased me in a good-natured way.

Schacker poked fun at me by saying in a hushed voice, "Professor, you looked like you were going to win the war by your own self today. It didn't look like you needed any help."

Scooter said the same, and that is why he had looked for cover while I was firing. I confirmed that I'd been trying to hose down the enemy fire, but I doubted that I killed anyone. Chris said that at the evening briefing the captain had asked who I was.

My curiosity caused me to inquire more about the gooks we had fought. I didn't like the answer.

"Those were hard-core NVA we were up against out there. Straight down the Ho Chi Minh trail to save their VC brothers from American oppression. They don't run from much. We shoot the shit out of them, and they still don't run like the VC do. You're in the big-boy war now. Not that simple shit around Bien Hoa," said J. B., who had been carrying the tube that day.

"That's why they transferred you to us from the Big Red One," added Gomer Sanderson, our hillbilly wit. The ribbing made me feel accepted. I liked it. I knew I would have to cut out the "This is the way the Red One did it" stuff. I was getting back a little of my own medicine.

There was never much getting used to contact. The first shots always caused a stabbing, hurting feeling. The noise seared through one's body and mind. It was usually sudden and shocking. Quick evaluations of how much fire and from where raced through one's mind. When the evaluation was complete, the mind had an estimate of the amount of personal danger present. This was a sort of fear quotient.

Anyone who has had a near miss in a car accident knows the feeling of sudden terror. The racing heartbeat and the sweat. Amplify that same feeling repeatedly, over and over again, for an extended amount of time, and the feeling of being in a firefight starts to emerge. Some of the reaction may be the body's physical response to danger, and some may be mental response. No one ever got used to it. Reflexes and instinct take over. Luck also plays a major part. Like any gambler, someone in combat tries to make the odds stack up in his favor. I would have loved to have had the big tree for protection, but that being denied, any tree, no matter how small, would have been appreciated.

At ground level, where the 11Bravo20 infantry grunt fought, the war appeared futile. We didn't feel we were fighting for anything. There was no home or family to protect. There didn't seem to be any glory or honor in any of our actions. There was bravery when someone in the unit needed help. And there was caring for the wounded and dead. Those were all natural emotions that seemed to flow easily. In Vietnam during 1970, no one was gung ho to win the war. Everyone had his own reason for doing what he did.

Those were often selfish motives. The hard-core, Regular Army lifers knew that combat experience was the best assurance of rapid promotion. They would joke, "It's not much of a war, but it is the only one we've got!" The drafted guys were just putting in their time. They didn't particularly care how or what they did. Graves Registration was a rear job, and more than once, I heard people say that they would volunteer for the Baggie Brigade to get out of the field alive. One year of duty, and we were out of there. We suspected that the war was scheduled to go on for a long time, and no one thought that any individual action, great or small, would make a tremendous difference in the grand scheme of things.

The *Stars and Stripes* reported that there were intermittent peace talks in Paris, but the discussions held little relevance for the grunts in the field. Any ground we captured wouldn't be kept, and any casualties we inflicted on the VC and NVA would be replaced by a new batch of gook kids coming down the Ho Chi Minh trail. So what was the use?

Sure, the United States had started a de-escalation of the war. That was why I had been transferred from the Red One to the 1st Cav, but each 11Bravo20 knew that, with his next footstep, he could be crippled or blown up, compliments of a land mine or booby trap. We cared little for the shape of the conference table in Paris or which delegation would be seated where. We just wanted out of that dreadful place.

Each mission was an endless calculation of danger. How old was a trail? How used was a trail? Had another unit encountered contact in the area? If so, how recent? We were never briefed as to the objectives of the next mission. Rarely did we know the significance of the "grand plan." We simply saddled up and moved out into thick jungle in stifling heat. No wonder guys smoked dope, got drunk, and lost themselves in letters home.

My letters to Karen and to my parents were my lifeline to sanity. They could also serve as a chronicle of my adventures should I ever want to write a book about my experiences in Nam. I had planned to use the year as a learning experience. I had thought that I would come back an authority on the war; I didn't have the faintest idea what was taking place.

The night after the firefight was another fitful one. No one slept too soundly. I slept next to the foxhole. If we were attacked in the middle of the night, I wanted to be the first one into the three-by-five, four-foot-deep piece of real estate. Certainly the gooks knew where we were. They could have easily followed us. I am sure that we didn't kill all of them, if we killed any of them at all.

The next morning the NVA gave us a wake-up call. They hit us with mortars. I was the last one to stand guard that night, and that meant that I was on guard as the sun came up. *Thump! Thump! Thump!* . . . I heard nine to ten thumps in all. I had never heard an enemy mortar fire before, but instinct told me that was what I was hearing. "Incoming!" I yelled and so did a half dozen other guards on the perimeter. The mortar rounds were leaving their tubes, but they had not hit the ground yet. The rounds were somewhere over our heads headed down.

I found the hole immediately. So did eight or ten other people. I was first in and, thus, on the bottom. The weight of the bodies above crushed me so I couldn't take a full breath. I loved the feeling. I could breathe later, after the mortars landed and the guys got off of me. I didn't care how long it took. All I wanted was the feeling of people above me.

The enemy must have fired fifteen rounds in all, and when they hit, we could tell that they weren't very close. The nearest was a tree burst fifty meters to our east and not close enough to cause anyone any harm. When they felt that it was safe, the top two layers of humanity crawled out of the hole, and my lungs started to function again. The FO called in the arty, but we had no distinct targets, and the explosion of 155 shells in the jungle put the NVA on notice that we could pop shells back on them.

The company packed up fast in preparation for scampering out of there. We knew that the gooks could come back at us at any time. They might choose to pop some more mortar rounds into a tube and adjust them so that they would land more accurately. They could also pull a ground attack on us. They certainly knew our general location and were funning with us.

We never made it outside our night perimeter. Alpha Company, which was on ambush two thousand meters to our west, was hit by a ground probe. The firing was intense. We could hear M-16s answered by AK-47 fire. Everyone selected a tree or piece of jungle for protection, but I had a fondness for the hole so in I went again. Scooter and Gomer joined me. We listened intently, trying to figure out which side was winning.

"That's AK fire!" someone would say.

"That's the machine gun working out!" It was almost like listening to the play-by-play of a football game.

The firefight lasted about an hour. We felt sorry for the grunts in Alpha. Some Bravo RTOs close to a radio could hear what was happening and passed the word on to the rest of us. Arty fired up a mission for Alpha. Then we heard the Cobra gunships come on station and start to work out. Next the fixed-wing rolled in and blasted the hell out of the jungle the same way they had helped us the day before. Finally, the medevac came.

After a while, the NVA melted away. Alpha Company got its wounded out and received a resupply. We left our area and looked for thick jungle in which to find a secure spot. We found such a good place that we stayed holed up for the next day. Then the command-and-control guys pulled us out and airlifted us to a fire support base. We were there overnight. Just long enough to get resupplied, cleaned up, and go to church. Every once in a while, a chaplain would hit the fire support base when we did, and he would hold worship services. He would have a little makeshift cross, and we would sit around it and sing hymns and pray. The praying we did at these services wasn't nearly as intense as that done in the field or when we were in contact. Prayer at those times lost all its formality and got to be real personal.

The army choppered us to an area very near Cambodia. Supposedly, we were about three thousand meters—three klicks—on the Vietnam side of the border. We started to hump. Once, we got on the wrong side of the border and some lifer in a helicopter had us pop smoke to mark our position. After he confirmed that we were then touring Cambodia, he made us hotfoot it back to the east and Nam. Scooter questioned in jest, "How are we supposed to know Nam from Cambodia? There ain't any lines drawn on the ground." He was, of course, right. But in the heat and with the weight we had to carry, no one gave him credit for his humorous insight. Besides, it didn't matter where we were until we hit the shit. Then we wanted to know exactly where we were located on a map and where the artillery would place its fire.

On the fourth day of the mission, a unique event took place. Bravo Company found a small clearing, and we called in for three more days' worth of resupply. Getting resupply was the most excitement we could count on of a positive nature. Between resupply and watching our mustaches grow, we had limited entertainment. On resupply days we received ammunition, C rations, cigarettes, water, and most important, letters from home. We often were giddy with excitement and sometimes got careless.

I had been designated 5-Mike for our platoon. The 5-Mike was the person from a platoon who helped unload the chopper and distribute the resupply and mail. It took time, and I was often the last one to get my personal stuff sorted out. That meant that I was usually the last one to open mail from home. The anticipation of reading mail from loved ones and friends was often more enjoyable than the actual reading of the correspondence itself. It was always nice to know that someone at home cared about you enough to take time to write. I was always fortunate as both Karen and my parents wrote numerous letters. I even got letters from former students.

One advantage of being the platoon 5-Mike was that I could share in the packages of cookies and goodies that the guys received from home. Since I gave out the stuff, I knew whose relatives had sent what. In skilled hands, one or two shakes of a package would give away the contents. On the other hand, since I opened my packages last, I was the object of everyone else's attention. While I didn't mind sharing other's goodies, I jealously guarded the cookies sent to me by my mother.

During this particular resupply, I received two packages. One was from Karen. It contained the usual Wylers lemonade envelopes and a can of hard salami. The other package was from my parents and a complete surprise. As I peeled off the brown wrapping paper, my eyes bulged. There, before me, was a box of Brach's chocolate-covered cherries! My mouth fell open in amazement. After eating all the junk the army called food, that box of real-world food was unbelievable. It was a wonderful treat that only a mother would think to send. Instantly, I tried to conceal my treasure from the other members of 4-6. No luck.

"Schneider's got candy, chocolate-covered cherries," Scooter squealed in delight. In his excitement he had broken noise discipline and had almost yelled the fact. The entire heavy-weapons platoon literally dropped what it was doing and crowded around me.

"Open it up!" J.B. demanded. Noise discipline was truly gone. "Open it up! Open it up, right now!" the rest of the platoon chorused. The tone of their voices varied from demanding, to pleading, to pure begging. They resorted to any method to get me to open the box and for them to have a taste of at least one piece of the candy inside.

In our minds, each of us could taste the chocolate. Each of us imagined how the cream would taste as he broke through the outer layer of milk chocolate. Each of us rolled the cherry out of the cream with his tongue and bit into it. Each of us savored the taste and the sensation. Then, as each of us finished that imagined piece, we reached back into the box for another.

I knew, just knew, that I had to share the chocolate-covered cherries with everyone in 4-6. That meant a whole lot less for me, and I was selfish enough to moan inwardly. I knew I had to share and that there was no way around it.

"Okay! Okay!! Get your butts back, and I'll give you some. But first let me finish getting my shit together." I tried to put them off to some vague point in the future. I placed the candy on top of my rucksack. Next, I went to work getting my Cs arranged and filling my canteens with water from the orange water balloons they had dropped to us. I fooled no one into looking away. In fact, perched on the rucksack, the box of candy took on the prominence of a mighty god placed on a shrine. Each glance in its direction was a moment of devotion. Each of us enjoyed the anticipation. Repeatedly, in our imagination we ate a piece of the candy.

The picture on the front of the box didn't help either. It branded the taste into our very souls. The morsels begged to be eaten.

At last, I could not postpone the opening of the box any longer. No one in the platoon had forgotten about it, and I couldn't hide it away. Every time I went near my rucksack, every eye in 4-6 followed my movement. "Open it!" the eyes said.

And open it I did!

With nearly religious ceremony, I slowly unwrapped the clear cellophane from the outside. With reverence, I lifted the lid of the box. The platoon crowded around. No one was on perimeter guard. One enemy hand grenade would have killed us all. No one cared as long as we died with chocolate-covered cherries in our mouths. Here was a treat from the real world, the US of A . . . . home. When the lid of the box cleared the top of the candy, our eyes fell as one on the contents.

Maggots!

The candy was covered with maggots! We stared in disbelief. Maggots! Maggots! As one we moaned, and as one we nearly broke down and cried. Tears of frustration, tears of disappointment, and tears of anger filled our eyes. Here we were, the lowest of the low, 11Bravo20 grunts humping the jungle. You couldn't get lower than that. Even the maggots had it better than we did; *they* were eating the chocolate-covered cherries!

"Damned maggots!" Homer said.

"Fucking maggots!" Scooter corrected.

"Son of a bitching maggots," I intoned.

"Motherfucking . . ."

On and on it went. The little white creatures were vilified with every curse word known to the English-speaking man. Each member of the platoon tried to find the worst adjective to describe Mother Nature's little garbage disposal units. We tried. God knows we really tried. So deep was our hurt that long, elaborate, and elegantly constructed strings of cusswords weren't suitable.

I closed the lid and put it back on top of the rucksack. At least twice, members of the platoon went over and looked at the box. They opened it, and the swearing began anew. Maybe the men of 4-6 thought that there might be one piece that didn't have too many maggots on it. No one could believe the incongruity of the situation. The picture on the front of the box looked so right, and the contents looked so wrong.

As a substitute, we tried to satisfy our sweet tooths with army SP candy bars, which were half paraffin wax and half chocolate. They didn't melt in the heat or get maggots. It didn't work. We knew we were eating army candy, not World candy. The Hershey's bar tasted like colored wax, and so did the Nestlé's Crunch bar. We would have gotten the same satisfaction if we'd been eating candles.

In the course of the afternoon, a grunt from the platoon that tied in with us to our west wandered by our area of the perimeter. His eyes caught the vision of the Brach's god resting back on my rucksack. "Number fucking one! Can I have some of those chocolate-covered cherries?"

"Not even!" I growled. I was, by then, in a very bad mood. "They are from my mom, and I wouldn't part with them for one hundred dollars. *Didi mau!*" I was really pissed. The box had great sentimental value. My mother had cared enough to send me a box of chocolate-covered maggots halfway around the world. What type of son would I be not to appreciate at least the thought?

"I'll give you ten bucks for them!" the grunt countered.

J.B. caught my eye and gave me a wink. "Get lost! They're ours. You guys in the line platoons don't do anything for us. Besides, we've already opened them," I said.

The grunt's eyes zeroed in on the box. He could taste the candy the same way we had before we'd looked inside. He walked up to the shrine and lifted the box. It had weight to it. We hadn't eaten too many, he reasoned. "Come on, man! I'll give you ten bucks for what is left!"

I restated the obvious: "You mean to tell me you'll pay me ten bucks to eat what is in that box of chocolate-covered cherries?" He could tell I was weakening. The platoon was dying. The men could hardly stifle their laughter. They were in physical pain. Scooter grabbed his groin. He was about to wet himself.

"Let's see the money."

The grunt fumbled into the inner pocket of his jungle fatigue pant leg and pulled out his wallet. He gave me ten dollars MPC. He was ecstatic.

I had one last word of admonishment. "Now listen, I sold you this candy, and I probably shouldn't have. It's yours. But if you ever meet my mother back in the world—don't tell her I sold this to you. They're special cherries!"

In an instant, the grunt was gone. Off he went with his prize to gloat before his platoon. Some of our guys fell to the jungle turf and split their sides laughing. They rolled and howled. *"Shhhhhhhh,"* J.B. urged. Noise discipline was gone on our part of the perimeter. The platoon to our west also had lost it. They were *"oooooooh*ing and *ahhhhhh*ing," and then cussing. We knew they'd opened the box. Of course, we broke down laughing again.

Immediately, the grunt who had made the purchase came back to our sector of the perimeter. He was a bit upset. "Asshole! This candy is rotten!" he said. "It's full of maggots, and I want my ten bucks back."

The platoon gathered around me and looked once again into the open box. "Hey, look. The candy is bad!" J.B. exclaimed in mock surprise.

"Isn't that the way it's supposed to be?" Lennie asked.

"Bad? That's the way we like ours in Kentucky," Gomer said.

Scooter pushed forward, and after looking once again into the box, looked the grunt in the eye and growled, "You said you would eat the contents of this box for ten dollars. Now do it, stupid!"

Our joke was turning sour. I knew that guys could get fragged, or accidentally shot, for less. Obviously, the grunt didn't have as keen a sense of humor as we did. I guess I could have returned the ten bills, but I was feeling mean, and that was my chance to take it out on someone.

"You bought it from me for ten bucks. Go sell it to someone else," I said and turned my back on him with the air of one to whom an incident was closed. It was a done deal. I hoped that he thought so, too. With the rest of the platoon covering my back, I walked back to my rucksack and busied myself with a minor detail.

The grunt must have reached the same conclusion. After surveying the glares from my buddies, he turned heel and left our area. That is, he left after calling us every name we'd called the maggots. It was refreshing to know that we hadn't omitted any Anglo-Saxon cusswords.

The incident would have ended there if the company had moved out on operations, but we stayed in the resupply area for some reason. About a half hour later, the same grunt showed up in our area again. This time he had his M-16 with him and two buddies from his platoon, each armed.

"Oh hell!" went through my mind. The heavy-weapons platoon sat up in notice, and some of the guys looked for their weapons. I saw J.B. pull the .45 out of his holster and hold it partially concealed by the back of his right leg. I was leaning against my rucksack rereading letters from Karen and my M-16 was somewhere behind me. I couldn't easily or quickly get to it.

The grunt towered over me. I pretended not to notice him, so he kicked my foot. I looked up. To hide my fear I tried an annoyed expression. "What do you want?" I tried to spit the words out of my mouth through clenched teeth to look angry and upset.

"Smart-ass! I should beat the crap out of you, but I sold the cherries for twenty bucks!" His eyes lit up, and he started to laugh. It was the same laugh we'd directed at him when he had bought the cherries. We all joined in. The tension was broken. He was pleased to have outsmarted someone from another line platoon and have made a profit. Each of his buddies told how he had helped. We joined him in his mirth. In Nam, it didn't take much to have a good time. Sometimes screwing over someone else was high entertainment.

Once again this incident would have ended then if we would have just moved out. But we didn't. We were getting nervous. We had been in the resupply area too long. Headquarters had some additional equipment that they wanted to get out to us, so we had to wait for the next available chopper to bring it out. We just sat.

As in the Red One during downtime, one person would stand guard or remain semialert, and the others would read or sleep or play cards. After the incident with the Red One where I had almost been zapped while playing cards, I was a devout believer in the evils of gambling. We were engaging in this kind of general relaxation when a guy from a platoon to our east walked through our part of the perimeter. In his hand he held a box, a box of chocolate-covered cherries. Could it be a coincidence that the brand name on the box was Brach's?

The grunt walked around in an obvious manner, displaying the box of cherries and talking to Scooter and J.B. At first no one said anything and ignored the box. Finally, Scooter broke down and asked, "Is that a box of cherries you have there? They look like they just came from back in the World."

"Yeah, my mother sent them to me," he confided. He almost got the words out of his mouth before the platoon roared. Noise discipline was gone again. Only this time the guys just let it rip. We laughed so hard we were helpless. We were as useless as the day the company had gotten drunk on the chopper pad and couldn't hump the boonies. We laughed so hard our sides ached. Then we laughed even more. The chump with the candy didn't see what was so humorous and looked around in bewilderment.

"Don't give us that shit! You bought those from somebody! How much did you pay for them?" Gomer demanded.

"All right, I did buy them. I got them for forty bucks, but I will sell them for thirty-five."

We could hardly breathe. We begged for mercy. The grunt was angry. He didn't like being the object of our joke. Whatever it was. Our levity came to an abrupt halt when the lieutenant who served our company as field artillery observer (FO) from the CP came over and chided us about our noisy demeanor. "What's wrong with you guys. You've been noisy all day. We can hear you all over the place. Shut the fuc— Say, what is that, a box of candy?"

Looks were hastily exchanged. "Maybe the CP and the captain would like some cherries!" Schacker suggested with a straight face. A chorus joined in, "CP! Give the candy to the CP!" Someone suggested, "Sell it to them for fifty bucks." In any case, the FO and the most recent owner of the candy headed in the direction of the CP for a talk.

I'm not sure where the cherries went from there. It was a very minor incident in a very major war, but Lord was it funny. The memory of those maggots wouldn't die. Later that day, after we had moved and found an ambush site, the rains came and Scooter observed that this war was not a box of chocolate-covered cherries. For the next week or so, everything was either a chocolate-covered cherry or a maggot. For instance, when a FNG soul brother took over point, he was called a chocolate-covered cherry. Everything that was disagreeable was a maggot. People were called maggot-face, maggot-breath, and maggot-dick. I never told my mother about the maggots in the candy. I did tell her not to send any more. "It melts too fast" appeased her good intentions.

We finished off three more days chopping our way through bamboo and cussing every thorn prick it produced. The company was then airlifted back to the company area at Firebase Buttons outside of Song Be. The company took up positions at bunkers around the airfield, and it became our duty to protect the fixed-wing aircraft and REMF from harm. What a cushy job. We loved the few days we spent there. Showers, a small PX, a MARS station, and the company rear area made it a wonderful place to be.

We were even provided ice cream. Of course, it had to be eaten quickly before it melted. Each person received a gallon of ice cream, and it became a race to see if we could consume it before the sun did. Snarfing down the cold ice cream at a record pace made our heads ache, but it was delightful. I didn't even mind that it was strawberry ice cream, my least favorite.

On the second night of our stay in Song Be, Ted Michaels, the company clerk, came down to the berm and asked for volunteers. He was in search of someone who could type and would be able to help him clean up some REMF-type records for the big IG inspection Bravo Company would be undergoing in a short time. No one seemed to want to give him a hand. First of all, we were comfortable for the first time in a long time. When the monsoon rains hit, we crawled into bunkers to wait them out. Next, most of the guys were catching up on sleep and beer and peace of mind. Not to mention that some heavy games of cards were being played. Only the short-time girls were missing.

But Ted had said the magic word, "type." For almost five months I'd been telling anyone who would listen that

I could type, but no one would listen to me or allow me to demonstrate my twenty-to-twenty-five-words-per-minute skills. I immediately volunteered. Damned fools who would volunteer to type seemed to be hard to come by in our infantry company, and Ted accepted my unselfish offer.

Ted and I spent the rest of that day and most of the night typing, filing, and straightening out company records. Due to the complexities of the way the army structures things, I was never really sure what I was doing, but I could follow what Ted told me to do with some degree of accuracy. The next morning, I rejoined the heavy-weapons platoon with the understanding that I could come back to the company area in the afternoon and that we could continue to work. I was eager to return. I was learning a whole lot about being a company clerk, sort of a crash course in how to be a MASH Radar O'Reilly kind of guy.

Later that day, Ted and I continued to work and drink beer. Drinking beer didn't improve my typing, and the old clunker of a Royal typewriter we had didn't help either. Eventually, Ted and I interwove work with talk of home and family. Ted had even visited St. Louis and dated a girl whom I vaguely knew. We discussed her ample chest and easy virtue. We were becoming friends. "Professor, I am getting really short. I mean *really* short. I'm shorter than Schacker, and the other day, he said he was shorter than a maggot's dick. I'll need a replacement soon. And I haven't even had my R and R yet. What would you think about coming in from the field and training as the company clerk?"

I couldn't believe my ears. Of course, when I'd started helping him, I had found out that Ted had only a short time left in Nam and that he would need a replacement. I had assumed that he would be replaced by some Stateside-trained clerk type. My typing for him had been a general suck-up for any future REMF jobs that would open up other than company clerk. To think to replace the existing company clerk would have been a dream that even my optimistic mind couldn't have fathomed. I was stunned by his words. I stammered my acceptance of his proposal. Pride prevented me from kissing his hand or foot, but the gratefulness oozed out of me. Ted knew what the offer meant; he had humped as a grunt too. He knew what it was like to be handed your life back.

I spent the next several days on dual duty. I sincerely tried to learn the army paperwork fiasco during the day and to stand guard duty on the berm at night. At times, I was so tired that I couldn't see straight. One night, the base went on full alert because a gaggle of gooks had been seen in our area, and we were told that they were going to try to overrun us that night. Firebase Buttons was so big and spread out that they could have had their choice as to where to slip in or force their way through. Our platoon guarded the break in the berm where the planes taxied to go to the base runway, so that seemed like a weak place and a prime target for an attack. Just my luck to be in a potentially hot area.

It was a long night, and we were never attacked, and the base did stay on full alert. I couldn't decide if I wanted to be in a fighting position, such as a bunker, or out in the open on the berm. If I stayed in the bunker, I would be safe from mortar shells and direct small-arms fire, but then the sappers could chuck in a satchel charge, and everyone in the bunker would be history. If I stayed in the open, I wouldn't get zapped in the bunker, but I might get shot by an AK-47 round or a B-40 rocket or hit by mortar. In the back of my mind, I could still hear Ted's words: "Now, Professor, don't get yourself killed before I can get permission to get you back in here!"

No attack materialized, but we were a strung-out group of grunts the next few days. I, of course, was the worst. I was experiencing a type of short-timer's fever.

All too soon, our fun in the sun at Song Be was over. We received orders to saddle up for the bush. A quick trip to the company area reaffirmed Ted's pledge to get me in from the field to replace him as soon as possible.

He repeated his warning and added, "I'm going to Australia for R and R beaucoup soon. I need you in here before that. There will be one condition that they will put on you. It will be that you must delay your own R and R until the very end of your tour of duty. Can you live with that?" I assured him that I could and that R & R in Hawaii would remain a fantasy until a later date. I would have promised him my firstborn son if he had asked.

I now busied myself with the real world of surviving in the bush until Ted could get me reassigned to the rear job. Little did I know that events were heating up in Nam. Nixon had decided to clear out the NVA and VC sanctuaries in Cambodia. The war was about to take a major step up in escalation at a time when all I wanted was to play possum for a couple of weeks.

Our company left Song Be, and after several uneventful days in the field working along the Cambodian border, command and control sent us to guard and then to help dismantle an ARVN fire support base called Judy. Our mission was simple. We were to guard the ARVNs while they moved their 105 artillery out of that area. Again, I don't know what the grand plan was. I simply knew that we would soon be without artillery support and would be out there deep in the boonies with a lot of bad guys. We didn't know about Cambodia then and, in fact, may even have been the last to know when the incursion finally did happen. We would have worried our butts off, if we had known. The days on Fire Support Base (aka LZ) Judy weren't that bad. We were kind of out of touch with things, and the firebase was secure for a while. We were working on the South Vietnamese schedule. That meant that everything took twice as long to do.

Bravo Company set up shop on the perimeter of the base, and we settled in. Schacker was back with us from Sidney, Australia, and hung a pair of red panties on a pole outside our bunker as our flag. Okay, that was juvenile, but what the hell. Schacker retold the story of how he obtained those red panties about seventy-five times. It was a slightly different story each time. At first I thought he had bought them, but then I didn't care. His stories and my personal fantasies overcame any logic that was left in my brain. Since we didn't have a TV, Schacker made for good entertainment.

It was at Firebase Judy that I nearly got into very serious trouble with the U.S. Army. Each of us had to take his turn on the berm guard duty. One night, after I had finished my portion of guard duty, I woke up Lennie, another grunt in the 4-6 heavy weapons platoon. Lennie was a sound sleeper and had a reputation for being a bit disagreeable. He was especially sour when awakened in the middle of the night. In any case, I woke Lennie and waited for him to go to the berm and take his turn at guard. The night was pitch black, and when I didn't hear or see him go to the guard bunker, I woke him up once again. He got really angry and cussed me out. I was tired, too, but I knew that he had to stand his guard. I wasn't about to cover his guard just because he was too lazy to wake up. Lennie had a previous history of falling asleep on guard, so I made one more effort to get him up.

"Let me alone, Professor! I can get up. I just have to put my boots on!" Lennie said. I guess I should have stayed up and personally walked him to the berm, but he seemed to be awake and was talking and swearing, so I assumed that he would go to the berm after he put on his boots. I wrapped up in my poncho liner and crashed.

About an hour later the officer of the guard woke me up and wanted to know why I wasn't on guard. I told him that it was Lennie's turn, that I had awakened him and that he was on guard. When we went to the guard station Lennie wasn't there; he had rolled over and gone back to sleep.

The next day there was an investigation. I was sweating bullets. Not only could I get in big trouble with an Article 15 punishment or worse, but I could kiss the company clerk job good-bye. When I talked to the captain, I told him my side of the story. I admitted that I should have realized that Lennie was irresponsible and that I should have been more aggressive in monitoring his going to the berm. The captain disagreed. He seemed to think that I had done all that was required and maybe more.

Lennie had a history and that worked against him. Lennie got an Article 15. He wanted to fight me over it. I really wasn't opposed to some kind of macho scuffle, but once again I didn't want to chance any trouble because of the impending clerk's job. Other people in the platoon talked to Lennie, and he calmed down after a day or so. We were never close after that, but generally our differences were forgotten. It still remained a source of worry for me. In both the Red One and the Cav, I had worked very hard to be considered dependable and someone to be trusted no matter what the situation. Now my reputation was at stake. I especially didn't need the captain to think I wasn't responsible enough to be the company clerk. I didn't need that kind of trouble just then.

While at LZ Judy, we practiced firing the 90mm recoilless rifle. It was a blast, literally. Two thousand flechettes came out the front, and the beast had a backblast that could kill. The person firing the weapon had to be to one side of it. We took a terrific picture of me firing it. Scooter loaded the shell. Schacker took the picture by keeping the shutter of his camera open while I pulled the trigger. It made a dramatic picture: the flechettes flying out the front and the backblast out the back.

We also practiced firing a gook 60mm mortar that the company liberated before I had joined it. At first, it had been useless, but we had since acquired ammo for it. From then on, we were going to carry it rather than the 90mm recoilless rifle because the 90mm recoilless rifle was too bulky, it was heavy, and the backblast made it worthless in average combat situations. The little gook mortar was lighter to carry, could be broken down into a baseplate and tube, and the ammo wasn't as heavy. We took turns learning how to load, aim, and fire the weapon. I had to hand it to the U.S. Army; if you enjoyed firing exotic weapons, they could entertain you.

One part of our assignment was to use up and destroy any old ammunition that was stored at Judy. We did that by holding "mad minutes." At a given time during the night, everyone would shoot his weapon toward the perimeter. Ostensibly, we did that to keep the enemy off guard if he was planning an attack. Sometimes mad minutes would cause the hidden NVA and VC to think that their plans had been detected, and then they would attack before they were ready. In reality, mad minutes were just fun, shoot-up-ammo times.

One night we blew up a pile of various kinds of outdated small-arms ordnance. What a fireworks display! The ensuing explosion was spectacular. M-60 machine-gun tracer ammo flew into the sky, and the whole area lit up. I had placed several dud 60mm mortar rounds on top of one of the claymores to the front of our bunker position for detonation. That night I selected what I thought was the correct claymore clacker and blew it, but nothing special happened. The next morning, I found that I had blown the wrong claymore. I had a history of doing that. I hid the dud mortar rounds, and the following night, I blew the correct claymore and shook our whole bunker. It was a dangerous game, but fun. I knew that I would never have so large an amount of explosives at my command again, so why not enjoy the big bang.

Midafternoon the next day, we discovered that I wasn't the only one who liked pyrotechnics. *Kaboom!* The first bunker south of ours lifted up and sat back down. Scooter, Gomer, Schacker, Lennie, and I were standing about twenty feet away, and the concussion buckled our knees. No one moved. I looked down my body to see where I was hit. I couldn't feel any pain, but I expected to see blood squirting out of holes in my chest and abdomen. All five of us were in a state of shock as we checked ourselves for leaks.

"Incoming!" Scooter shrieked, and instantly I dove into a sleeping position bunker with overhead cover. Even though I was older than the other four, I was the fastest that day. The other four grunts piled in after and on top of me. Once again, I was happy for the company. We hunkered down and waited for more rounds to hit.

"Anyone hit?" I stammered, still checking myself in disbelief. With such an explosion so close, I had to have several wounds but, probably because of the adrenaline pumping through my body, I couldn't feel anything. A second body search produced another clean bill of health.

In the meantime, no additional incoming rounds hit the base. There had been just one explosion. After about five minutes, we grunts-turned-groundhogs emerged into the sunlight. A survey of the area showed some of our guys running over to the bunker and searching through it. Sims, a soul brother with the first platoon, had occupied that bunker. He was lying on the ground. The concussion had gotten him. He was groggy, but unhurt. Members of his platoon were laughing and joking. "You got twenty-four at one time, we think!" came a report from one of the grunts in his squad.

Chagrined that we were diving for cover when others went to the bunker to help, the five of us grabbed our M-16s and raced over to the bunker. "Thirty-four seems to be the final tally!" someone yelled from inside of it.

"Thirty-four what?" Gomer asked.

"Thirty-four rats! Sims got thirty-four of them at one time."

By that time the brass from the fire support base had huffed over and demanded an accounting.

Since Sims was still a little goofy from the explosion, one of his buddies bragged for him. "Sir, these bunkers are full of rats. You know that the ARVN don't police up their areas as well as we do, and these bunkers are overrun with the creatures. Sims hates rats. He really does. So he put a C-4 in each of the holes in the bunkers where he suspected there were rats. At first, he was just trying to get the rats to eat the stuff and die. When that didn't seem to work, he hooked some of the holes together with det cord and slipped in a detonator cap. He hooked that up to a claymore wire and clacker. When he squeezed the clacker, he tried to blow up the rats in their holes. I guess he had too much C-4 in some of the holes, because it made quite a pop."

By that time, Sims was being helped over to the aid station. I thought he might try for a medical profile or discharge. He could always say, "Yo, Bro, I got thirty-four before they got me! They was real rats." It would have made a good story back on the block.

Of course, the command-and-control guys didn't see the humor in the situation. Actually, neither did Scooter, Gomer, Schacker, Lennie, or I. We were a little embarrassed and angry. But anyone could understand Sims's frustration. When on guard in a bunker, we saw rats whenever an illumination flare popped. They would be right there silently beside you in the dark, and when a flare brightened the area, they would dive for cover. It was disgusting. Sometimes in the middle of the night rats jumped on your chest or stomach while you were asleep. That is why many people, me included, chose to sleep outside rather than in the sleeping bunkers despite the overhead cover the bunkers provided. Choosing to get hit by incoming rounds at night or sleeping with rats was a matter of personal choice.

Word came that we were almost finished tearing down the base. The ARVN had left, and Bravo Company was without direct artillery support from our own base. We would have to leave in the next day or so. The executive officer, who was in charge of the rear area, came out to talk to the captain. On his way back to the chopper pad, I caught up with him and asked if I would be going out with the company or hopefully joining Ted and him at Song Be. I didn't like the answer: Ted was trying to get me back ASAP, but the captain wouldn't release me until the end of the month. Our platoon, 4-6, had been assigned a new sergeant directly out of shake-and-bake NCO school. He was green, and there was some talk that I might be more suited to act as platoon sergeant for 4-6 until the shake-and-bake sergeant could get some field experience. In any case, I would have at least one more mission in the field.

The time on Fire Support Base Judy had been good time. Despite the goofy things that had happened, it had been safe time. Now we were going out to hump. All I wanted was an easy, no-contact time in the jungle. "Just do what you've always done. You'll be safe." I tried to get myself up, but no amount of mental gymnastics could erase the thought that it could be my last mission. How many times on television and in the movies had I heard that Joe Doe got killed on his last mission. Nam had its own crop of such tales. The shorter one got, the worse the case of nerves. I still had about six months left in country, but I could see that with a job in the rear, I could make it out alive. All I had to do was make it to the end of April.

The next morning, we got bad news and then worse news. An NVA soldier was seen outside the perimeter of FSB Judy. Since we had no arty, the enemy must have thought that we had left already. The mortar platoon was told to rush over to the west side of the base with the tube, baseplate, and ten rounds. We ran like hell to the appointed bunker. The ell-tee for the 2d Platoon pointed to a break in the jungle where the NVA soldier had stepped out. Proud of our newly acquired skill at firing the 60mm mortar, we laid down ten rounds in the surrounding area. I don't think we got him, but we did send a message: "Let us depart in peace." I couldn't believe how brazen the NVA were. They were ready to move in as soon as we moved out. They would police up anything we left behind.

If the enemy being on our doorstep was bad news, worse news was that we were going back to the area where we'd made the contact on March 20. Wherever that special piece of Vietnam was located, it was not a place I wanted to revisit.

Later that day, we loaded up on choppers and headed out. Every aspect of the mission took on special significance. I kept telling myself, "This is your last mission. This is your last air assault. This is the last time you will be on operations with your buddies in the 4-6 platoon. After this, you will be different from them." Then the notion that I might get killed or wounded would jump into my mind. The bloodlust barbarian in me wanted to kill gooks. The civilized educator of young children wanted to hide in a deep hole for the next few weeks.

CHAPTER 11

By the Skin of My Teeth

Sometimes it lasted under twenty minutes. Sometimes it lasted for thirty or forty minutes. But whether it was longer or shorter, the ride in a chopper to the drop zone was always enthralling. Words can't explain the thrill of riding into combat in a Huey helicopter. Other men in other wars may have felt the same way when they rode their chariots, horses, or tanks into the fray. I just have to believe that flying into a landing zone in a slick has got to be the best way to get to work. I never heard a grunt complain about a helicopter ride, especially the ride back to base camp from a mission, but the outbound flight was also a kick.

Prelight preparation for a mission was totally unique for each person. Every 11Bravo20 addressed his emotions in a different way. Before going out, many of us went to a makeshift church. Sometimes, just a few guys stood around two twigs tied together to form a cross. We would say a prayer, and then do last-minute busywork for the mission. There were always last-minute items to occupy my mind. Routine helped make boarding the choppers easier.

Usually we were at the helicopter pad long before the Hueys arrived. In the interest of fuel economy and the most efficient use of limited resources, it was better that we wait for them than for the aircraft to wait for us. That dead time was just torture. Sometimes I would just think. Sometimes I would write another "last letter" home. Each man tried to make this time a no-brainer. The command-and-control guys had learned their lesson about visiting us before we went out, and they certainly didn't want to bring us any beer. We had blown that kind of VIP treatment on the mission earlier that had put more puking drunks in the field than able-bodied soldiers.

Riding to the area of operation in the choppers was great sport. First of all, the birds would appear over the horizon. The sight of inbound helicopters quickened the heart.

"Off and on!" the ell-tee would yell. "Off your butts and on your feet," was the translation. Reluctantly, we would get up and start putting on our gear.

There were two methods for donning one's pack. Some people preferred the piecemeal method. The grunt stood up, then bent over and picked up his pack, and in one fluid motion, swung it up to his shoulders. Since most packs weighed from forty to sixty pounds, that maneuver could serve as a last-minute check for hernias. Unfortunately, no tickets out of combat were ever earned by that method. Another method of hefting the load was to sit on the ground and slide into your rucksack strap one arm at a time. Once the pack was in place, the grunt would stagger to his feet like a camel.

I disliked the latter method. It felt awkward so I rarely used it. I was a piece-by-piece man. The ritual started with my pistol belt; it held everything I considered essential for a last stand—a one-quart water canteen, a pouch that held two fragmentation grenades and a first-aid pack. Then, hernia method, I would put on my rucksack. Finally, I looped over my left shoulder a claymore bag full of M-16 ammo magazines.

I had formulated a personal survival plan in the Red One and had carried it over to the 1st Cav. If our company ever got wiped out, and I had to take off running, I could drop the rucksack and *didi mau* into the jungle, carrying only the pistol belt and claymore bag of M-16 ammo. That way I would have water for survival, and if necessary, ammunition to make a fight of it.

The grenades were the last resort. I swore that before the

gooks would take me prisoner, I would take a hand grenade, pull the pin, stick it under my chin, and release the safety lever. I doubted that I would know what happened when the grenade went off. I wasn't up for a prolonged prison stay in any Hanoi Hilton. I was just too chickenshit for the kind of torture the VC and NVA were said to practice.

As the inbound choppers neared the ground, some grunt would stand out in front of them to guide the pilot down. I'm not sure why the chopper pilot needed the assistance, but I have seen the same thing in major airports in the States with large passenger aircraft. It is as if the pilot doesn't know which way to turn the plane once he is within the last thirty yards of the gate. Some guy with lighted batons always has to guide him in. Thank God the pilot can get to that last thirty yards using his own eyesight and radar. The guy on the ground must feel all-powerful with his prestigous job.

In any case, once the choppers were on the ground, the blades continued whirling. We would bend over and fight through the downdraft to board the bird. Usually the Hueys held six to eight grunts, depending on weight and equipment. I always hung back. I wanted to be the last person on the helicopter. Because the choppers didn't have doors, I wanted to be the one who would sit on the floor on my side of the chopper bay. I loved riding over Nam with my feet dangling out. Looking down at the countryside as it glided below my feet was a thrill I looked forward to. I must have taken twenty pictures showing my feet hanging out of chopper bays. I considered these photos dramatic and hoped to use them to project a macho image to the folks back home.

The pilot would hover and test the lift of his helicopter to be sure that it wasn't overloaded. When he was satisfied, we would be off into the air. God, it was dramatic! As we took off, we would look at one another and grin and smile. We would flash a thumbs-up or a V-for-victory sign to those on the ground or in another chopper. Some guys would grimace. Flying and the prospect of a combat mission didn't always go over big with anxious people.

In the air, we would pass over a variety of terrain; at this time, we enjoyed a bird's-eye view of the fire support base from which we had just departed. There might be Vietnamese people in white cone-shaped hats innocently working in rice paddies below. It was considered bad manners and a major breach of international decorum to drop a smoke grenade down on them and frighten them, which is why we did this only a dozen or so times. The little critters sure could scurry. Besides, if they were VC, they were counting the number of choppers in our lift and marking the direction that we were going. Later, they would report it to their own command-and-control guys. They were not all that innocent.

Sometimes we might fly over a river. Some rivers were broad, but in our area, from the air the Song Be River looked like a snake. We flew over deserted fields and over jungle. Sometimes we flew high. Sometimes we flew low and fast. I loved the masculine feel of the flight; it was what real men did. At times, if I leaned out of the helicopter a little too far, I would experience vertigo. What would it feel like to fall or jump? I liked the giddy sensation.

Looking around, I could see other choppers. Often, the helicopters flew in a slightly staggered formation, two abreast. I took pictures of other GIs in their slicks, and they took pictures of me. Once on the ground, we always promised to exchange photos when we had them developed. We never did. I ended up with ten pictures of ten guys whose names I didn't remember. Somewhere in the United States are ten ex-grunts trying to remember who I was and why they have my picture in their Vietnam albums.

Always too soon, the flight ended, and we would head down. If we were the first lift in, the door gunner would flip his M-60 machine gun off safe and start shooting into the tree line as we landed. That was to keep the gooks' heads down until we were off the bird, on the ground, and into cover. Sometimes, a Cobra gunship or two would run the tree line and fire up the area. We liked to see that stuff; it showed that we had support, and that gave us confidence that we could make a good safe landing. I also theorized it might chase off any wanna-be gook heroes.

In this part of Vietnam, the 1st Cav continued to work in company-size operations. Of course, I loved the idea of one hundred and twenty guys being in close proximity. In my head, I always figured that the other one hundred and nineteen would get killed first. Besides, I was still in 4-6, the heavy-weapons platoon. We always walked second. We didn't rotate to the point element as the other platoons did. We were special. We pulled security for the captain and CP. We took care of the captain, and he took care of us. Kind of a scratch one another's back thing.

I was now a man with a mission—not to get killed. I had to stay alive until the captain released me for the company clerk job. It all seemed so simple. So simple. Just stay alive, and I would get back to the World, back to home and family. I would be back to a real life. I was now in such an enviable position that a million-dollar wound would do me no good. Oh, a slight scar on my arm and face might look nice if it could be managed without too much pain or blood. That way, when I caught people back in the World staring at me, I could say "Yeah, got that one in the Nam!" A small, obvious wound would be better than a tattoo.

New day, new mission, and 1st Platoon took the point. We walked second, carrying the liberated 60mm gook mortar instead of the 90mm recoilless rifle. The mortar was our new toy, and we wanted to play with it. We had practiced shooting it on Firebase Judy, so why waste all the effort. The fact that we were in triple-canopy jungle and that we couldn't get a mortar round past the foliage over our heads without detonating it on top of us didn't dampen our enthusiasm for using it. We carried twenty rounds, the tube, and the baseplate. We had left the tripod legs back at the company rear area. The legs were just extra weight. We would fire the mortar freehand as we had practiced.

On the ground, the routine of moving through the jungle began. For several days prior to April 23, our sister company, Delta, had made contact. Each time, I prayed for them. Then I prayed for me. I would be going to the rear soon, but did that mean the end of April or the start of May? The word "soon" can mean an eternity.

To occupy my time, I wrote letters to the companies that made Cybris salamis, and Hunts Snack Packs. I told them how much we grunts in Nam enjoyed the taste of their products. I hoped to mooch a case or two off them. I did this for the platoon because I was tired of having people watch me eat the World food that Karen and my parents sent me.

Reading and writing were favorite pastimes; I worked at being a grunt full-time. On April 24, we took our turn at adversity. We knew we were deep in Indian territory because there were signs of VC and NVA activity all around. Once we crossed a major trail the gooks used to bring supplies into Nam from Cambodia. I couldn't believe the width of the road. It must have been eight to ten feet wide, and it showed evidence of recent use.

One of our line platoons set up an ambush along the road, and sure enough, they popped a 'bush on a contingent of NVA. They got a couple, but unfortunately, the NVA got one of our guys.

The captain was worried about the ambush platoon's position and ability to move. He wanted to bring the company up to them rather than have them pull back to us. Probably it was good thinking, but at the time I would have preferred the opposite. In any case, the captain ordered everyone to drop his rucksack and form up! We were going to help the disabled platoon.

We would have to handle most of this situation on our own since it had started raining in sheets. No air cover could be on hand. Artillery could help, but with us moving, and the fact that we really didn't know exactly where the platoon on ambush was located, the coordination with arty would have been really tricky.

Word came down that all of us were going. I had assumed that the heavy-weapons platoon would stay to protect the rucksacks from NVA who might try to sneak up on us from the rear. But no, we were all going. I buckled on my pistol belt and looped the claymore bag holding my M-16 ammo over my shoulder.

I was really angry. In the past I would have seen helping the frightened and debilitated guys in the line platoon as a really noble thing, but by late April I considered myself just too damned short for that type of stuff. In any case, we would accompany the CP and the two other line platoons. The rain and the prospect of the mission had severely dampened my spirits. As we started, I turned to Gomer Sanderson and started bitching.

"I'm too short for this shit!" I complained.

"Aren't we all!" he replied. My anger turned to shame. Sure I was trying to stay alive during this encounter, and my motives were selfish. In a few days, or weeks, I had the prospects of procuring a rear job. Gomer and the rest of the guys would hump until thirty days before they went home. They had less time left in country than I did, but they would all spend more time in the field. They weren't getting out of the boonies this time, or the next time, or the time after that.

I bucked up. Playing mental games, I again told myself that things weren't that bad. In my mind I said, "You're a grunt! Airmobile Infantry. An ass-kicker! We are still only walking second. Second Platoon will lead the way. Now go help these guys."

The self-administered pep talk partially worked. As we moved out, the rain was coming down so hard that I couldn't see out of my glasses. In an effort to clean the lenses, I took the end of the towel I constantly wore draped around my neck and started to wipe the moisture from the lenses. Mistake! The towel was so dirty that I only smeared mud on them. My glasses were unusable. We started to walk. Once we had our intervals between men, I again tried to clean my glasses, this time with my shirt-tail. Even worse! The lenses were caked with more mud. I was getting more desperate. For all practical purposes, I was now blind. I tried a pant leg. It also was too wet and muddy.

Still, we moved through the jungle. I couldn't really see anything and thought that I would be better off without my glasses. Wrong! Every wait-a-minute vine, every root in my path, knew I didn't have my glasses on and reached up to grab a foot. The rain made seeing hazy, and with no glasses, I could only discern people a few meters in front of me. I could get lost, or take a wrong turn, and the rest of the column behind me would follow into oblivion.

I groaned, moaned, and swore. As in the past, mouthing my misery didn't stop the rain or alter the situation. In addition, I was angry with the captain. He really should have left some part of the company back to guard the rucksacks. The NVA could be putting booby traps under every one of them at that very minute. It just was not a good situation.

Not being able to see was my own personal hell. I finally ran my hands over my body in the hopes of finding some part that was not dirty, or at least not caked with mud and grime. But there didn't seem to be any place or item on my entire body that was clean.

My hands felt my wallet. Maybe something in my wallet was dry! As we walked, I opened the button on the pocket of my pant leg where I kept my wallet and took it out. Stumbling around, I searched through it for anything that was clean or dry. Hidden in the back, in one of those semisecret compartments that supposedly no one knows about, was an American ten-dollar bill. It was wet but clean. We weren't supposed to carry American greenbacks. I should have turned it in when we in-processed into the country. I had hidden away one ten-dollar bill in the belief that it might come in handy someday. I guess I thought that I could exchange it for a taxi ride home, if needed.

The bill was semiwet but free of mud and grime, so I used it. My sight was restored. The company stopped, and we set up a perimeter. The point element hooked up with the platoon in need. Together they cut thick bamboo to use as supports, and then made a litter out of ponchos and shirts. The KIA was placed on the litter, and we moved him back to an evacuation area. As it turned out, because of the weather, he couldn't be medevacked that day anyway.

Now the company did an about-face and started back to where we'd left our rucksacks. Word was passed to be careful when we got to that area, that it might be booby-trapped. We were reminded to check our gear before we picked it up!

Sure, I thought, now I'll bet he wishes that good old 4-6 would have stayed back to guard the stuff. Despite having my sight restored, I was still bitter.

In anticipation of a break in the weather, we moved to a clearing in the jungle; the break never came, and we had to dig in for the night. We dug an especially fine, deep hole that night. Because the heavy-weapons platoon was close to the CP, the corpse was situated to our rear. He was covered, and we did everything we could to protect him from the rain. I didn't know the kid who had been shot, but like all Americans in Nam, he must have been a good guy.

That night, I took first watch. Instead of sleeping on line at the perimeter, I decided to guard the body. I did this not so much out of respect as out of the thought that if we were mortared or overrun in the middle of the night, I would be the first one into the hole, and I would pull the body in on top of me.

Nothing happened. The KIA and I had a restful night's sleep. Still, the sight of a dead GI was a terrible, terrible thing. The term "body count" was only good in the third person, "theirs." The first person, "ours," sucked. A lot of good men died in Nam. And if they were not good men before they died, the very fact that they died in that god-forsaken place fighting for who-knows-what cause made them good in my opinion.

The sun eventually came up. An early-morning lift came in and dropped a stretcher, and we medevacked the body. By then, it was no secret to the resident VC and NVA that we were in the neighborhood.

Once again, we moved out. This time, two of the line platoons set up an ambush. Two NVA, probably fresh from a trip south on the Ho Chi Minh trail, carrying heavy packs and unaware that GIs were in the area, walked into it. This time the good guys shot them up. We had one enemy KIA and one NVA, minus his rucksack, who set the record for the jungle one-hundred-meter dash.

Third Platoon popped the 'bush on the two NVA just about the time I was preparing a gourmet evening meal back at the company perimeter. I'd been heating some soup that had come in an envelope from home. The firing from the line platoon was close and intense. Incoming bullets cracked and popped over our heads. I dove for cover in the mortar pit. We had dug a hole from which to fire the mortar should we have need. My rifle and helmet were nowhere to be found. But I was ready to drop some mortar rounds into the tube should we have the need.

We lay in the hole for some time awaiting orders. I asked if anyone saw my rifle. Gomer located it behind him and threw it over to me. I didn't want to leave the hole. The "all clear" was passed, and we stood up. I looked around for my warm soup, only to find that Schacker was wearing it. At the outbreak of the firing when we all dove for cover, I dumped the noodle soup on Schacker, but he didn't discover that fact until I had started an inquiry as to its whereabouts. He looked funny in jungle fatigues covered with Lipton noodles. Following the precedent of the earlier incident with the chocolate-covered cherries and the maggots, Schacker's fashion statement became the topic of conversation. We were a closed society, and it didn't take much to open new avenues of entertainment at someone else's expense.

Schacker became known as Lipton boy. He was told to "use his noodle" at various times. Following the precepts of good grunt humor, "his noodle" began to mean other parts of his body, and a wet noodle, or limp noodle . . . it went on and on for a while.

No calendar had to tell me the next day would be April 26. I was a master at keeping track of time until the end of the month. "Just stay alive until the end of the month!" That thought echoed through my head every five minutes of every day.

The company spent an uneventful night. The next morning, we prepared to move out. The grand plan was to follow the gook who *didi mau*'d. We moved out in that direction. We didn't walk the trail but generally followed its course. We were all tense.

About 0800 hours, our lead platoon got hit. The whole Oriental world opened up on them. They returned fire. The lead platoon had just gone over the crest of a slight incline that could be called a hill, and they were on the downward slope. The CP and our platoon hadn't quite achieved the crest. I was at the front of the heavy-weapons platoon and on the right side of the column.

When the firing started, I did what everyone did. I hit the dirt! From the volume of enemy fire, I was sickened at the thought that we would be in another major firefight. I could identify a lot of enemy machine-gun, AK-47, and RPG fire hitting just on the other side of the crest of the hill. Bullets flew everywhere. I dutifully sprayed bullets into the jungle to my side of the perimeter. As I changed magazines, I tried to locate exactly the origin of the enemy fire. To my relief, it all seemed to be coming from the downside of the incline over the crest. Our part of the perimeter wasn't receiving any direct fire. Bullets were cracking over our heads, but they were eight or nine feet up. The angle was such that the NVA couldn't put a direct line of fire on the CP, the heavy-weapons platoon, and the two line platoons to our rear. I sprayed the jungle again. I knew we were up against hard-core NVA and this would be an all-day affair, so I took the luxury of pausing a moment to see if I could improve my fighting position.

Eight feet in front of me was a tree about eighteen inches in diameter. It would stop most bullets. I immediately low-crawled to that tree. Because the terrain in front of me fell off to a slight incline, I wanted to secure that tree for cover as well as a base to bring fire onto the enemy should they try to maneuver around us to my side of the company.

Just as I made the tree and jerked off my rucksack, the leaves and vegetation in front of the tree hopped with bullets. Impossible, I thought. How could there be gook bullets hitting from that direction? But I crawled back away from the tree and surveyed the jungle.

Once again, I was in the open. Of all the bamboo

thickets that grow in Nam, why couldn't God have put one in front of me? The bullets from the firefight raged to my left, and the front of the column continued to bear the brunt of the action. I could hear AK-47 rifle fire answered by M-16 fire. By then, I certainly had enough experience to distinguish the difference. RPGs were answered by M-79 grenade fire. Machine gun answered machine gun. Yet no fire was coming directly into my position.

The tree! That tree just looked so damned good, I had to try to repossess it. Once again, I crawled forward. I knew I was slightly out in front of the rest of the guys, but to no great extent. Once again, the vegetation in front of me was bounced around by gunfire. This time, I noted that it bounced from my right to my left. The fire was coming from someone on my right down the hill. I looked down, and about twenty meters to my right a new guy from the second platoon was shooting up the hill in the general direction of the enemy fire. His bullets were useless since if they cleared the incline, they would have been twenty-five or thirty feet over the enemy. He fired a lot of rounds directly into the ground in front of me. Having shot up a tree myself in my first firefight, I understood his frightened firing. He stopped to reload, and I started yelling and throwing rocks and leaves at him.

"Stop! Stop shooting up the line!" He was deaf to my instructions and obviously scared out of his wits. He was firing at nothing and denying me a position behind a really nice piece of foliage. Once again, I crawled away from the tree as he unloaded another magazine load of useless ammunition in my direction.

I was pissed and turned once again to tell him to hold his fire. I threw some more rocks and leaves and even one of my spent M-16 magazines at him. Suddenly, the vegetation on his left side danced, and he yelled, "I'm hit!" I saw him take the bullet in the fleshy part of his left thigh.

Impossible! How could this be happening? The enemy had the point element pinned down on the other side of the slope. How could this guy get shot? We were not taking any fire. It was inconceivable that he could be hit.

The cherry, in a show of guts, turned over on his stomach and emptied another magazine of bullets up past my tree. Upon hearing that he had been hit, someone farther down the line immediately came to his rescue, and started bandaging the wound.

No, this is impossible! I thought. But at least I get my tree back! and I crawled out and secured it. Settled beside the tree, I listened to the sound of the battle raging on the other side of the hill. I tried to make sense out of what was taking place around me.

It was clearly a bad firefight, but at the present time I had limited options as to what I could, or should, do. All I could do was watch to be sure that NVA did not flank us. I had already fired maybe four magazines of ammo. I knew that I should save the rest for when I would need them. I prayed for each new crescendo of fire from the enemy to stop. I could hear the field artillery observer calling in arty. The captain was on the horn with the lead platoon. He was also requesting helicopter and fixed-wing support.

I wanted the support, and I wanted help. I really wanted the whole U.S. Army and Air Force to rain down death on the bad guys. Maybe that would coax them from their bunkers and spider holes and maybe entice them to run away.

As was SOP, the artillery came on line and started blowing up the jungle. But artillery can only get so close, and the NVA were nose to nose with the GIs in the lead element.

Someone came over from the CP with an order. "They're running out of ammo up front. We've got to get them as much as we can. A kick-out supply is inbound. How much have you got left?"

I lied. I felt that if I gave up ten magazines, or 50 percent of my ammo, that was sufficient. Others farther behind could do the same. They shouldn't have fired a shot yet.

"Good! Gather up what you can. They are passing some more up from down there. Take it forward!" As he spoke, I could see to my right that people were passing up a vestful of M-79 ammo, a can of M-60 machine-gun ammo, and assorted bandoliers of M-16 ammo. Looking, I saw that the confluence of this material was headed to me.

"Heavy weapons does security for the CP, takes ammo forward, and brings back the hurt and dead!" A voice in my head repeated what I had heard when I came to the unit. I had written those words of reassurance home to Karen and my family several times. I had just never really believed them. I was about to live them. The realization swept over me in a wave of panic. I was to be the one who would do it. It was my job, and I was strategically in the right place in the line. I looked around for someone else. The wounded guy and the people who had helped him had cleared out a sizable hole in our line to my right. Maybe I could just stay there and guard the area? No, that excuse would just not work. I had to be the one who would take the ammo forward.

At that moment, I considered myself a dead man. I could have written my own toe tag. All I needed was the physical pain and agony to finish it off. And in a way, they only seemed secondary. Thoughts of the company clerk job, Karen, my mom, my dad, my brothers, school, a future, and life back in the World were gone. I would be killed on the other side of this hill.

It was just a matter of routine. Somewhere on the other side of the incline was an enemy soldier, away from his home, too, who had a bullet in his weapon that would kill me. All either of us had to do was to go through the motions. No thinking was involved.

In a way, the panic subsided. You can't come back from the dead, and I knew that I was dead. Sure, the sweat broke out. I know I fumbled with the M-79 grenade vest as I put it over one shoulder. I would carry the machine-gun can full of ammo by its handle. The M-16 bandoliers I draped on my chest and back. Although I was wearing my glasses, I had lost the ability to see. I couldn't hear. I'm not sure if the CP guy stayed, or not. I just knew that I had to go, and go now!

There had been an intermittent lull in the firing for several minutes. In every firefight I had been in, there was shooting, then rest, then shooting, then rest, then shooting, and then quiet. Once in a while, a random shot would spark an exchange of firing from both sides. It was quiet just then. I began to take deep breaths, and on the third one, I told myself, I would go. One—two—three!

I was up and running!

I ran over the crest of the hill. There was really no order. People were behind trees, in depressions, everywhere and anywhere. I started throwing M-16 bandoliers at people as I ran. I guess they were grateful. I did hear a rude "Get down!" as an acknowledgment of thanks. But I ignored it. I was too fired up to stop and talk. I didn't know exactly where the machine gun had been placed, but I had a general idea from the earlier sound of firing. With eyes that saw nothing and saw everything, I located a place where the M-60 should be. It wasn't there, but Frenchy, one of the guys I knew, was there and had been bravely firing the M-79 grenade launcher. He was out of ammo. I threw him the vest. He was wounded in the left arm, but had stuck it out, and kept firing.

My style of ammunition distribution was "close enough to someone is good enough." Sometimes the ammo landed on top of them, and sometimes within five or six feet, I covered a good part of the perimeter on the right side. I saw the machine-gun team and heaved the ammo can in their general direction. All had been quiet. No shooting yet!

I off-loaded my last supply of M-16 ammo to three guys down in a depression behind a tree. It wasn't great cover. As I chucked them the remaining bandolier one of them yelled, "Get this guy out of here!" Lying next to him was a grunt with bandages around his head. I couldn't tell if he was dead or alive, but I knew I couldn't carry him back alone. He was just too big. I hesitated.

Suddenly from the corner of my eye another grunt came up and yelled, "Drag him! I'll help you drag him!"

Without another thought, I grabbed the grunt's right arm. I knew that the inert form was a corpse. Life had ebbed from him sometime before I had arrived. The other guy took the left arm, and we started to pull him back. We sprinted through the jungle, trying to avoid trees, roots, and junk. It wasn't easy. During this whole time, not one shot had been fired by either side. The grunt didn't groan, and this confirmed my belief that he was a KIA. In my mind, I marked the crest of the hill and safety. If we could drag him back over that crest in the next thirty or forty seconds without getting killed, I would consider myself to be alive again.

A world of noise opened up behind us. Enemy bullets cracked and popped around us. The leaves and vegetation from trees fell in front of us. Dirt kicked up beside us. I focused on making the crest. The other grunt helping me drag the dead guy up the hill took the lead in our run for cover. Never a great athlete myself, I always expected to see someone run faster than I could. Sure enough, he gained ground in our race to the top of the hill. I could see him clearly out of the right corner of my eye. Slowly, more and more of his body came into view. He was definitely outrunning me. I envied him his speed. He made the top of the hill and disappeared. Five or ten seconds later, an eternity in combat time, I was over the crown of the hill, too. I was safe!

As I crested the hill, I saw a group of GIs huddled behind a large tree. I wanted that tree, too! I deserved that tree, and would take it by force if necessary. Bullets flew harmlessly over our heads, and I knew I had come back from the dead! I virtually collapsed.

The grunts behind the tree recoiled at my intrusion. I didn't give a damn.

"Get that dead guy out of here!" one of them admonished. "Take him back to the CP!"

"Medic! We've got a KIA here," one of them yelled.

For a moment, I thought they meant me. I wasn't used to being alive yet. I don't think I fainted. I didn't lose consciousness. I just withdrew from reality for a while. I caught my breath. I was sweating buckets. I shook and I stared. I must have been in some kind of shock. A medic came forward and asked where the KIA was shot.

"In the head," I stammered, still in a daze. An examination of the body showed that he had suffered multiple gunshot wounds all over his body. Some of them, I suspected, were inflicted as we pulled him back.

"How did he get here?" asked the medic.

One of the grunts behind the tree informed him that I had brought him back! By now, some of the CP group had come up and wanted to get the body even farther back and eventually medevacked out. There were other wounded and dead starting to pile up.

"This guy pulled him back!" one of the tree huggers proclaimed.

Still in shock, I mentioned that the other grunt had helped. I wasn't up to a debate over who or how many people had helped pull the dead grunt back. Frankly, I didn't care. The ammo was up front, the KIA was back, and I was safe. Nothing else seemed to be important.

I got up and went to my area of the perimeter and the tree I had staked out as my own. In exhaustion, I replayed the scene on the other side of the hill in my mind. The other grunt wasn't an apparition. There had been another person helping me drag. When the shooting erupted, he had started to run the same as I had. I forced myself to reconsider what had just happened. In my mind's eye, I saw him ahead of me. He had been running faster because he wasn't dragging any weight. He had been smart enough to break his hold on the corpse. He had run full speed, unimpeded. I had been so transfixed by fear that I hadn't thought to let go of the dead GI's arm. I had run away from the firing behind me while dragging the body with me!

I never knew who the other person was who helped me pull the KIA back. I didn't know the KIA either. I blanked the whole thing out of my mind.

Around me, the company was going about the task of getting resupply in and wounded and dead GIs out. I watched in a trance. I saw eight wounded and six KIAs evacuated.

The battalion had sent a scout dog and a handler along with us on that mission. Both had been with the point element when we had hit the shit and had been wounded. The handler was medevacked, but there was a debate over whether to send the dog back or shoot it. Death and misery were all around us, yet there was compassion for man's noblest friend. I'm not sure that anyone in the company could have shot that scout dog that day. We would have easily killed NVA on the other side of the hill, but to shoot a dog—that was just too inhumane.

The medics strapped the dog to a stretcher board and hauled the poor thing up into the chopper. It clawed and bit at the straps as it was pulled up through the jungle canopy. We held our breath in fear that it might get out of the bindings and fall to its death. Days later, we received word that the dog was okay. I don't know if the army retired him and gave him a pension or not. Just the fact that the dog was alive made us all feel that we had accomplished a minor victory.

For the most part, I was kind of out of the rest of the battle. Others did heroic and silly things. If anything, the chaos of battle produced highs and lows in human behavior. One of the new shake-and-bake sergeants from the CP came over to the place where the grunt who had been wounded in the leg had been lying. "I got myself a dink! Right here!" he boasted and pointed to the ground.

He was very proud until he discovered the GI bandages and wrappers surrounding the bloody area. With a look of astonishment, he realized the truth. He had shot another American. The sergeant looked around for affirmation. I was close enough to make eye contact with him. He knew that I understood what had happened. I didn't say anything. It wouldn't have served any purpose. The war was tough enough. He would have to carry the mental scars of his actions the same way the guy who got shot would have to carry the physical scars. Reporting it to the captain wouldn't have done anyone any good. Accidents happened, and I wasn't in a position to be critical of people who made mistakes under pressure. Besides, we still had a long day ahead of us.

CHAPTER 12

The Cambodian
Incursion Mess

It was about 1500 hours by the time the wounded were lifted out of a hole in the triple canopy, the company resupplied, and nerves nearly under control. The NVA had not fired a shot at us for some time, so most of us reasoned they had left the area or been killed; they had been under a terrible volume of firepower from artillery and gunships. Fixed-wing aircraft had also fired up and bombed the complex for the last several hours. The company was licking its wounds when the order came to move up. Our orders were now to go into the NVA bunker complex and search it.

Our lead platoon was all shot up and not up to the task of being able to lead us into the complex itself. So 2d Platoon moved up from the rear to take the point. My heart went out to the point men. Because we walked in three lines abreast, there had to be three of those guys, and I am sure that booby traps were on each of their minds. How the grunts in 2d Platoon got up the courage to take the lead, I will never fully understand. Maybe they had a taste of the blood lust in them, or maybe they, as I had earlier, already considered themselves dead. In any case, we moved into the bunker complex.

I had been in perhaps seventy-five bunker complexes in my life. Most had followed the VC model, spider-hole fighting positions. The VC complex where I had found enemy ammunition and matériel had been extensive, but it was fairly old and infrequently used. I had never seen anything as elaborate as the NVA complex we were about to enter, a virtual jungle city. It had huge bunkers that would sleep fifteen to twenty people. Each bunker had at least two feet of overhead cover built from logs, bamboo, and mud. It would have taken a direct hit from an artillery shell or a bomb to damage the bunker and hurt its inhabitants. Each bunker had several gun ports about eighteen inches long and six to eight inches wide. The enemy could fire out, but it was hell for us to fire back through such a small opening. They had been safe in their holes. The complex even had its own well for water.

Most startling was that over each bunker there was a roof of bamboo and leaves for camouflage. It would have been impossible to detect the complex from the air. Under each roof were benches and chairs, that is, they were NVA classrooms. Clearly we'd stumbled upon a major Communist staging, indoctrination, and rehabilitation complex.

Considering the size of the complex, we found relatively little. We had tipped our hand that we were in the area by our noisy arrival and by the shooting up of one of their guys earlier, so the NVA had removed most of the transportable supplies and left behind a determined group of people to inflict maximum casualties. From the looks of the complex, we had probably gotten off easy with just six dead and eight wounded.

Overwhelmed by what we were seeing, we moved silently into the complex. Everyone was on alert for mines and booby traps, and no one was eager to explore the area. Several people did go into bunkers while others of us formed a perimeter. The searchers found some propaganda papers and some records, and in several bunkers they found blood trails. We had killed or wounded some of the NVA, but we had no idea how many. At one point, the shake-and-bake sergeant spotted an NVA pith helmet lying on the ground. "That's mine!" he cried, and lunged for it. Gomer grabbed him just in time.

Gomer took off on him. "I can't even fucking believe

you, man! What did we just say? Leave any gook souvenirs lay! It's booby-trapped, man!"

The shake and bake looked him in the eye and said, "It's mine!"

It was a bad scene. Schacker and I intervened. "Let's look it over. Step back!" Schacker said in a calm voice and motioned for me to join him.

I sighed and went with him. We started by looking for trip wires around the helmet. There were none. We then looked for any kind of land mine that could be around it. We found none. The area around the helmet seemed to be clean and clear. A debate broke out as to whether there could be a grenade under it. The pith helmet was too light to hold down the spoon of a fragmentation grenade, but the gooks could have devised some other clever method to booby-trap it. Gomer solved the problem by unwinding a length of claymore wire. With Schacker on one end, and me on the other, we dragged the claymore wire across the helmet and cringed, waiting for the big boom. Nothing happened. It was safe.

Schacker was the first to react. He went over and picked up the helmet.

"There it is! Now it's mine!" he stated.

The candy sarge was shocked.

"Wait a minute! I got a part of that thing, too!" I interjected. Suddenly, the desirability of the souvenir took hold of me. Lying on the ground, it had looked useless, and I didn't want it. Once it was safe, it began to look pretty valuable.

The FNG sergeant found his voice and began to swear and yell. Noise discipline disappeared, and a general argument ensued. It was a really bad one. In a way, everyone and no one had a right to the pith helmet. In the past, we had rarely argued over souvenirs; usually, no one wanted to hump them. The brass took any items of military value. The guy who shot the VC or NVA got first choice. That was when we knew who killed someone. With the exception of Super Sarge, who was a walking antique store and VC cheap-gift shop, most of us veterans did not want to lug the extra weight. I think we also had a bad feeling about taking stuff that belonged to the enemy, that it was kind of unlucky.

Now that I thought I was on my last mission, I believed that I should have something to show the folks back home. So far, all I could claim were some minor items, such as a machete, a silver spoon, and some VC and NVA uniform pieces that I had squirreled away when I was with the Big Red One. I did have an SKS (a semiautomatic and thus a legal "trophy" in the States) with my name on it in the storeroom at the company area. Everyone had been given one as a souvenir from a cache the company found just before I joined it. The NVA helmet would be a grand prize, and it wouldn't be heavy to carry.

But, with the thought that I hadn't called for it first, I reluctantly relinquished my claim. My mind was too focused on other things to construct a persuasive argument. I just wanted to get out of the bunker complex and dig in for the night. Eventually, all claimants except Candy Sarge relinquished their claims. He got the helmet. Needless to say, that was a bad start for him in the platoon.

After a quick once-over, we moved out of the NVA bunker complex and found a place in the jungle to dig in and hide. On our side of the perimeter, the jungle was so thick even the red ants would have had a difficult time making their way through it. The NVA must have known where we were. In any case, the heavy-weapons platoon dug one of the best holes I have even seen in Nam. It was deep and would hold at least five of us comfortably. In a pinch, seven or eight guys could get into it. All during the digging, tempers were short and flared. Often shovelfuls of dirt were "accidentally" thrown at someone rather than piled up in front of the hole for protection. There were no happy sky troopers on our side of the perimeter that night.

Another miserable night followed, the kind when a person got little sleep and thought too much. In my mind, I replayed a videotape of my ammunition run and of dragging the KIA over the crest of the hill. I went over at least one hundred things I could have, should have, and would have done differently. Next time . . . But there might not be a next time for me. I'd just try to stay alive.

April 27, the sun came up in Nam. A check of meteorological records would show that every day during America's involvement in Vietnam the sun rose and set. And every GI in the country would count that day. For some, it would be an arrival day in country. For some, it would be a going-home day. For some, it would be another routine day. For some, it would be a day to die. For me, it would be another day of anxious waiting.

April 27 started off okay. Everyone in the unit seemed to be in better spirits, and stories of personal heroism broke out. I blushed and told mine. I didn't even have to embellish it.

The guys in 4-6 knew about my run. They half teased and half applauded my actions. Spirits were high, we were going back to the bunker complex, when word circulated that the first platoon had movement outside its sector of the perimeter. The NVA were probing to find out exactly where we were. In an instant, we were armed and took cover. I liked the hole and chose it immediately. Three other people piled in beside me. Quietly, we waited for some type of action. None transpired.

Instead, a terrible odor seemed to permeate the hole. It smelled like human feces. I looked at Schacker next to me.

Schacker looked at me. "You fart, Professor?"

"No, you shit in your pants?"

Something was amiss. The smell of human fecal material filled the air. Together, we looked to my left at the shake and bake. He denied that the smell emanated from him. At last, foul odor overcame fear, and I stood up. My eyes followed the direction that my nose gave them, and I looked down at the area directly beneath me in the foxhole.

I had human feces on the butt of my rifle, my boots, and the legs of my pants. I was covered with human shit.

Schacker exclaimed, "Professor, it was you!"

"Not even!"

Then Schacker and I realized the truth. In the middle of the night, someone had taken a dump in the middle of the hole and had barely covered it up with loose dirt. I was now standing in it. Nam was great for humbling a person. I crawled out of the hole and started a general cleanup. I could have thrown up, too.

It was as if we had called a time-out in a football game. We expected the enemy to cooperate with our dilemma for the next few minutes. Some of the guys helped me and gave me spare toilet paper packets that they carried in the headbands of their steel pots. There was no water. I rubbed dirt on some areas of my clothing. I knew I would have to live in these clothes for some time yet. This was disgusting.

"Who would shit in the hole?" became the major question. Everyone in the unit knew better, except one person. Candy Sarge was still in the hole. He was pretending to guard the area.

My buddy, J. B. Paris, was pissed. "Who would take a turcott in the hole? That is so disgusting. I could kill the guy who would do such a thing."

With that, he took out his bayonet and began to sharpen it. "If I ever found out who did that, I'd cut their throat in the middle of the night!" he growled.

Schacker, Gomer, and some of the other veterans caught on to his intended message.

Gomer was chewing tobacco and spit onto the dirt over the new sergeant's head. "We stick together out here, and no one screws up like that! We cover one another when we need to take a shit, and watch out for one another. Only some kind of pervert or rookie wouldn't go outside the perimeter to take a dump."

All the ire didn't go unnoticed by the new sergeant. The NVA helmet the day before, and this bowel movement had put him in his own pile of deep shit. Everyone grumbled and moaned about the incident until we mounted up and left the area.

We humped to another resupply point. There we received a kickout resupply of additional matériel, food, and water. Because it was a kickout, the chopper didn't set down, and I couldn't get out on it. Nor did they bring me a change of clothes. So I started another three-day mission humping an odor that separated me from others of my kind. Every time I had thought that Nam had done its damnedest to me, it came up with some new degrading trick.

It was the end of April and the first of May 1970. I had the promise of a rear job as company clerk ahead of me. What could go wrong? Besides, I was already in Nam. What more could they do to me? Send me to Cambodia?

I was really getting worried. Ted missing his R & R to Australia filled my mind. What if he snagged someone else to be the company clerk in the meantime? What if a Stateside clerk type showed up? Thousands of possible and impossible scenarios played out in my mind. One such grim thought was running through my mind during a break, when a single shot rang out. It sounded like an M-16, but the company went down and got ready for a firefight. Everyone found cover and waited. As it turned out, it was a single-shot affair; one of the guys in 3d Platoon accidentally shot himself in the foot. We had to find a clearing and medevac him out. That caused us a delay, and the chopper also helped to mark our spot in the jungle for the boys from "up north."

The next day a second person accidentally shot himself in the foot. He too had to be medevacked. The company was having an epidemic of foot problems. The last incident happened while the grunt was cleaning his M-16. It may even have been a real accident. Two foot wounds in two days did open the door for speculation about how bad can a foot wound feel? Just what part of the foot would one shoot? How would you do it so as not to make it seem intentional and get court-martialed? Not that any such thoughts ran through my head or anything. Some of the other guys must have thought them in my presence.

On April 30 at 2100 hours, people back in the real world turned on their televisions to hear the president of the United States, Tricky Dick Nixon, inform them in somber tones that as commander in chief, he had authorized the use of United States and South Vietnamese forces in

Cambodia. There was a general feeling of shock and dismay among the American public. Yet there was an element of support. Many people understood that we were going after NVA sanctuaries and supply bases. We were taking offensive actions that could help us withdraw from the war earlier and destroy the enemy's ability and will to fight. Many Americans saw it as a positive action. Others, including the students and antiwar elements in America, saw the Cambodian incursion as an unauthorized invasion of a foreign country. Congress hadn't officially approved the expansion of the war, and there was some feeling that Nixon had overstepped the boundaries of his authority. Student protest broke out, and the Kent State shooting took place. The United States news media went into a feeding frenzy.

The effect of that news on my parents and on Karen was devastating. My family knew I worked along the Cambodian border, but that had meant little to them. Nam was Nam, and they knew I could be zapped anywhere. Now, with the new focus of activity on Cambodia, new worries and dreads developed for them.

For the most part, the troops in the field did not know much about the grand plan of action that was taking place. We had given up hope of the war's ever ending before our tours of duty were finished. Hell, they had even argued for so long over the shape of the table at the peace talks in Paris that we had a strong suspicion that any true going home meant on an end-of-tour Freedom Bird or in a body bag.

In the bush, the radio operators who monitored the command-and-control radio frequencies were the first to pick up the news about Cambodia. They didn't know the who, what, or how, but we were definitely in for something. By and by, the word got out, and we, too, were shocked. The United States was going into Cambodia to clean out gook supply bases and kick butt. As each person heard the news, a groan issued from his throat. Cambodia, the ultimate bummer.

The rumors became fact, and I became despondent.

There was just no way that they would take me out of the field to be company clerk. First, I was a seasoned trooper with some degree of leadership and courage to my credit, and two of our NCOs were cherries. Second, Cambodia had to be at the far end of a pipeline of supply for men and matériel. Once in Cambodia, it would be next to impossible to get back to Nam and Song Be until withdrawn. Third, the company would need every person it could muster to help fight. A company clerk, important as he is, just doesn't do much for the company when it hits the shit. I knew I was doomed.

Bad luck had struck again. Drafted thirty days before I would have been too old. Sent to Nam instead of to Europe. In the boonies humping despite my master's degree in educational administration. And now, just when I had the promise of the company clerk job, off we go into Cambodia. There is "bad" luck and then there is "bad, bad" luck and then there is that kind of unspeakably bad luck.

On guard duty the night of May 1, I went over my options one more time. In a way, I cursed the damned rear job; if I had just had no hope, I would have hated the Cambodian mess, and then done what they told me to without any feeling. The promise of the company clerk job had given me the demon hope, and it had turned around and bitten me. The night was jet black. As usual, a person could hold his hand up six inches in front of his face and not see it. Just for fun, I put the business end of my M-16 on my foot. How much could it hurt? I adjusted the point of the barrel from the top of my foot to my third toe. Then I considered turning my foot sideways. Maybe a glancing blow.

One bang and "Oh no! I'm shot. The M-16 accidentally went off. It's not my fault."

I practiced my lines in my head. I even considered the trauma I would undergo lying there all night until the medevac could pick me up the next day. Surely, they wouldn't suspect someone of shooting himself on purpose in the middle of the night, who had to lie there the rest of the night waiting for the chopper. It was a good plan. It might even be a great plan. It just wasn't me. I just couldn't do it. "Cambodia here I come!" I thought.

The next day we didn't move. The army needed every helicopter it could get ahold of to carry troops and matériel to Cambodia, so it put us on hold. For the time being, we were to stay put. We got a hasty kickout of supplies and water, and that was all.

That dead time allowed the rumor mill to fire up and run full speed.

RUMOR #1: We would be fighting hard-core NVA from Hanoi.

RUMOR #2: Those were the best troops that Ho Chi Minh could muster.

RUMOR #3: The NVA would booby-trap every square inch of a complex.

RUMOR #4: Cambodia had a notorious snake called the "three-step-snake," the venom of which was so potent that once a person was bitten, he would die before he could take three steps.

Upon hearing rumor #4, I firmly decided that should I be bitten by a three-step snake, I would under no conditions take more than two steps. I didn't care who would have to carry me around for the rest of my life, I wasn't going to take the third step.

Rumor #4 made everyone snake conscious. I had seen only one snake the entire time I had been in the field, and that had been a little red one I had unearthed while clearing a place for sleep with a machete. The red snake had been only about eight inches long before I divided its head from its tail in one stroke of the machete. I guess I could have used the machete to toss the snake aside and spared its life, but mankind and snakes do have an adverse history. Besides, daily living in the jungle can put one in a mean mood.

After I had related that minor incident, a wave of snake stories erupted among the members of the 4-6 platoon. No one could be outdone. The stories included the traditional one about the water skier who skied into a nest of five thousand poisonous snakes all rolled up into a ball in the middle of some lake, then died horribly. An autopsy had revealed that the skier had not died of the five thousand snake bites, but of fright before hitting the pile of snakes.

There were at least three snakes-in-the-sleeping-bag stories, one snake-in-a-kitchen-knife-and-fork-drawer story, and one snake-in-the-fan-belt-of-a-car-to-keep-warm story. Gomer was the unofficial winner of the storytelling contest. His story was about his three uncles who had been frog gigging at night in a rowboat along some Kentucky river. One uncle was in the front of the boat with a frog gig. The second uncle was holding the light, and the third uncle was in the back of the boat, paddling. In the course of the evening, a snake fell from a tree limb into the boat between the uncle with the light and the uncle who had been paddling. The paddling uncle dropped the oars, grabbed the 12-gauge shotgun on the seat beside him, and attempted to shoot the snake. Instead, he blew a hole in the bottom of the boat, it sank, and the snake swam away.

It was the first time that I had heard that story. Sometime later, when I asked Gomer to repeat the story for a different audience, he enhanced it, saying that it had been a metal-bottom boat and that all three uncles were full of buckshot. But I liked the original version better.

Rumor #4a eventually extended the three-step snake rumor to having the snakes live in trees and packs. It was said that they would jump from the trees and float down through the air in packs of twenty to fifty and that whole columns of guys were killed by them.

With such forms of merriment, we killed time in the bush waiting for our orders and a helicopter ride to exotic Cambodia. Of course, it rained every afternoon at dinnertime and ruined the C-ration meals we had so artfully prepared. It seemed to be raining all the time, or perhaps our spirits were just gloomy. In any case, on May 2, we were due for another resupply, so the company found a decent-size clearing in the jungle and enlarged it. The log birds started delivering supplies. On previous missions, there was a fifty-fifty chance that the resupply helicopters could even set down; frequently they just kicked out the supplies from ten to twenty feet up. Due to the enlarged LZ, the slicks did set down, and some personnel who were scheduled for rotation home or for R & R climbed aboard. Their grins as the chopper took off were sickening. I especially remember watching as two soul brothers got on board one of the choppers and waved good-bye.

With each chopper that came and went, my heart sank even deeper. Foolish pride prevented me from begging the captain to let me board one to Song Be. Then—I got word to report to the CP! I hurried to where the captain was holding forth while monitoring incoming log birds and the reorganization of several FNGs who had come in on the last lift. He beckoned me to him, and we squatted down. "Professor, I want you to go in on the next lift if they can set another one down. Ted is clearing out for R and R and wants to finish training you before he goes. The top sergeant wants you back, too. They have an inspector general evaluation coming up, and they think you are the best man for the job. Get ready to go back to Song Be!"

I could have kissed the man on the lips. With that he turned his back on me in dismissal, but I couldn't let it go at that. "Sir," I said and touched his arm. I wanted to look him directly in the eye. He turned around and looked at me with a puzzled expression on his face. I had the eye-to-eye personal contact I wanted. "Thank you, sir. I'll be the best company clerk you'll ever have!"

He smiled slightly and said, "I know that, Schneider, or I'll have your ass back out here pronto!"

With these words of encouragement, I retreated to 4-6's area of the perimeter and announced, "I'm going in! Ted needs me back at Song Be, and I've got to get on the next chopper out." It was definitely a bittersweet parting. There were handshakes, a backslap, and too many envious looks. I began to feel really guilty about leaving. We divided up my load of munitions and stuff. As a farewell gift, I gave out some of the food I had recently received from home. With a heavy heart that sometimes raced with joy, I carried my very light rucksack over to the landing zone to wait for the next inbound bird. I sat down next to the RTO who was on the battalion radio network and waited for the next lift. Rain started, and the bird was delayed.

Patiently I waited. Then all hell broke loose to our east. One of our sister companies had walked into an NVA ambush and started slugging it out. The firing was intense. We all got down behind cover as stray bullets cracked and popped over our heads. Then the RTO said they had canceled my lift to take ammunition out to the company in contact. They took about an hour, and the rain started again. By then, it was late enough in the afternoon that visibility was getting poor. I sat and suffered at each piece of news.

Finally, we were told we would have one more lift of supplies and that it was inbound soon. That was the longest "soon" of my life. I suppose I heard the *whomp-whomp* of helicopter blades a thousand times. About 1700 hours, the fantasy *whomp-whomp*s became reality, and a chopper sat down. I quickly ran over and helped unload C rations and water. I worked with a will. Then I hopped on. I sat on the side of the deck and dangled my feet, even though there was room in the interior of the chopper bay. The guys from 4-6 platoon came over and waved goodbye. That would be my last ride as an 11Bravo20 infantryman. From then on, there would be an invisible barrier between us. They would be grunts, and I would be a chairborne Ranger.

CHAPTER 13

Transition to REMF

It was raining when the chopper set down on the tarmac of the fire support base. I was on the last chopper that would fly that day, and the crew was anxious to get back to their base. They didn't know that they had delivered me, and the future generations of Schneiders that I carried in my loins, to relative safety.

The fire support base was the usual type. A perimeter of bunkers and red dirt turned to red mud for the duration of the rainy season. I surveyed the fire support base as a condemned man must survey his cell after a reprieve from a death sentence. It looked great.

The chopper was out of there in a minute, and I was left standing. I didn't know what part of the United States Army owned that particular fire support base. I had no friends or connections there. It was just an overnight stop for me until I could snag a ride to Song Be and Firebase Buttons.

As I stood in ecstasy, I became the object of attention of some top sergeant in charge of the command and control of the base. Out he came in the rain.

"Get off this chopper pad right now! Who the hell are you? What the fuck are you doing here, and what unit are you assigned to?" His barrage of questions had broken my tranquillity and had snapped me back to reality. I stammered who I was and that I just needed overnight accommodations.

It was obvious that I was a grunt in from the field, so he

immediately put me on the bunker line and guard duty. Putting his face into mine, he informed me in his best drill-sergeant voice, "Tonight your ass belongs to me!" With a parting, "Don't eat in my mess hall. And get shaved!" he tried to dampen my spirits, but I was still too euphoric to let that happen. I nestled into one of the bunkers with some dopeheads who were happy to have someone else with them. I declined the offer of a joint; I was on a personal high and didn't need any of that junk. I ate some leftover C rations. They were delicious. It rained all night, but wrapped up in my poncho and poncho liner, I was in a world of my own. I thought of home and family. For the first time, I seriously considered that I would see them again.

When I awoke the next morning, it was a new day and a new life. I still hadn't shaved and was still filthy. I made my way down to the chopper pad and started trying to hitch a ride to Song Be. It took some time, but eventually I caught a ride out. Just in time, for the top sergeant had been cruising the area by the bunker to which I had been assigned the night before. Without official written orders, I was kind of like a duck out of water. The command-and-control guys would have had to trust that I was going in the right direction. That would have been hard for them to do. In any case, I departed the fire support base and flew into Song Be.

I wandered around until I located the Bravo rear area and found Ted hard at work in the company tent. He was bent over the Royal typewriter, knocking out some report. I walked through the front tent flap and announced softly, "I'm here!" With my back to the sun and in the shade of the tent he squinted his eyes and could not make out who I was.

"Who are you?" he inquired and my heart shot up into my throat. Had there been some mistake?

"It's me, Schneider, the Professor!" Recognition filled his eyes, and he nodded a greeting.

"Get out of here fast! Go to the chopper pad and wait

until 1600 hours; then come back up here. Go out the back flap! Move!"

To my stunned look, he continued, "I'll explain later. Now move out!"

It didn't take a genius to understand that he wanted me out of the company area for some reason, either good or bad, so I *didi mau*'d out the back tent flap and headed in what I considered the direction of the chopper pad. I was wrong and spent the next three hours in a general tour of Firebase Buttons. One lifer-type accosted me about my status, but I acted confused and asked directions to the Bravo Company area. He pointed and talked, and I nodded. It was really hot, and we both just moved on.

About 1530, I got serious about returning to the company area. Ted was still in the tent, but his greeting was more cordial. He explained that if I had been seen in the company area earlier, he would have been required to put me on bunker-line duty. He didn't want to do that since we needed to work that night preparing for the inspector general's (IG) visit. That kind of inspection, I was to learn, was the army equivalent of a detailed income tax audit. Everything had to be counted and accounted for. We had lists of items to line up and present for inspection and a list of items that were lost or stolen. The items on the latter list would be written off as combat losses. We also had many items deemed to be unauthorized that we would have to hide. Officially, *I* was on the unauthorized list.

That night, and many days and nights to follow, I immersed myself into the paperwork side of army life. Usually, I worked during the day and at night stood perimeter guard. The IG inspection was important and pressing, but even more so was the fact that Ted had delayed his R & R to be company clerk. Now he was due, and he was headed for Sydney, Australia, come hell or high water. That meant that I would soon run the company by myself.

Well, almost by myself. We did have a top sergeant, an executive officer, a mail clerk, a supply sergeant, and two or three short-timers with under thirty days left in Nam. Each of those people had his function and duties, yet I did marvel at the control and power exercised by the company clerk. The film *MASH* hadn't been wrong in its characterization of Radar O'Reilly as the nerve center of the company.

On the surface, I didn't seem qualified for the job of clerk. I had no formal training in the paperwork maze that the army had constructed. I had no idea about army regulations, procedures, or protocols. Basically, I was an educated guy who at twenty to twenty-five words a minute could outtype most of the other members of the company.

My military education was to be of two kinds. One part would be the formal way that the army demanded things be done. The other part was the informal way that things really got accomplished. In addition to the Cambodian incursion, the army and the war were going through a dramatic transformation. First, because everyone, even the lifers, understood that the war was useless, no one was committed to it. Everyone fought to get a safe job and then go home. "One year and out" was the goal. Second, racial problems were developing. Black soldiers had gotten the idea that Vietnam was a white man's war. Third, dope had grabbed the attention of many of the younger troops. Lifers were generally more into alcohol. Fourth, the army was about to change from an army of draftees to an all-volunteer army.

How to effect such a change in the middle of an unpopular war would create myriad problems. Among them was the idea that the troops felt they had democratic powers and, at times, should be allowed to vote as to what military actions should be taken in the field and in the rear areas. One way that the troops got the attention of the brass and expanded their role in the decision-making process was through the fragging (attempted murder, occasionally with a fragmentation grenade, hence the term) of officers. Furthermore, the antiwar movement at home and the bias of the strongly antiwar media had influenced recruits in Nam.

The first week I was in Song Be was hectic. We got mortared at least once a day. The gooks didn't like the fact that American troops were in Cambodia and they wanted to let us know that they were still around. Song Be was so big that mortar rounds could land on one side of it, and the people on the other side wouldn't know Buttons was being shelled. To prevent injuries, the army was using a new kind of radar and would sound an alarm that indicated the troops were to take cover. The siren would sound, and we'd dive for overhead cover.

Our company hadn't yet joined the Cambodian incursion because of something about a change in command at the lieutenant-colonel level. I was never sure who was our head guy and who wasn't. The six-month rotation system, which gave officers six months of combat command, then six months of REMF command, seemed silly. Just when they were learning their jobs they got rotated to the rear. With only six months to make a name for themselves, they often got gung ho with troops who wanted to go gung slow.

The company did have several contacts with the enemy, and we had several KIAs and some wounded. My heart went out to the guys in the field. I felt like a dog every time word came that the company was in contact. I was beginning to adopt a motherly attitude toward "my company."

Because we usually called one another by nicknames, I found out that I didn't know people's real names. At times, I was astonished to find out that someone I had called J. B. Paris was really Jonathan Basal Paris and that Bubba was Melcome John. Ted sometimes would have to help me make the connections between a person's field name and his real name. That was especially important if they were "line one," KIA, or "line two," WIA. Contact between our guys and the enemy left me cool inside. Despite my feelings of guilt, I noticed that each time our company was in contact, my typing ability went up five to ten words per minute. Contact was a definite incentive for me.

Not only did we get mortared in those first days, but I was on hand to witness members of our company refusing a direct order to go to the field. Some of our guys had quit the war. Two of the people who refused were the two soul brothers whom I had seen leave on one of the flights ahead of me when the captain had said that I would go to Song Be on May 2. They had simply boarded the chopper without permission and departed from the company. When they reached the same fire support base I had gone to, they hid out with some soul brothers. When they were missed in the field, word was sent to the fire support base, and they were rounded up and sent to Song Be. They said that they couldn't go back to the company because they thought that the white grunts in the field would kill them because they had deserted. I'm not sure that would have happened, but I wouldn't have blamed anyone in the field if they had buzzed a couple of M-16 bullets over their heads as a warning during the next firefight.

Ted taught me paperwork, U.S. Army style. We typed up requests for three hardship discharges, one compassionate leave, two AWOLs, one battalion Article 15, and gave orientation to fifteen new recruits, one of whom was a Sigma Chi FNG. As company clerk, I began to realize the gravity of my position and the impact that I would have on the lives of the men in the company. Two of the hardship discharges were really phony. One was not. The compassionate leave was heartrending. The poor grunt had humped the field for five months. The Red Cross let us know that the guy's house had burned down, that his grandfather had died of shock, and that his wife was badly burned. With that news, he was useless in the field and requested to go home and get things straightened out. I typed up an impassioned plea, and the army granted him the compassionate leave. Later, it was turned into a hardship discharge.

The two AWOLs were for the two blacks who had skipped out on the company. At first it looked as if they would receive a slap on the wrist and nothing more. But the brothers wouldn't let it drop. One of the two refused to go on berm guard and got a battalion Article 15. All this uproar set a bad example for the new guys. Some of them began to think that they, too, could get out of going to the field by just refusing to follow orders. "What are they going to do to us? Send us to Nam?" they would say to themselves. I understood the attitude. I had been there once or twice myself. Yet it had become my duty to get them to the field as fast as possible. The company needed them, and I needed to get them out of the company rear area. Lifer brass were constantly looking at our roster to see where we had men placed, and the status of each man. Ted showed me several tricks, and we were able to hide a few guys.

Ted had been in the field and had a general policy that I agreed with wholeheartedly. Any grunt coming in from the field should not have to stand berm guard on his first night in the rear. He should get two things: a good night's sleep and a beer or soda upon arrival in the company area. Usually, we could fill the beer and soda from company rations, but at times Ted, and later I, had to use personal money to stock our supplies. Because we kept the beers and sodas in an unlocked cooler, most people used the honor system and at times even popped for a case or two themselves. In general, the system worked well.

That was until the slacker who had the battalion Article 15 decided that the cooler owed him a continuous drunk. He drank beer in a two-handed manner and became more obnoxious with each beer. His constant references to Nam as the "white man's war" were really irritating to us white draftees. About the third day of this stuff, we had heard enough. He was a sick wacko, and each day he got drunk or stoned. Ted and the executive officer locked the cooler and put the beer off-limits for a while. Tension was running too high.

The next day, when the Article 15er went to start his daily drunk he couldn't get into the cooler. He came into the company tent and demanded beer. I told him that I didn't have the key, which was true. The incident might have passed except that he stormed out of the tent. About an hour later, rifle shots filled the air. I thought that the Viet Cong had gotten into the company area and hit the floor of the office. I grabbed the .45 automatic I kept in the right-hand drawer of my desk and jacked a round into the chamber while hell raged in the area behind the tent and people were running for their lives. I was fortunate enough to find cover behind some C-rations cases, and when I poked my head over the top, I was ready to kill a gook.

Others were showing up with assortments of M-16s and pistols. There was no VC, just the drunk, who was loading another magazine into the weapon and getting ready to fire up the area again. The executive officer grabbed the man's weapon and wrestled it away from him while yelling, "Don't shoot! Clear your weapons!"

His remarks were directed at those of us who had the drunk covered. Several people were yelling, "Do the bastard! Kill the motherfucker!" and other threats. The XO placed himself between the gunners and the drunk, and his order to clear weapons was reluctantly followed. One grunt warned, "XO, get him out of here, or he won't see the sun tomorrow! He's going to get killed."

I think that most of the people present agreed. In any case, the drunk was on the next plane to LBJ, Long Binh jail. There he would be given a military trial, some kind of sentence to hard labor, and a dishonorable discharge. He owed his life to the executive officer. Later that night as we discussed the day's events, some of us, white and black, came to the conclusion that some Americans were as useless as the gooks.

Excitement aside, like most REMF jobs, being company clerk could be dull, and that was one reason guys blew smoke. For me, working all day and standing guard at night made each day a blur. Yet there were lulls. Usually in the afternoons when the sun caused the temperature in the main tent to soar to astronomical heights, I tried to perform official duties, but generally, I just sat and sweated. I didn't perspire. I sweated gallons of liquid.

One of my unofficial duties was to watch over the unauthorized Bravo Company mascot. Max was a dog named after the Blue Max, our Cobra helicopters. When we were in contact in the field, to have the Cobra helicopters come on station and start blowing the shit out of the enemy was one of the most reassuring things that could happen. Grunts called this "Bring in the Max" on the enemy. Max was a Vietnamese mutt. He weighed about thirty pounds and had a short brown coat. He was arrogant. He loved Americans and hated Vietnamese and potheads. Ted's final words as he left for his R & R in Sydney had been, "Don't screw up too much before I get back. And Max is your responsibility now."

Max generally took care of himself. At mealtime, he could be found outside the mess tent, where people fed him scraps. I never saw him eat C rations, and he refused the tough water buffalo meat that the cooks fed us on Thursday nights. We would try to trick him by tossing him a piece of the tough meat as we left the cook tent, but he would spit it out. GIs had been trained to eat anything the army served, but Max had better taste.

Max had character flaws. One was that he loved to fight other dogs. He wasn't a pit bull, it was just in his nature to teach other dogs their lower status.

Men away from home sometimes do things that they wouldn't do if they were in the company of their mothers, wives, or first-grade teachers. One of those things was to bet on dogfights. As it was second nature for Max to fight, it was second nature for some Bravo Company personnel to bet that Max could beat any other dog in Song Be. The contests weren't fights to the death or anything. The winner was determined by which dog chased which off. Quite simply, Max never lost, and we often used his winnings to keep the beer and soda ice chest full.

Max loved to ride any form of transportation. We couldn't get the company jeep started without Max jumping into the backseat. He loved to ride on the motorized flatbeds we called MULEs. He lived to travel around Song Be and see the sights. But if we went somewhere and he did not join us for the return journey, we knew that he would find his way home to our mess tent by mealtime.

During one of our journeys to the chopper pad, three dogs from another part of the base started chasing our jeep. Max and the dogs exchanged challenges. At a place in the road where I had to slow down, Max jumped out and fought all three dogs. I had tried to warn him, but he didn't understand the "But there's three of them!" warning as he jumped out. Within seconds, he had each of them running in a different direction. After dispatching the three canines, he came to the jeep, jumped in, and looked at me disdainfully. His expression seemed to say, "You mean *only* three dogs."

Max had been and would be passed from Bravo Company clerk to Bravo Company clerk for as long as there would be a Bravo Company, 1/8th Cavalry, in Nam. Every six months or so, he formed a new bond with the new clerk. He slept in the clerk's hootch, rode with the clerk, and generally was the clerk's companion and aide. I don't know what happened to Max, but I hope that when the last Bravo Company clerk left country he had the guts to shoot him. I don't believe that Max would have done well with a Vietnamese master. He was too Americanized, and immigration laws being what they were, it was hard enough to get a Vietnamese wife back to the United States, much less a Vietnamese dog. Otherwise, I would have tried.

Before Ted left on R & R, we had been subject to the inspector general's inventory. We had passed. We had lined up everything that we should have had and hidden everything that we should not have had. I wasn't officially supposed to be in from the field yet, so I was one of those "should not have" items. During the IG, I took my M-16 and Max, and we guarded our illegal stash of VC and NVA weapons and equipment.

With Ted on R & R, I became the boss. I know that the top sergeant might have thought that he was running things, and sometimes the executive officer made noises like he was in charge, but Max and I knew the real truth. Between us, we controlled that small segment of Song Be, South Vietnam.

Sometimes people become jealous, and so the Alpha Company REMFs got a mascot of their own. It was a small spider monkey their company clerk bought at the trash dump from a Montagnard boy who was about seven

years old. The kid usually sold souvenir Montagnard
crossbows to GIs, but one day he had a monkey with him.
The Alpha Company clerk purchased the primate for a
carton of Camel cigarettes. The kid had already developed
a substantial smoking habit and really liked American
brands. In any case, Alpha Company had its own mascot.
The monkey was just as much against regulations as
Max, but it sure was cute. The monkey was named Crossbow, after the connection with the Montagnard kid, and
was the darling of the battalion. Max took a backseat to the
little rascal.

Crossbow had the run of the battalion area and often
came over to our tent to visit. He—I just assumed that it
was a he—took to teasing and tormenting Max. Between
1400 hours and 1700 hours, the heat in Nam was so oppressive that no one did anything. We generally looked for
a shady spot to do little duties. Max was no exception, and
he often found a place in the shade of a tent flap to zonk
out. His twitching and occasional low growls were
probably dreams of past fights or visions of future ones. It
was at such times that Crossbow would aggravate Max.
Taking to the commo wires and tent ropes, Crossbow
would sneak up on Max from above and bombard him with
rocks. One time I saw him simply drop an old C-ration can
on Max. Of course, Max jumped up in surprise and bewilderment. I was never sure that Max even knew that
Crossbow was the culprit who disturbed his afternoon
slumbers.

That is, until one day when I was sitting in the company's main tent. The typewriter was in front of me, and I
was trying to make up the guard duty roster. Mainly, I was
just a victim of the heat. I had my shirt off and sweat glis-
tened off my muscles, which is just another way to say that
I was sweaty and smelly. I was very lethargic as I looked
out the front tent flap. Max was walking past the corner of
the Alpha Company tent. His tongue was hanging out, and
I assumed that he was looking for a shady place to take a
nap. Chance would have it that Crossbow was approaching the same corner of the tent from the opposite di-

rection on one of his rare appearances at ground level. Had they been humans they would have bumped into one another at the corner of the tent, excused themselves, and gone on their way.

As I watched, each animal rounded the corner of the tent at exactly the same time. Each was surprised by the appearance of the other. But Max's fighting instincts took over and in a flash he grabbed Crossbow by the head. The entire head of the spider monkey went into Max's mouth, and Max violently shook the little creature like a rag doll. Max uttered a low growl as he tossed the helpless little body back and forth. Then he spit Crossbow out.

I half rose from my seat. I was sure that Crossbow was dead; the spider monkey had to have suffered a broken neck. I realized the trouble that was about to take place between the two companies. Alpha Company REMFs would come over and tell us that Max had killed their mascot. Our guys would defend Max and start saying rude things about Crossbow and make comparisons between Crossbow's parents and the genealogy of Alpha Company troopers. A fight would break out. Each company would defend the honor of its animal. Sillier fights had happened. Entrenching tools, knives, and even firearms could come into play. People would be hurt.

This was serious. In a panic, I quickly searched my desk and immediate area for a shoe box or towel or something with which to conceal the corpse of Crossbow and sneak it out to the trash dump. On the chance that I would meet someone from Alpha Company, I sure as hell didn't want to be carrying the dead monkey's body out to the dump in plain sight.

To my surprise, Crossbow hit the ground and gained his feet. He wasn't dead, but he was disgusted. His whole head had been in Max's mouth and was covered with dog saliva. Immediately he set about cleaning it off. The monkey wiped his hands across his face and rubbed them on his side. He cleared the saliva out of his eyes. The expression on his face was one of utter disgust and loathing. He continued to work furiously at the job. He didn't run or make any attempt to run; his primary need was to get that dog juice off his face. Eventually, Crossbow cleaned up his face enough to feel semipresentable, although I bet he would have liked a good shower. With a quick look around to see if Max was near, he took to the tent rope and his second-story domain.

Max strutted away. He had gotten his evens. I breathed a sigh of relief. There wouldn't be an intercompany recreation period. After that incident, I don't remember ever seeing Crossbow mess with Max at nap time again.

My path and Crossbow's were to intersect many times, yet only one other incident was significant. After the dog-monkey confrontation, my curiosity got the best of me. How had Crossbow's neck survived such a brutal shaking? Several times in the next few weeks when Crossbow came to our tent, I secretly examined his neck and head. They seemed to be okay. In fact, I noted that Crossbow could turn his head almost completely around—180 degrees from the front.

One afternoon, I wanted to test my observation. When Crossbow showed up at our tent, I coaxed him into a back storage area. There I opened up a can of pineapple C ration and gave him a piece. Crossbow and I were on generally familiar terms, so he didn't comprehend that I was about to try something kinky with him. After presenting him with a second piece of pineapple, I said, "Crossbow, let's see how far you can turn your head to the right." With that I took his head in my thumb and fingers and turned it to the extreme right of his body. Astonishingly, Crossbow could almost look directly behind himself. His head turned 130 to 140 degrees.

"Now, Crossbow, let's see how far you can turn your head to the left." I was holding a third piece of pineapple, and Crossbow obliged. Only this time, I really turned his head. I twisted it almost all the way to the rear, 180 degrees! But I must have twisted it a little too far, because he let out a squeak and bit my right thumb. His sharp little teeth met in the middle of my appendage. Pain shot up my thumb into my arm, and in a reflex reaction, I jerked my hand up into the air. Crossbow went flying across the tent, landed unharmed on the other side, and took off up a tent rope out of reach. I was in serious pain, and blood flowed freely from the wound. I held my thumb and danced around the company tent growling every cussword I had ever learned in the army.

"Make it bleed!" I thought. "Make it bleed!" Blood gushed. Looking around, I spied a bandage pack, broke it open, and covered the wound.

I've got to go to the aid station! I said to myself, and off I went. The aid station was about two hundred yards from our tent. During the first hundred yards, I thought of how I could turn this injury into a Purple Heart. No reasonable story presented itself. Then the truth hit me. What was I going to tell the medics?

"Well, I took this contraband spider monkey into one of the company storerooms and tried to unscrew its head." I could already hear their responses:

"One, you shouldn't have a monkey as a pet on this base. Two, you shouldn't be taking the monkey into store-rooms and doing God-knows-what perverted thing to it. Three, just how stupid are you?"

A few steps before I got to the aid station, my pace slowed. The pain had subsided, and when I looked, the bleeding had stopped. There was little that the medics could do for me, and a lot that they could do to me. I turned around and walked back to my hootch. I dropped onto my bunk and thought about what I had done. I promised my-self that I would never, never, never tell anyone about how dumb I had been. Then I thought about tetanus shots. I'd had a booster not long before, when I had cut myself while working in the company area, so I was safe on that ac-count. Sleep had started to overtake me when the thought of rabies popped into my mind. I bolted upright in bed. Do monkeys get and carry rabies? I didn't know. How could I ask one of the medics? And get real, like they would know anything anyway. I knew that if you got rabies, you be-came afraid of water or something like that. I vowed that each day for the next fourteen days I would get up and drink a lot of water each morning. If I was afraid of it, I would go immediately to the aid station, tell my story, and demand to see a medic or a veterinarian. I would throw pride to the wind.

The army doesn't have veterinarians, I found out. Weeks later, after I was sure I had survived the monkey-bite incident, I noted that Max had a growth over his left eye. One of the medics thought it was a cancer and suggested that we kill him. The supply sergeant and I talked long and hard about what to do, and, more important, who would do it. Each of us made a firm case for the other or someone else being the one to shoot the mascot. Max had been with the company long before we had rotated in from the field, and he should, by all means, stay with the company until the end of the war. We developed a plan to save him.

First, I typed up orders for Max and Sergeant Long, the supply sergeant, to go to Bien Hoa and Long Binh to have the cancer removed. Off they went on a chopper. To my knowledge Max had never ridden on a chopper before, but he willingly boarded. The chopper crew was less than enthusiastic, but we talked them into accepting the unauthorized passenger. Once in Long Binh, Sergeant Long had a terrible time getting anyone to look at or work on Max. The army medical personnel simply said, "No way!"

That is, "No way" until the supply sergeant offered to give each of the doctors an SKS rifle. The supply sergeant passed back word that I should send down two rifles with the mail clerk, and Max would have his operation. The next day, the rifles went south to Long Binh, and that night Max was escorted in the back door of some hospital and knocked out. He had the tumor removed and the doctors each had a souvenir weapon. I am sure that the physicians each made up a good story for the folks back in the World about how they acquired the enemy rifles. We didn't care. Max came back alive and well. We thought that Max deserved a medal, so we secured a Purple Heart for him. Sergeant Long made Max a dog collar out of a rucksack strap, and I pinned the medal to it. Max didn't like the collar or the medal and lost both within a week.

We had a change in top sergeants. The new top sergeant was a lifer and a nice guy. The week before he was to assume his duties, he came in from the field with a really high fever. I was on guard duty, so they put him in my bunk. The poor man sweated so badly during the night that he literally soaked my army mattress. The next morning when they took him to the aid station, my mattress smelled very badly. I tried airing it out, but could not use it again. Because mattresses were in short supply, I was dismayed that I would have to do without. Finally, someone from Delta Company left for the World, and I liberated his mattress. So as not to feel too badly about taking the good mattress, I left the smelly one. Compared to the boonies, a mattress problem was small change. Being a REMF wasn't all that bad, and I should have been happy. Yet in the darkest part of my soul, I knew I needed one more Vietnam adventure. I wanted to experience once again the emotional rush of a firefight.

CHAPTER 14

Chairborne Ranger

Although being company clerk had its lighter moments, it also had its sadder side. One of my duties was to in-process new guys and send them to the field. They were the same kind of frightened that I had been. I tried to ease their fears, but there was just no way. Each replacement was a potential KIA or WIA, and I tried not to look into their eyes. Sometimes, when they were on perimeter guard with me, I would tell them stories of our firefights and the daring actions of members of our company or some other company. I tried to answer their questions honestly. The war was winding down, and they wondered, as I had, whether they would serve a full year. What effect had the Cambodian incursion had on the enemy's ability to wage war? They envied me my REMF job. What were their chances of getting one? Those and a thousand more questions poured forth. Many were the same questions I had asked so many times when I was new in country, or when I had been transferred from the Red One to the Cav. I knew their anguish and could do little to alleviate it.

As company clerk, I was responsible for securing emergency leaves for guys who had trouble at home. Each time I applied for some type of special request or discharge, I put my heart and soul into it. I tried to make the situation sound as bad as possible so that the applicant could go home. Also, we had members of Congress send congressional inquiries about the status of men in the company. Congressional inquiries were a pain in the butt and usually didn't accomplish much for either the grunt who had complained or the parent who filed them. The congressmen thought that they were helping constituents, but in reality all they were doing was making work for some desk jockey like me. Often congressional oversight got in the way of meaningful work.

On one occasion, one of our guys was killed in combat. That meant we had to dig through the storage conex and find his personal effects. This was always a sad and miserable job. It was always hot, and the individual's personal gear always seemed to be at the bottom of the conex. In that particular case, the parents requested that we send home their son's K-bar knife. Little in the way of personal effects was ever sent in from the field. I knew from experience that it was the general policy to send in as much as possible, but that the logistics of the situation often only allowed for a small bundle of pictures or a wallet. The KIA's military equipment was divided up among others, and sometimes the KIA had told a buddy, If something ever happens to me you can have my . . . whatever.

We couldn't find the K-bar knife anywhere. I really wanted to find it, and communicated with the people in the field, but to no avail. Eventually, we had to answer a congressional inquiry and explain that the knife had been lost during combat. I took the fact that we couldn't produce the K-bar knife as a personal slap in the face. I knew the grunt's parents must have thought that someone had stolen the knife, and someone in the field may well have kept it for his own use. I do know that no one in the rear had it.

If possible, whenever we had a KIA or a serious WIA, we tried to send home an enemy souvenir weapon from our storage to the family or to the individual who had been wounded. The weapons left Song Be, but I don't know how many made it home. I suspect few did.

That was before anyone had thought of a Vietnam Memorial Wall, so I always tried to type up letters of comfort for each family that were truthful and expressed appreciation of the sacrifice that their son had made. I signed the captain's name. Of course, the captain was far too busy to write those letters in person, and I did a good job for him. Besides, in many cases, I knew the guy better than the captain did. Besides, I was an English teacher and a good writer. They were really sad letters. Using the old Royal clunker of a typewriter, I sometimes typed and retyped them trying to make them letter-perfect. I hoped that they would be of the quality that could be framed and put on a mantel over a fireplace. Anyone killed in Nam was a hero in one way or another.

I wish I could honestly say that all the deaths in our company and in Nam were combat related; I am afraid that wasn't the case. I would guess that about thirty percent of all the deaths were noncombat related, and sometimes just a stupid waste of life. One of the battalion mail clerks shot himself in the head while cleaning his .45 automatic pistol. Dumb. Three guys got zonked on dope and went to sleep under a deuce-and-a-half truck. The truck driver returned to the deuce and a half, started the truck, and ran over them. Some guys got too much dope and overdosed. Mixed with combat deaths, one dumb thing after another took place. Each was so sad.

From personal experience, I knew that accidents do happen and that stupid things do take place. That monkey thing wasn't the only inane thing I did. One other incident was far worse.

Basically, I hadn't eaten World food in many months. Karen continued sending me packages, and I blessed her. But she was limited as to what she could put in them. The chocolate-covered cherries were an example of a no-no. Our mess hall's cuisine lacked imagination and, often, taste. When I had been humping the boonies, it seemed like a hot meal was sent from heaven, but once I got used to being a REMF, even hot mess hall food was boring. I had not eaten pizza, real hamburgers, or popcorn in nine months. I could get wet dreams just thinking about those food groups.

One day a package of food from home produced a pan of Jiffy Pop, a pan of unpopped popcorn wrapped in aluminum foil. I now unwrapped all packages from home in the security and sanctity of my hootch so no one knew I had received treasure in the mail. Immediately, I secreted it away deep in the confines of my abode. The next night, I put myself on the perimeter-guard list. There was a method to my madness. If I cooked the Jiffy Pop in my hootch, its pungent odor would travel to other hootches, and I would replay the chocolate-covered-cherry scene again.

"Not even!" I told myself. Instead, I would go to the bunker line early, use heat tabs to cook the Jiffy Pop, and there, by myself, eat it all alone. No one went to guard duty early. If they made it on time, it was a miracle, and usually, thirty minutes late was an allowable standard.

That evening, I was first to arrive at Bunker 14. I was soon ready to cook the popcorn. I squatted down over the blue heat tabs and lit them. I then held the Jiffy Pop over the flame and tried to pop it. Nothing happened. The heat tabs didn't produce enough heat. They did produce a string of swearing and consternation. It was getting close to guard time, and it would be just my luck that people would start arriving on time. I moved my cooking operation inside the bunker and out of the wind. I considered taking a claymore apart. The puttylike C-4 explosive used in claymores created a perfect cooking flame. But stepping on the C-4 to extinguish the flame would cause it to explode, thus blowing off parts of a foot.

In the Red One, we had used C-4 for cooking all the time, but the Cav really frowned on it. In addition, there was always the chance that the claymore I took apart for cooking fuel would be needed later that night for defense against the enemy. It might seem a false—and dangerous—economy to use a claymore, but there were also trip flares that had been placed in the wire to alert the perimeter guard that a ground attack was in progress.

The trip flares burned phosphorus, and they burned hot. Just the opposite of the wimpy heat tabs. Without another thought, in the confines of the bunker, I picked up a trip flare, popped it, and aimed it at the Jiffy Pop. But the damned trip flare spit out flame and phosphorus. A phosphorus burn is terrible. Each time I tried to hold the Jiffy Pop over the trip flare, I had to pull it back because the flame and the spitting phosphorus were just too hot and dangerous. To compound the situation, the trip flare got really hot, and I had to drop it.

Drop it on top of some detonation cord! Det cord looked like a plastic rope and was used to hook one claymore mine to another. With det cord we could daisy-chain claymores so the whole line would blow up within a millisecond.

Det cord was just another form of explosive. It was there on the ground because no one ever cleaned up the bunkers. When guard duty was over, we just threw the claymores, det cord, and spare ammo into the bunker and walked away. They would be the problem of the next night guards. Not the best practice, but keeping a tidy bunker was never a guy thing.

The trip flare had hit the dirt, where it spit smoke and fire on the det cord. An explosion was imminent! I had two choices. Run out of the bunker or get the det cord away from the trip flare. In a panic, I kicked the det cord away from the flare. There was a lot of it, and the stuff wanted to maintain its original position and shape, so it kept springing back to rest where it had started. I continued to do a quickstep with the det cord and, at the same time, kept trying to kick the trip flare outside of the bunker door. Fred Astaire never displayed quicker feet or better dancing ability. Smoke filled the bunker, and I began to choke, but one last kick at the flare sent it out the door. Coughing and gagging, I followed. I was still not sure that the bunker wouldn't blow up at any second.

As I moved away from the bunker, I realized how stupid I had been once again. I had almost blown myself up trying to pop some Jiffy Pop. I looked at the Jiffy Pop, but I couldn't fault the popcorn. Instead, I hid it. I took the handle of the pan and tucked it in the back waistband of my pants where the handle of the Jiffy Pop was held firmly and the pan itself, warmish but not hot, rested in the small of my back. I covered all with my jungle fatigue shirt. To the outside world, no one could tell what I had in the back of my pants and against the small of my back.

Sure enough, the captain of the guard was making an inspection of the bunker line. He roared down on Bunker 14 in his jeep. He was pissed.

"What in the hell is going on? Why is there smoke coming out of that bunker?"

I still didn't have my wits about me enough to exercise common sense, so I took the offensive. "This bunker's a mess! There's stuff lying around all over it. Are you in charge of this perimeter? Why is that stuff just thrown in there? I just went in there and tripped a flare. It sparked all over the place. I could have been killed. Somebody is going to hear about this! This is exactly why they have inspector generals. Who are you?" I was shaking with fright and horror. The hot pan of Jiffy Pop was starting to burn the small of my back. I was in deep trouble.

With a general look of dismay and, oh shit, I don't need this, the captain of the guard said, "Okay, okay, get this place cleaned up. I'll be back later."

"Well, I'll clean it up this time. It don't mean nothing anyway!" I growled.

He drove off, and I went back into the bunker. It was a mess. I sorted out a few things, then went outside. Other people were arriving, and I went back to my hootch to hide the Jiffy Pop. Then I went back to the bunker and stood guard. It was a miserable night. Not everyone who should have come down to guard duty arrived. We were short one man. Then two of the guys went and sat on the berm and smoked dope. They were useless, and crashed. I stood my own three-hour guard plus one for the dopers. And then half of another one. I considered the extra duty punishment for the Jiffy Pop fiasco.

Perimeter guard was never fun. Two people would stand a three-hour guard together. Usually they would face one another, and one guy would sleep sitting up for an hour and a half while the other guy stayed alert. Then they would switch. If a captain or sergeant of the guard came up to the bunker, the guy who was awake would kick the sleeping person, and both would pretend they had been alert. Sometimes both guys would fall asleep, and if they were caught, Article 15 punishments were handed out.

In addition to boredom and lack of sleep, we had the opportunity to mingle with mosquitoes and rats. From time to time, aerial flares lit up the sky so that we could look out and see if any gooks were sneaking up on us. At night, we would wrap in a jungle poncho liner to combat the lower temperatures. The night temperatures were not really cold, except when compared to the daytime degrees of misery. Of course, rain made guard duty just a little extra special, too.

More misery hit our company. One guy set out an automatic ambush and his buddy walked into it the next day and was KIA. The grunt who had set out the ambush went crazy. The captain sent him to the rear, and we were supposed to watch over him. He kept saying he wanted to join his buddy, but it was next to impossible to keep knives, guns, and explosives away from someone in a combat zone. Even so, we locked up as much stuff as we could. But when he kept saying, every night, that he wanted to go on perimeter guard, I realized that he wasn't getting better. Finally, we obtained permission to move him to a hospital in Bien Hoa.

Next, three blacks refused to go to the field. The white-man's-war syndrome had struck again. I acted as an official witness to their refusal to follow a lawful order to go to the field. I knew that I might have to testify, which would get me a few days in Bien Hoa or Long Binh. But the MPs came for them, and I don't know what happened to them. White man's war, my butt!

One of our guys was caught with some dope in his pocket by the MPs in Bien Hoa. He had come back from R & R and swore that he had put on the wrong shirt when he had gotten out of the showers. Since we rarely wore shirts with the correct names on them, that could have been the case. True or not, he was court-martialed. We sent him to Long Binh under the guard of a grunt with only twenty days left in country. The guard got drunk and the prisoner took the guard's .45 pistol and kept it for him so he wouldn't hurt himself. The prisoner came back to the company with the gun and his papers—reducing him in rank and fining him some money.

The guard showed up two days later and swore that five Saigon cowboys had hit him over the head and taken his gun. After listening to his story and questioning him about the details, I produced his gun, holster, and pistol belt. He looked sheepish, and I gloated. I wasn't a big enough person not to tell everyone in Song Be that story.

J. B. Paris came in from the field for a trip to the dentist, which he stretched into a two-week tour in the rear. It was really good to see one of the guys from 4-6, my old platoon. It was from him that I got the straight facts about one of the KIAs I had written up as a combat fatality. In real life, our guy got his head cut off by a helicopter blade. He had been playing cards, and when the chopper came in, he was supposed to unload it. He was pissed that his card game had been interrupted and wasn't looking where he was going. He walked downhill, and because of the way the chopper was sitting, the blades were closer to the ground than normal, and he walked right into them. Such a waste.

While at the dentist, J.B. heard that there was going to be a Mormon meeting, and demanded that he be allowed to go. I knew for a fact he was a Southern Baptist, but he said he had converted. For some reason, the regular chaplain didn't do Mormon services, and they held special meetings in Long Binh every month or so. J.B. was off to the meeting. He stretched that into a ten-day religious experience in Saigon. He came back with the Book of Mormon and the dates for the next meeting. I asked J.B. what he knew about Joseph Smith. J.B. said he had never met him but that he might have traded drinks with a guy in a bar in Saigon with a name similar to that.

Rumor had it that our battalion was going to move from Song Be to Phuoc Vinh, a more civilized area away from the Cambodian border. We began to pack for the trip, and I began to think in earnest about R & R in Hawaii with

Karen. Each day and night, I envisioned some lewd aspect of that five-day rendezvous. But before I held Karen in my arms, I would have to weave my way through a variety of complicated situations.

During the first week of September, I became entwined in a minor international incident. One of the South Vietnamese Kit Carson scouts had come in from the jungle. Generally, the Kit Carson scouts were former Viet Cong or North Vietnamese who had decided to switch sides. They were part of the *Chieu Hoi* program the United States had established to entice enemy deserters. They generally worked with the company, but usually the term "scout" was stretching their duties a little. Rarely did they walk point, and rarely did they walk anywhere near up front. A few did and were very brave, but most of the time, if the point man thought there was trouble up front, he would call up the Kit Carson scout, who would either confirm or deny the suspicion, and return to his place in the rear of the column. I had seen good Kit Carson scouts and bad ones. Sergeant Hoa had been so-so. But when he came to the Bravo Company rear area, he had a request. He wanted to go to Vietnamese Officer Training School. He wanted to advance himself.

We all complimented him on this. The general attitude of the average GI in Nam was that the United States had sent the unwilling to help the ungrateful do the impossible. Now here was a Vietnamese who wanted to advance himself to better fight the war. Wow!

I typed up a glowing recommendation and forwarded it to the South Vietnamese Army headquarters at Song Be. Sergeant Hoa waited for an answer. He waited for two weeks. One day, I noticed he had a Timex watch exactly like mine. Time, tide, and sweat had eaten away the leather wristband, and he had replaced it with a rucksack strap just as I had done. The similarities between our two watches were astonishing. Too much so. When I looked in the drawer of my desk, where I kept the watch, it was not there. Sergeant Hoa had liberated it. I was deeply offended. I had taken extra time and patience to type up a really effective letter to get the guy a promotion, and he had repaid me by stealing my watch.

Realizing that the Vietnamese were not as fortunate as we capitalistic Americans, I employed diplomatic courtesy and the next time I saw him I told him. "That's my watch! You put back in drawer!" He started to protest, but I looked him in the eyes, repeated my statement, and walked off. The next day the watch was back in my desk drawer. The incident would have ended if I hadn't told the XO, who told the Vietnamese military contingent at Song Be. They summoned me before some kind of military court. Sergeant Hoa told them his story in Vietnamese, and I told them my story in English. I doubt that they matched.

Somehow the court got the impression that I had given Sergeant Hoa the watch, or that I didn't want it, or that I had thrown it away. They asked me questions in Vietnamese, which, of course, I didn't understand. Their command of English was equal to my command of Vietnamese. Sergeant Hoa glared at me the entire time. He clearly considered me some kind of traitor, even though I had typed up such a good evaluation for him. It was a screwy affair, and I was pleased when they dismissed me and I left the Vietnamese tent.

I don't know what happened to Sergeant Hoa, but he never returned to our company. I had my watch, and I was happy. I did worry about Hoa's chucking a grenade into my hootch some night, but then I had Max with me, and he hated the Vietnamese. He would have barked up a storm if Hoa had come into the Bravo Company area. Max had become my shadow because he had recently gotten into trouble and felt he had best stay in our area for a while.

Max's trouble was not really his fault, that time. He and a jeep full of Bravo Company grunts had gone off to perimeter guard, a nightly occurrence. Max usually made his way home sometime after dark. He would push through the mosquito netting that covered the entrance to my hootch and zonk out at the foot of my bed. There he would remain throughout the night, unless disturbed by

someone entering the sleeping quarters. If he recognized
the person, they passed unharmed. On the other hand, if
the intruder was a Vietnamese or someone who had been
blowing grass, Max went wild. He would growl and bark
and raise the dead. In the dark of night, he could give the
impression of being five times his size. If the army had
given me a one-day drop for each day I had remaining in
Nam for each of the times Max nailed someone, I would
have gone home at least two months early. Grunts zonked
on weed would come back to the company area, and the
next thing I'd hear would be, "Professor! Help! Call him
off!" Max hated the smell of pot and wasn't above
showing his feelings.

The evening Max got into trouble, he had jumped on the
jeep with the guard detachment. Bravo Company grunts
loved to take him along. The bond between man and dog is
a natural union no matter the country or situation. This
night the guard detachment headed for the berm, and
somewhere along the way, when they slowed down to ne-
gotiate a bad part of the perimeter road, Max spied a large
white dog that must have somehow shown him some sign
of disrespect. Max jumped out of the jeep, ran at the white
dog, and after a brief skirmish, chastised it severely. The
white dog ran for the safety of its home area, another battalion's cook tent.

Into the cook tent Max went after the dog. Seconds later
out came Max on the run. Behind him was a three-hundred-
pound black cook with a meat cleaver. Max made the jeep
and jumped in. The cook took one swing at Max with the
meat cleaver as he jumped and cut part of his left rear leg.
It was not a bad cut, but it was a cut. The Bravo grunts,
who had been roaring with laughter and not a little pride as
Max chased the white dog, turned sour. One of the guys
stuck his M-16 up under the cook's chin, then locked and
loaded a round. It was a reflex reaction, but one made with
deadly intent. The cook's eyes bulged. He was looking
at death. It clearly wasn't a race relations situation, as
one of the Bravo Company blacks kept yelling, "Do him,

man! Off the motherfucker!" Others in the jeep felt the same way.

Tension was high, but luckily an artillery captain witnessed the incident and intervened. He ran up to the jeep, and ordered the Bravo Company grunt to put down the M-16 and clear it. He told the others to shut up. Backed by the captain, the cook got his courage up and tried to hit the driver of the jeep with his fist. His blow missed, and he hit the captain. At that point, the cook was in *big* trouble; he had assaulted an officer. To make matters worse, the captain's hat had been knocked from his head and had landed in the mess hall grease pit—except for a latrine, the most disgusting place on the base. The captain was furious.

Other officers and personnel arrived, and amid, "I'll get you later!" and "Watch your back, sucker!" the three sides parted and went their ways. The captain involved reported the incident to me in detail. He wanted immediate action and severe punishments for the Bravo Company grunts. He was red in the face when he related the incident. Suppressing a smirk, I started typing up a series of statements and charges. During the next few weeks, we delayed doing much about them, and the captain rotated to another job. I buried the paperwork, but not the memory. I used it as a threat against Max when he didn't behave himself. The story made its way around Song Be and even out to the field. Grunts coming into the company area would pop a beer or a soda, see Max, and start teasing him about it. Max was a real morale booster.

If Max did his part to boost our morale, so did the traveling Miss America USO show. I never would have thought that Song Be was big enough or important enough to merit a visit from Miss America 1970 and some of her lovely court, but one day, there she was. On a makeshift stage, they sang and danced. Due to the press of bodies, it was hard to see and harder to hear them. We just did not care. I justified watching the show on the premise that I had missed the Bob Hope show so the army owed me entertainment. The sight of round-eye women drove us crazy. Their visit had been quick and kind of unexpected, but it was a glimpse of what the World still held in store for us. God bless their souls!

The executive officer said it would be okay if I went out to the company during the next sit-down resupply. I had some paperwork that needed attention, and to be honest, I needed some adventure. The trip out was uneventful. I was carrying the pay for the company in a money belt, so that was a worry. Paying the company was the XO's job, but we worked things out. He had been a good leader in combat, and he trusted the people around him to do the right thing. He trusted me, and we got along well. Besides, I could forge his name better than he could write it.

The grunts were astonished to see me. Company clerks usually didn't visit the guys in the field, and that visit was my second trip out. I had gone once while the company had been along the Cambodian border. The main purpose of the first trip had been to qualify for a Cambodian campaign medal if one was issued. Now I just wanted to reacquaint myself with members of our company. Both the FNGs and the short-timers liked it that I came out. It was good public relations. Secretly, I knew that I wouldn't stay the night. I didn't take my M-16, not even a rucksack, just a .45. In addition, I typed myself priority orders so that I'd have first chance at any chopper transportation I wanted. I was going in style.

I was on the first resupply chopper out to the company and on the last one to return to Song Be, which allowed me maximum time in the field. The company had received a sit-down resupply, and we had arranged for them to have a hot meal. The U.S. Army tried whenever possible to provide a hot meal for units on operations, and that was always appreciated. Large insulated containers of food were loaded onto helicopters and ferried out to the troops. After the men had eaten, the containers were ferried back into the fire support base. I rode amid the sloppy pots and containers on the last chopper back to Song Be.

Rather than sitting on the floor in the doorway the way I had on the flight out, I perched myself on top of a pot that had contained buttered whole corn. Butter and leftover cooking water leaked out the gap between the pot and the lid on which I had parked my behind and my butt got soaked. More important, so did the floor of the chopper, which became a slippery, greasy mess. The weather was a bit rough and the chopper started weaving and jerking from the left to the right and back again. One pot slid out of the right door and fell. Evidently, the pilot was enjoying watching my consternation over whether I would accompany the next pot going airborne; he looked back and grinned. He probably was just funning with a REMF, but my dignity was injured. Maybe other chairborne Rangers deserved to be messed with by the air wing of the army, but not me; I was a former 11Bravo20 grunt. With pants soaked in butter and corn juice, I knew I didn't look combat ready, but I set my dignity aside and cautiously eased off the pot of corn and onto the floor, where my behind had a better grip. As the chopper hit the tarmac at Song Be, I slid out the door, off-loaded, and without a look back, I headed for Bravo Company and a shower.

The calendar was never one's friend. At the start of our tour of duty, 365 days seemed like an eternity. Now ninety days seemed like they would never pass. Rumors were flying. Nixon would soon be allowing troops to go home early. People were getting seven- to ten-day early outs. Short-timers' calendars now had another factor to take into consideration.

And, finally, the predicted move from Song Be was about to take place. We would pull up everything and move it by road and chopper to our new area in Phuoc Vinh, a major city and a major post located in the middle of the country. Nixon and the Joint Chiefs of Staff didn't consult us. We just got ready to move. I was packed and ready to go in more ways than one. I had at last secured permission to go on R & R, and I was to meet Karen in Hawaii. Karen had been my mental and physical support throughout my tour. I looked forward to the time we would spend together. My poor mom had hinted that she might enjoy seeing Hawaii, too, but Karen tactfully talked her out of it. I loved my mother, but . . .

Time can play dirty tricks on a grunt. It passed super-slow while you were in Nam and superfast while you were on R & R. In letters that had probably scorched the mailman's hands, I had encouraged Karen to wear a low-cut dress when she met me at the R & R center. In her replies, she had seemed hesitant, but when I got off the army bus, she was there, and I was more than pleased with the white scoop-neck dress she wore. Karen had fulfilled my every fantasy. We kissed and necked our way through the thirty-minute orientation given to R & R–bound troops headed for civilization in Hawaii. Then, formalities completed, we headed for our hotel.

Hawaii is rich in culture and American history, and Karen and I did Hawaii proud. We almost saw parts of it. And kind of saw other parts. But we missed the Pearl Harbor Memorial. Our patriotic intentions dissolved when Karen chose that afternoon to perform her exotic dance of the seven veils. I'm afraid Karen saw a lot of the ceiling in our hotel room. As with any newly married, reunited couple, we created our own entertainment.

For me, the airplane ride back to Nam was sickening. I promised Karen I would be safe and wouldn't take any chances. And when I made the promise, I meant it. "All I have to do is lay low," I reassured her.

By my return to Nam, the company had completed the move to Phuoc Vinh. They had missed me. They had missed me so much they had put in a requisition for a real company clerk to take my place. I was officially short enough to be declared useless. It felt really good.

Of course, having been away from my duties for ten days, I found the paperwork and mischief had stacked up. In addition, setting up a rear area in a new location had its challenges. I threw myself into my work with all my heart. In Hawaii, I had seen the World. It was still there, and all I had to do was keep myself busy until it was my turn to catch the Freedom Bird home.

Busy I was. We had a new executive officer, and he needed to be trained. He often thought that he should sign important papers. After practicing his signature, I convinced him that he was wrong, and that I would handle signing his name for him. He soon concurred.

J.B. came in from the field because the scheduled Mormon meeting was about to take place. J.B. had clearly become a powerful influence on the religious sensibilities of the company, because he brought with him four new converts who had had reputations as slackers and malingerers. But, thanks to J.B., they had seen the errors of their ways. Off all five went to Bien Hoa.

J.B. was getting short, too. He had won a Silver Star during a firefight, and the captain was watching him less. So when he came back from his religious obligation and requested another trip to the dentist, I felt safe in sending him. Upon his return from the dentist, he set up shop to repay me for my kindnesses. J.B. had a good heart and a knack for seeing opportunities to make money where others did not. He did stuff on the black market and never got caught.

When the army changed the color of the military payment certificates (MPC) we used for money, he saw a way to help himself and others. He went to the fence where the South Vietnamese were waiting to get the attention of any guy who could help them. Changing the color of the MPC virtually changed the banking system. The old colored money was useless. From then on, only the new-colored Monopoly money would be acceptable tender at PXs and other United States military installations. That meant that Americans could go to exchange points and trade old money for new money. The South Vietnamese could not. They weren't supposed to have GI money anyway. Yet they all did; GIs paid in MPC for sodas, beers, food, hootch cleaning, and sexual services—just to mention a few items. All the money the South Vietnamese had earned from the GIs would become worthless if they couldn't get it converted from old MPC to new MPC. The changeover also made old MPC money useless to the Viet Cong as well, which was one of the main purposes of the system.

Some guys took pity and converted the money dollar for dollar for the Vietnamese; that was illegal and defeated the purpose of the switch, but it was done. Some GIs took the Vietnamese money and disappeared. They converted the money and kept it, reasoning that the Vietnamese would have had nothing if they had kept the old money, so no one was hurt. J.B. was different. He honestly exchanged money, for only a 50 percent cut. "They deserve the money no matter what color it is," he stated. "I get half because I'm taking a beaucoup chance, too." He made sense.

J.B. was now spending as much time in the rear as I was. And he was not a Cheap Charlie. He started buying his share of beer and soda for the cooler that supplied the grunts coming in from the field. While I had been on R & R, no one in the company had stocked the cooler. J.B. became aware that I was the guy who usually put up part of his personal spec four fortune to buy supplies, so he devised a system to build a fund for future beverage purchases.

He arranged to sneak girls onto the base and into the back room of the main company tent. There, in a makeshift room with spare mattresses, he went into business. When the word got out that he had two girls and that they were available at night, our company tent became very popular. Because that might seem an immoral and illegal activity to some, I put myself on guard duty on the nights when he and the girls held forth. I didn't want any part of the project. One night when I did return to the company area, I noticed that not only did he charge for short-time, but that for fifty cents you could also be a voyeur and watch other people through a peephole in the tent. J.B. may have been the inventor of the adult porno arcades.

The executive officer and the top sergeant rarely visited the company area at night, so they were not aware of the transgressions taking place. Having Vietnamese inside the wire at night, male or female, was a really bad no-no. Running a string of girls was also forbidden. One night the XO put in a rare appearance. J.B. came running back through the tent and tried to hustle the girls out the back flap while others detained the XO up front. "Beaucoup lifer coming!

Beaucoup lifer coming!" he told the girls. His meaning was, "Get out of here. The brass is coming and will catch us. Scram!" The girls misinterpreted. One grabbed her crotch and said, "No! Me sore!"

The other pulled down her panties and said, "Five dollar more, I try." They'd thought that J.B. had been talking about a lifer with a large male organ. Sometimes multilingual communications between grunts and the natives was difficult.

J.B. paid the girls, kept some of the money, and forwarded the rest to the beer and soda fund. My conscience hurt me about that, but by then, I was really, really getting short. I borrowed Ted's phrase and told people, "I am so short, that every morning I have to climb a ladder to get into my shoes." On October 2, I learned just how short I really was. My replacement walked through the front flap of the Bravo Company tent.

CHAPTER 15

Back to the World

Things were happening in Nam. More units had been designated to close down and take their colors home. That meant fewer guys back in the States were being sent to Nam as replacements. For us, it meant that we would get a rash of experienced grunts who had served with other in-country units. That was good and bad. The transferees knew combat and, in most cases, were seasoned veterans. Little or no training was necessary to get them oriented to operations in the field.

Unfortunately, as experienced grunts, they also knew the ropes. Over 60 percent of them walked through the tent flap and demanded to see the doctor, the dentist, or the chaplain. I had been in their place, so I knew what they were trying to do. I appreciated it, and when possible tried to see that they got the attention they desired; it cost the army only a few days of service per man. In addition, many of the transferees were looking for REMF jobs. Pete had walked in with a group of about twenty guys and announced up front that he could type. Was there a clerk job available?

Pete had humped for three months with the 3d Brigade of the 9th Infantry Division. They had worked in the delta country down south. He described their operations as patrolling during the day and sleeping at a fire support base at night. It sounded cushy to me. He said they had only one guy killed in a year and a half. Eventually, he had taken over the company clerk position in the same manner I had.

I held a brief conference with the top sergeant and the XO. We decided I was overworked and could use some help in the rear. Pete could train to be my replacement. With the scheduled drops coming through, I would be due for rotation back to the States within a few weeks. Someone would have to take over Bravo Company.

I took on the role of tutor, showing Pete the ropes much the way Ted had done when I came in. Then I became semiuseless. Pete already knew about morning reports and army paperwork, so I was free to dream more of home. Life would have been ideal had the army not decided that our battalion should move back to Song Be! For some grand reason, we were chosen to pack up and and move north again. I'm not sure why. Once again, we were part of some grand strategy, but who cared? I was very short. My tour of Nam was nearly done.

Once again, I noticed something about myself. When the day came to move, I elected to go via ground transportation rather than fly. I could have easily assigned myself to a chopper, but I put Pete on it instead. He went ahead to set up our company area, which was located exactly where it had been before the move to Phuoc Vinh.

Sergeant Long, a grunt nicknamed Chief, and I loaded up a jeep and its trailer, and went to what we thought was the designated assembly area with a convoy of trucks headed back up the highway to Song Be. I wanted one last look at Nam up close and personal, and maybe one last tempting of fate, one last firefight. It was a goofy thing to do.

Moving day started out badly. We waited in the assembly area for two hours for the convoy to show up. It never did. Our radio communication was poor, and we didn't know the convoy had already left, or that we were stranded. Eventually, it dawned on us that something wasn't right, and we went looking for information. Sergeant Long found some people he knew from supply and learned that we were two hours behind the convoy. "Don't worry. I've got a map. Besides, how many highways are there in Nam?" he said.

With that, he beckoned Max to jump into the jeep. Chief and I hopped in as well. To be honest, I had expressed great enthusiasm for a trip north with a convoy of trucks and GIs. A solo trip with two other grunts and a dog didn't fit into my original plans. But Long was optimistic. "Professor, don't you worry. You and Chief are security, and I'll drive. Keep your M-16 ready. You have a full field load of ammo. There shouldn't be any problems. How fast can a convoy of trucks go, anyway? We can catch them in a half hour. No problem. You just have short-timer's fever."

I agreed with his calculations. How fast could a convoy of trucks go down a Vietnamese highway? Besides, I knew that Long with his M-16 and Chief with the M-79 grenade launcher would be dependable guys in a firefight. The adrenaline pumped as Long started the motor, and off we went to catch the Song Be–bound convoy.

At first we made great time. We were on a paved highway, and swinging in and out of Vietnamese traffic, Long showed great skill as a driver. Driving in Nam, like any Third World country, was half guts and half horn. Bluff and honk was SOP.

We flew past Vietnamese Lambrettas and buses. Bicycles scattered. For about twenty miles, we felt no pain. Yet we didn't see the convoy. The paved road gave way to a hard-packed, red-dirt road, deeply rutted and terrible to navigate. All Long could do was stay in a line behind Vietnamese traffic. At times, he attempted to pass; sometimes he could, and sometimes he would encounter a part of the road that was so poor that traffic could only go one way at a time. So, slowly we made our way down the road. We still hadn't caught up with the convoy.

Noon came and went, and we were in the scenic countryside, the kind of place where tourists pay to see the natives in their natural surroundings. And the army was giving all that to us for free. We passed through small Vietnamese villages that were marginally protected by irregular Vietnamese guards that we called Ruff-Puffs from their abbreviation, Regional Forces Popular Forces. One was never

sure if the RFPFs were on our side or on the side of the
Viet Cong. At each encounter, a glaring contest took place.

Once we stopped to remove a stick that had been snared
by the undercarriage of the jeep, becoming wedged in
such a manner as to rub against the right rear tire. "Wow,"
I exclaimed. "I'm glad that didn't pop the tire. The time it
would take to change that would have put us really behind.
Do we have a jack?"

"Not even, Professor, we don't need a jack. We don't
have a spare tire," Long explained. We were touring Nam
over some of its worst roads, and we didn't have a jack or
spare tire. Long continued, "Don't sweat it! I'm more
worried about the road being mined than getting a flat
tire."

On we continued down the road, and at about 1500
hours we caught the tail of the convoy. I was never so
pleased to see a column of trucks in my life. At least if we
broke down, we could get help. Or so I reasoned. I knew
we had reached the end of the convoy, because there in the
middle of the road was a truck that was being serviced by a
squad of army mechanics. A classic motor pool sergeant,
greasy, potbellied, and sucking on the stub of a cigar, was
cussing them out. He wanted certain things done and done
now! The squad of mechanics jumped when he gave directions. The day was getting late, and they didn't want to be
on the road after dark any more than we did. Once we had
passed the sergeant, his wrecker, and his fix-up squad, we
felt better. Surely they wouldn't leave us out there with
mechanical troubles. I hoped. From the look of the sergeant, I would have hated to test the issue.

Although we were deep in the boonies, the villages we
passed were used to seeing GIs come through in convoys,
so the kids ran out into the road to give us the V-for-victory
sign, their way of begging for food. We had little to offer,
so we felt like dirty American capitalist pigs because the
only thing we could leave them was a dust trail through
the village.

Riding in the jeep was hard on one's kidneys, so we
made frequent comfort stops. During one, Max wandered

over a small hill to the left of the road. He was out of sight for about thirty seconds. Then, barking and running, he scurried back to the jeep and hopped in. Since we were out in no-man's-land, I offered, "Gook?" Chief grabbed his grenade launcher and Long his rifle. Spreading out, we retraced Max's path. There, about fifty meters off the road on the other side of the hill, a group of Vietnamese woodcutters was moving wood to the next village via water-buffalo cart. They seemed as surprised to see us as we were to see them. One of the papa-sans offered his Vietnamese ID, but none of us knew anything about identification papers, so we examined it and gave it back to him with an official look of approval. I took a quick picture, and we hustled back to join Max in the jeep.

We still hadn't passed the main part of the truck convoy, just the rear element and several disabled trucks, each of which had a driver beside it, usually alone with his M-16, protecting the contents from the VC and from the local inhabitants. It was a lonely, hazardous job, and I gained new respect for those who had the "easy" job of driving a truck. If nothing else, I sure as hell wouldn't have liked to explain to that motor pool sergeant why my vehicle wasn't highballing down the road. Given the choice of facing the motor pool lifer or the VC, I'd have chosen the VC.

At one sharp bend in the road, we saw the Alpha Company storage conex, not on top of the flatbed truck where it belonged, but upside down in three feet of water beside the road. It had somehow broken the bands that held it on the truck and had flipped over. Our better-Alpha's-than-ours attitude was un-Christian. We didn't even stay to help extract it. Daylight was leaving us, and we wanted to be off the road as soon as possible. About ten more miles down the road, we entered Song Be and Firebase Buttons. It was nice to be home.

Our former area in Song Be wasn't what it had been. The tents were messed up and torn. The wood platforms that had formed the floor of the tents and had kept us dry during wet weather had been liberated by other units when we left, and all we had were dirt floors. We didn't have electricity, and the small fan I'd used to circulate air in my hootch had been misplaced or stolen. Sleeping without it was a bummer.

I was curious to find out what time the tail end of the convoy got in to Song Be. The motor pool wasn't far from the company area, so the next morning, I wandered over. After talking to one of the mechanics, I found out that the last truck had been repaired on the road and limped into Song Be around midnight. The motor pool sergeant had gotten all his chickens into the coop. That wouldn't be the last trip for him or the convoy. They were headed back the next day. Sometimes, we grunts didn't respect the role played by support units.

Reconstructing a company area in Song Be was no dream. But basically, it was not my problem. Battalion kept sending us drop notices, and we were yanking people in from the field and rotating them home two and three weeks early. GIs were out of their minds with glee. On October 27, another list of personnel who could leave Nam arrived. My name was on that list. Since men do not cry, my eyes filled with wet drops of emotion. There was my reprieve from Nam. I could go home just as fast as I could get released from the company, packed, and down to Long Binh and Bien Hoa. We had a saying that went something like, "When I die, I know that I will go to heaven, because I've spent my time in hell!" Pete was looking over my shoulder at the list of drops. His name would not appear on one for several months, so I could guess his feelings. Once again, I experienced the mixture of giddiness and guilt I had felt when I left the guys in the field to come in as company clerk. It was difficult to explain to Pete, so I didn't try. He would find out when it was his turn.

"I'll type up your orders," he offered. "We'll get you out today!"

"No, thanks, I'll go tomorrow morning. Put me on guard duty tonight."

That night was the best guard duty I ever had. I sat up almost all night under Vietnamese stars. The Southern Cross was a sight I thought that I would never see again. The guys on the bunker were a combination of new guys and seasoned grunts in from the field and soon to be homeward bound. We talked about our anticipated homecomings and told war story after war story. We were experiencing the joy of survival. In a way, we were also getting all our data banks set up for years of memory use. What we remembered as we left Nam would be what stayed with us for the rest of our lives. We practiced relating the information to friendly ears first. They were a kind of test market for the world to which we were to return.

In the World, our stories would grow and be embellished in millions of homes, around thousands of campfires, in hundreds of classrooms, and in any suitable social situation for as long as there were Vietnam veterans alive to remember and tell them. If Vietnam vets had anything good from their experiences, they had their stories and memories and photographs.

The next morning, for the first morning in almost a year, I wasn't tired. I sat down in front of the old Royal typewriter and took a deep breath. I started typing up the paperwork that I would need to go home. That included authorization for the Chicom SKS rifle that I would take with me. I had put a special SKS aside. Our company had always kept the rifles it found in Nam, and we had a large supply. Every member of the company was entitled to one. A returning GI could take only one semiautomatic weapon back to the States as a souvenir, and this was mine. I had cleaned and relished it. Now all I had to do was to watch over it so some REMF didn't steal it. I had already sent other VC and NVA items home. I hadn't carried a lot of souvenir stuff, but while with the Big Red One and the Cav, I had accumulated several minor objects to send back. Most of my bounty consisted of uniform items and other incidentals. In retrospect, I wished that I had sent back more, but those things did not seem important at the time.

At 1000 hours, I shook hands with the people in the company rear area. I wished them good luck. Because we were used to a constant ebb and flow of personnel, relationships were never all that deep. I patted Max on the head, and told Pete that he should watch over him. To tell the truth, in the last few days Max had gravitated to Pete the same way he had gravitated to me. Somehow, he had known after our adventure on the trip back to Song Be that I wasn't to be in his future much longer. Although I took pictures of the Bravo Company rear area, I took one last look at it. I wanted to freeze it in my memory. Pete drove me to the shack that served as the Song Be airport terminal. I was truly homeward bound.

Stepping into the darkness of the hut from the bright sunlight, I couldn't see anything. As I waited for my eyes to adjust, I heard a voice that I recognized but couldn't place. "Schneider? Is that you?"

Then, standing up from a bench full of men and stepping into my rapidly clearing vision, was Joe MacCord. Joe and I had gone through basic training at Fort Leonard Wood together. We had gone through advanced individual training at Fort Gordon, Georgia, together. Luck would have it that each of us had independently decided to report three days AWOL at Oakland. We had flown to Nam together, and we had in-processed at the 93d Replacement Center together. MacCord had gone to the 5th of the 7th Cavalry when I had gone to the 1st Infantry Division. He had humped with Echo Company, which was primarily a recon platoon. Now we were going home together. Joe was alive. I was alive. Hollywood couldn't have written a better script. In the semidarkness of the shack, he stepped over to me and we almost hugged. It was an awkward moment. We each felt some strong, mushy emotions at seeing one another alive, but there were other grunts in the shack. So we settled for shaking hands warmly.

Then, as we had done coming into country a year earlier, we started our long journey. Our first stop on the trip home was Long Binh. There we presented our papers to the proper authorities and were scheduled on a manifest to board a Freedom Bird home. As a company clerk, I knew how careless some REMFs can be, so I checked over my

201 file carefully. I made Joe do the same. I was pleased to see that the army had not totally messed up. Under the decorations, medals, and badges sections they had listed my National Defense Ribbon, my Combat Infantryman Badge, my Vietnam Service Medal with two bronze stars, my Vietnam Campaign Medal with 1960 device, my Army Commendation Medal, my Bronze Stars with V device and two oak-leaf clusters, and my Air Medal for twenty-five or more combat assaults. They also listed the 1st Class gunner, (M-60), Sharpshooter (M-14), and Marksman (M-16), and Expert (in pistol and hand grenade) Awards. I was also authorized to wear two overseas bars on my sleeve, one for each of the six months I had spent in Nam. Army paperwork being what it was, I hadn't turned out too bad. I was the most proud of the Combat Infantry-man's Badge, because it told the world that I had humped and fought. The Bronze Stars and Army Commendation Medal were for action during firefights.

The division clerk informed MacCord and me that we would be on one of the next available Freedom Birds home. He must have had a neat job. "But," he continued, "the main airline that services Tan Son Nhut from the States is on strike. Go down to the 93d Replacement and wait for your name to be called and posted. You may be there for a few days. Sorry about that."

MacCord and I looked at one another. We were alive. We were not hungry or cold. And no one was shooting at us. So all we had to do was wait. And wait we did. It took almost one week for the army and the airlines to settle their differences. During that time, people stacked up in Long Binh and at Bien Hoa. There were people all over the place. At night, MacCord and I often slept on outside tables. The dead time created some bad attitudes among the troops, and the gooks could have done some damage if they had hit us with mortars or rockets. Fortunately, the NVA were concentrating on fighting in the north and in the Delta at that particular time.

On 9 November, MacCord's name and mine were posted. We were to leave at 0900 hours the next day. So as not to miss the flight, we went over to the terminal and stayed there all that night.

The next day, we went through customs, where we discarded anything such as ammo or weapons or dope that we might try to sneak back into the United States. I had none of that stuff, but I did have a U.S. Government ballpoint pen that I realized I had been using, and tossed it under the table just in case.

In the newly built Tan Son Nhut airport terminal, we waited while a new group of cherries off-loaded our Freedom Bird. I remembered my first feelings and impressions about Nam. The smell of the country, the humidity, and, in my case, the erroneous impression that we were under attack all came back to me. Some of those guys would be casualties of this war, one way or another.

But I was headed home. The crowd in our homeward-bound section yelled and screamed, "Short! Short!" We made gestures with our thumb and forefinger showing just how short we were. Just like the returnees who had greeted our plane a year earlier, our behavior was utterly unmilitary and disgraceful. We were a wild mob about to storm the airplane.

I remembered one of the most sacred promises I had made to myself on that first day as I entered Nam. After seeing the mob of people who had greeted us, I had promised myself that if and when I left the country, I would do it with dignity. I might not have shown much dignity at times during my tour, but by God, I would show it as I left. A very brave air force REMF stepped to a microphone and informed us that if we lined up orderly in single file and passed through his turnstile, he would allow us to board the plane while the ground crew serviced it. Single file! No way, man! Orderly—ha-ha. Paperwork was thrown at the airman. People jammed the turnstile and pushed and fought to get through. I had been to the front of the mob and, after handing my paperwork to the airman, started to walk to the Freedom Bird.

My head held high, I was leaving Nam with dignity and poise. GIs pushed past me and ran for the plane. Others followed. Two hundred–plus men were running for the Freedom Bird.

I looked down at my legs. To my astonishment, they, too, were running. I was the model of decorum from the waist up, but I was running from the waist down. When we hit the steps of the plane, I fought to be one of the first people up the steps. Once on board, we screamed, "Get this plane out of here! Get it off the ground!" The plane shook violently.

Stewardesses, older, round-eye women, grimaced and tried to appear calm to quiet us down. No way! Not even! We wanted off the ground. The plane became hot and stifling. The time dragged by until the captain came on the intercom and said we were ready for takeoff. Then the plane taxied to the end of the runway and stopped. Mac-Cord asked me if I had heard about VC snipers that sat at the end of the runway and shot at Freedom Birds as they took off. I told him that those stories weren't true. I thought. I hoped.

The engines cranked up. The plane started to coast down the runway, gained speed, then made a steep climb to avoid snipers—just in case. We were homeward bound. After an initial cheer, the plane fell dead silent.

It took about twenty-three hours to fly home. Our route was Vietnam to Guam, then on to Travis Air Force Base in California. I would look at my watch, read a book, sleep, talk to MacCord, and look at my watch again. It would be ten minutes later. Time literally stood still. Maybe it had to do with the international date line, I don't know.

Now I thought of home and family. Karen didn't know when I was due to arrive in the States. I would call her. In my mind, I'd thought that if I could get home during the day while she was still teaching school, I would visit her during her last class. I would walk into her classroom and in a dramatic gesture sweep her off her feet and into my arms. I would turn to her class and declare, "Class dismissed!" I envisioned the kids screaming in joy and crowding around us. They would hug and slap the back of the returning hero. Wow! What a scene!

In real life, I realized that after I in-processed, got fitted with a dress uniform, and made reservations for a seat on a commercial airliner to St. Louis, I would be lucky if I made it home before midnight on November 12. I decided not to call ahead. I would surprise Karen at her parents' house, then go over to my parents' house and surprise them. I relished the thought of the look on their faces.

At Travis Air Force Base, we disembarked. I kept an eye on my SKS as it came off of the conveyor belt from the plane. The air force wouldn't let us put covers or cases on the weapons, so they got really scratched and nicked up. The stock on mine received a deep gouge. I hated to see that. I had taken such good care of it up until then. But that was only a minor problem.

Returnees were fitted with a dress uniform. We returned to the same building we had used to go to Nam. I could see guys going to Nam, throwing their dress uniforms into the same bin that I had used eleven months and seven days earlier. They, too, were being told that they would not have to pay for their dress uniform upon return. That was a lie. The clerk at my next duty station charged me for my lost uniform.

MacCord and I parted company. He went back to Kansas and I caught the first flight out to St. Louis. At Lambert Airport, I flagged a cab and sat back and relaxed. I couldn't wait to see the look on Karen's face when I walked into her mom's house. How would my mom and dad and brothers look? How should I act?

Actually it wasn't very kind of me to surprise Karen. The cab pulled up in her parents' driveway, and the cabbie got out and got my baggage from the trunk. He asked to see the SKS rifle. I really wanted to get inside the house, but I was too proud not to take the time to show him. We spent several minutes talking about his nephew in Nam. He said that he admired all of us who had been to Vietnam and that we were heroes. But he still charged me for the cab ride.

About 10:00 P.M., I knocked on the front door of Karen's parents' home and was greeted by her sister. She held her astonishment well and, after a quick hug and a kiss, called Karen from her bedroom where she was doing lesson plans for school the next day. At first, Karen didn't want to come to the door to greet a late guest. She was in her housecoat and curlers. When she did come to the front hall, she stood there in amazement. "What are you doing here?" was all she could say. "You should be in Vietnam! What are you doing here?"

"I'm home! I got an early out!"

Her mom heard the commotion in the front hall and came to see what was happening. The poor woman almost fainted. She had to sit down and recover.

Karen called in sick to school for the next day, and we dropped Karen's lesson plans off with a teacher who taught in her department. There was a Holiday Inn conveniently close, and we headed for it immediately. This was where I experienced my first brush with discrimination against Vietnam vets. When I told him that I was just off the plane from Nam, he demanded to see proof that Karen and I were married. Karen was wearing the R & R dress, and the clerk may have observed that I had a wild look in my eye. We produced the required identification and then ran to the room he assigned. We spent a night of ecstasy. After all, we now had a future.

Our next stop was my parents' house. They had been forewarned. I had called them a few minutes after greeting Karen. At my parents' house, we parked the car and climbed the front steps. I started to hide my left arm in the sleeve of my coat to make it look like I had lost an arm, but Karen rightly said that I would give my mother a heart attack. Since Mom had a weak heart, that was good advice. Mom cried. Dad's eyes filled with wet drops of emotion. My brothers shook hands and immediately wanted to see the SKS. The greeting was wonderful! I was home. My year of war was over.

Reflections

All my life, I've remembered that year in Nam. For me it had been a growth experience comparing to none other. I had reached down inside regions of my physical and mental reserves that I didn't know existed. I hadn't done great deeds of valor, but I had done a little. Nam helped define who I was and who I would become. Later in life, when I met bad times, I could always say, "I'm not cold, I'm not hungry, and no one is shooting at me." I also found the company and the companionship of other Vietnam veterans comforting. No matter what our assignments had been in Nam, we shared a bond and closeness. We shared a common language and an understanding of the importance of living a full life.

I went back to teaching and building America. I became chairman of the unified studies (combined English and history) department and coached track and football. I was fortunate enough to teach eighth grade for thirty-four years. Most parents hate the time that their kids are in eighth grade because that period is one of the most traumatic times in a young adult's life; I loved that age group because I knew I could have a positive impact on young people. I knew how to fight what at times seemed a losing battle.

Vietnam had taught me the concept of mission. My mission was to prepare young Americans who would be strong in academic skills as well as strong in the knowledge and appreciation of our country's history. When I returned from Vietnam, I was rehired in the same school I had left. In fact, I was eventually reassigned to the classroom that I had used the year before I had been drafted.

Once, when our school principal had made a particularly bad educational decision that harmed the students and teachers in our school, I became infuriated. One of my fellow teachers, who had served in Vietnam, wisely advised me in the language of our experience. "Ches, you've been to Nam. This guy 'don't mean nothing to you.' After Nam, every day is gravy for the rest of your life. Live it that way!"

His sound advice, based on our mutual Vietnam experience, stayed with me. Vietnam is billed as the war that America lost. Yet, in retrospect, Americans went to Nam to give the South Vietnamese a chance to construct an army and a society with which to stop the spread of Communism from North Vietnam. I think we did give the Vietnamese their chance. We just couldn't build their political and social institutions for them. When Saigon fell, the bulk of the American troops had long been withdrawn. America couldn't win a war for a country that didn't want to fight for itself.

While in Vietnam, American forces didn't lose any major campaign or battle. The enemy was able to inflict tragic losses on small groups of American troops at platoon and company level, but Americans devastated whole regiments and divisions of the Viet Cong and North Vietnamese Army. Even the 1968 Tet offensive was only an illusory victory, one that was measured in days and hours for the Communists and which cost them horrendous losses. In fact, after that offensive, the enemy's ability to wage a major campaign was destroyed and the Viet Cong ceased to be a viable force throughout most of South Vietnam.

Americans were sent to Vietnam to prevent the domino effect, countries collapsing and being taken over by Communist governments. After Vietnam, and eventually Cambodia and Laos, succumbed to Communism, not another country in the world fell to Communism. Shortly after

Vietnam was united under one Communist government, it fought its two Communist neighbors, China to the north and the Khmer Rouge in Cambodia to the west. Communists started eating up other Communists.

Perhaps the most important lesson that America learned from the Vietnam War was not to get into situations such as that again. Before Desert Storm, when Americans were unsure of our role in the Gulf region, President Bush reassured the country that "this will not be another Vietnam!" Vietnam draft dodger President Clinton had the specter of Vietnam looking over his shoulder when he sent troops into Haiti. This is also true of the missions in Somalia and Bosnia.

By learning the lessons of Vietnam, America may have saved the lives of many of its present and future young men and women. In that regard alone, Vietnam was an American victory.

Glossary

air strike   When fixed-winged aircraft were called in to hit the enemy with rockets and bombs. Including the use of B-52 bombers to blow the hell out of the jungle and anyone or anything therein.

AIT   Advanced infantry training. I had mine at Fort Gordon, Georgia. AIT followed the basic training I had at Fort Leonard Wood, Missouri.

AK-47   Made a sound you didn't want to hear. By 1970, it was the main weapon of the VC and NVA. Communist made; it was a 7.62mm automatic assault rifle.

AO   Area of operation. Could include a local area that was being worked by a small unit or a large area that was the center of attention by the command-and-control part of the army.

Arc Light   B-52 bombing missions that devastated the enemy.

Article 15   Similar to when the principal gets really angry about what some kid has done and gives an after-school detention. Punishment under the Uniform Code of Military Justice. Basically, a slap on the wrist.

Artillery   Cannon in civilian terms. Could be 105mm, 155mm, or 175mm artillery pieces used to support infantry and to fire harassment and interdiction missions. Also known as red leg. One of the first forms of support for a unit in contact with the enemy (God bless them).

ARVN   The South Vietnamese Army (Army of the Republic of Vietnam). Generally considered useless by many GIs.

AWOL   Absent without leave. AWOL could get a person an Article 15. But before going to Nam, everyone owed themselves at least three days of AWOL.

basic training   The eight weeks the U.S. Army needs to tear a person down and rebuild him (or nowadays—her) in the correct military fashion. A needed training period, but something to be enjoyed only once in a lifetime.

beaucoup   A word that I had never heard of before I became multilinguistic in Nam. Taken from the French "very many," in Nam it meant a big or large amount as well. Example: too many VC—beaucoup VC. Surprisingly, this word has entered the American lexicon with educators. Example: "Kid, you are in beaucoup trouble."

beehive round   Fired from 90mm recoilless rifle or artillery. Thousands of small two- to three-inch darts fired in one time from a shell.

berm   An earthen levee surrounding most large, permanent U.S. bases. It was part of the defense perimeter. Usually, bunkers were placed along it as fighting positions.

black market   Underground commercial system that sold anything you wanted to buy.

blasting caps   A silver device about three inches long that is inserted into claymore, plastic (C-4) explosives, satchel charges, or anything a person wants to go bang. Caution was needed when carrying them.

blood lust   A secret emotion best kept in check. When the primitive side of a rational human being surfaces. A strong desire to kill.

blood trail   A trail of blood on the undergrowth of the jungle that indicated a wounded soldier had passed (or a dead soldier had been pulled away) from the area of contact. Sometimes the only indication that the enemy had suffered casualties.

boonies   GI cute talk for the jungle and combat zones. A place to be avoided if one had typing skills.

boozers   A term borrowed from civilian vocabulary meaning drunk or heavy drinkers. Example: civilian—"My boss is a boozer"; military—"My top sergeant is a boozer."

bunker   A protected fighting position. The VC and NVA dug them into the ground and constructed overhead cover and camouflage. U.S. bunkers were built into berms along perimeters at fixed fighting positions.

burning the shit   Since there wasn't a raw sewage system in Nam, we used outhouses and cut-off barrels with a board over them as latrines. Once a day, someone had to mix the contents of the barrel with fuel oil. It was then burned and stirred. This was not a pleasant task.

bush The same as boonies. A place to be avoided unless you really like multicultural exchanges of gunfire with people from another country and culture. Same as field, Indian country, jungle, boondocks.

C-4 Plastic explosives. Used to blow up things and to cook food. Once it starts to burn, caution should be used when putting out the flame. Let the flame burn out. Don't step on it, or it will blow your foot off. Used as the explosive to fire small ball bearings in the claymore mine.

C & C Command-and-control personnel. Usually lifers who needed points for their next promotion. Directed personnel in the field.

CA Combat assault. A free helicopter ride to work. Twenty-five CAs would get you an Air Medal.

cammies Camouflaged jungle fatigues—shirts, pants, and hats. The forerunner of an entire industry that now supplies hunters and burned-out, drugged kids with clothing.

canister round Used in the M-79 grenade launcher and other weapons. In the grenade launcher, it was filled with double-aught BB shot. In the 90mm recoilless rifle, it had three thousand minidarts.

Cav Short for the 1st Air Cavalry Division.

chaplin's assistant Assisting the chaplin or army religious leader to do his duties. A job for the really religious or those smart enough to avoid the infantry.

Charlie The U.S. soldier's name for the Viet Cong. Also Chuck, VC, Sir Charles, Victor Charlie, etc.

Cheap Charlie A Vietnamese word for a GI who would not part with his money easily. (See Saigon Tea girls and short-time girls.)

Cheiu hoi When a VC or NVA saw the error of his ways and surrendered to U.S. forces. Usually waving a dollar-bill size piece of paper that indicated his intentions. In many places in Nam, the jungle floor was covered with these get-out-of-Communism-free passes.

cherry A new guy. Same as an FNG (fucking new guy). Inexperienced in combat, different units had different philosophies as to the value of a cherry's life vs. the value of a seaoned grunt.

Chicom Matériels made in Communist China.

chopper Helicopter.

chopper pad A designated place where helicopters landed and took off.

CIB The Combat Infantryman Badge. Awarded to a person who had been in a firefight or contact with the enemy. On a dress uniform, it is a silver rifle on a blue background surrounded by silver trim. The first and often the most meaningful award given to an infantry grunt.

CID Criminal investigation unit.

clacker The gray-blue handle for firing claymores. When the handle was squeezed, an electrical shock went down the claymore wire and detonated the claymore mine.

claymore mine An antipersonnel mine used extensively in Vietnam to ambush trails and protect permanent and semipermanent fighting positions. Slightly larger than a standard house brick and about half as thick, the claymore could saturate an area from ground level to six to eight feet above the ground and over an area sixty degrees in width with 750 steel ball bearings. The claymore could be hand-fired using a clacker or wired to a battery and trip wire for use as a booby trap along a trail.

claymore wire The wire that connected a claymore clacker with the blasting cap that was inserted into a hole in the top of the claymore mine itself.

CO Commanding officers. At the company level, the CO would be the captain of the company.

Cobra gunships (God bless them.) Helicopter gunships that provided close-in support for infantry units in contact with the enemy, using rockets, grenades, and machine-gun fire.

commo Grunt talk for communication.

commo check A practice transmission to ascertain if the radio was working and that the signal was being received. Another spin-off from Vietnam, in the 1980s, CB enthusiasts used commo checks as an excuse to talk to their "good buddies" along highways to find out about "smokies." Replaced by cellular phones in the nineties.

concertina barbed wire A type of barbed wire that is similar to a Slinky toy. Used to protect fixed positions.

conex A large steel container used to transport and store military goods, supplies, and equipment. Specially designed so that whatever is being sought is on the bottom, necessitating an hour of hard work in the sun to move items on top. At

times, the item being sought evaporates from the bottom of
the conex, causing one to wonder if it was really there in the
first place.

contact   A dreaded, yet magical word to describe a firefight between a unit of GIs and the VC or NVA. The word contact can
send shivers down one's spine and at the same time provide a
feeling of excitement and adventure.

C rations or **Cs**   Army canned food. Powdered eggs were the
worst. Beans and franks were filling. Mixing peanut butter
with grape jelly and smearing this goop on a can of pound
cake was almost as good as a package from home.

CS   Tear gas. In the field, it was used to flush VC from tunnels
and bunkers. In the rear areas, it was used to harass lifer types.
One CS grenade tossed into a hootch could serve as warning
to quit messing with the company personnel. The next
grenade might have a bang to it.

DEROS   Date of estimated return from overseas (with all
limbs and organs in the proper anatomic places).

det cord   A plastic-type rope made of explosives, used to hook
claymores together so that they fire at the same time. Can
be used in a variety of other situations where a big bang is
desired.

deuce-and-a-half   Two-and-one-half-ton military truck.

didi or *didi mau*   Another multilingual term learned in Nam by
GIs to increase their vocabulary. Vietnamese for "get the hell
out of here."

dink   A term for the Vietnamese enemy. (Used by GIs who
hated being in Nam and who lacked multicultural sensitivity.)

dopers   Another multilingual term. Borrowed from the drug
culture to mean someone who uses drugs. Usually referred to
a guy who blew pot (smoked marijuana for those not of the
sixties and seventies culture).

double-canopy jungle   Multilayer jungle growth.

drafted   The United States military estimates how many men
it will need to conduct a war and, after they get volunteers,
conscripts young men to join the military. Alternatives to
being drafted were to go to Canada, pull a Cassius Clay, or
kiss the recruiting sergeant on the mouth.

Dustoff   A helicopter used for medical evacuation.

early out   To terminate your term of enlistment before the
contracted date. Usually because of medical or educational
considerations.

EM Enlisted man; not an officer.

escape and evasion Course taught at AIT on how to get away from the enemy.

ETS Estimated termination of service, or when your tour of duty with Uncle Sam was over and you could start living your life again.

extending time Volunteering to serve more time in Nam so that one could leave Vietnam and the army at the same time. (DEROS and ETS at the same time.)

extraction The removing of troops from the field, usually by helicopter.

F-4 (Phantom) McDonnell Douglas fighter-bombers that saw heavy use in Vietnam. Also called fixed-winged aircraft or fast movers.

FAC Forward air controller.

fast movers Fixed-wing fighter aircraft.

firebase or **fire support base** A place usually cut out of the jungle that housed the artillery that supported infantry units in the field. Targets for the VC and NVA to overrun when they felt that they could. Every so often, a unit would come in from the field to guard the artillery and the fire support base. This usually was rest and recovery time from the ordeals of the boonies.

firefight Something you were never ready for. A shoot-out between U.S. and VC or NVA forces using small arms.

fire mission When the artillery fired in support of a unit on the field or to harass the enemy in suspected positions.

firepower Constructing a wall of lead. Establishing which side has the most guns and ammunition.

5-Mike (Five Mike) Someone in charge of resupply for a unit.

flak jacket Vests worn by U.S. soldiers to stop bullets and shrapnel. Usually only worn in rear areas of fire support bases. Some units used them in the field, but they were fairly heavy and too hot to carry on extended missions.

FNG You could be a fucking new guy for only a little while. Also called cherries by veterans. Anyone with more days left in country than the person he is talking to.

FO Forward observer. An artillery officer who traveled with grunt units and who called fire from 105, 155, or 175 artillery. The FO would also coordinate Cobra and fixed-wing strikes.

frag Short for fragmentation grenade. Also, to "frag" an officer meant to throw one of these grenades into his hootch.

Used as a term to threaten someone rather than to actually do. Example: "I'm going to frag your ass!"

Freedom Bird   After 365 days in Vietnam, the prettiest sight in the whole world. A Freedom Bird was the commercial aircraft that took one back to the United States.

free-fire zone   An area declared off-limits to all the good South Vietnamese people. Anyone in this area was assumed to be the enemy and could be fired upon immediately. No questions asked.

GI   Government issue. A World War II term for the infantry soldier.

goofy grape   The slang for purple smoke.

gook   The politically incorrect term for Viet Cong (VC) and North Vietnamese Regular Army troops. Also used in general GI talk to designate any friendly South Vietnamese person not in earshot.

graves registration   Army bookkeeping of men killed in Vietnam.

grease trap   Area outside a mess hall where used grease from cooking and food junk is thrown.

grunt   Proud to have been one. An infantry soldier.

gun ports   Holes cut in the side of a bunker through which one could fire a rifle. Usually about eighteen inches long and eight inches high.

gunship   Heavily armed helicopter used to support infantry troops or to stage independent attacks of enemy units. First used in Vietnam as major component of battle.

H & I   Harassment and interdiction. Artillery would fire up suspected enemy bases and staging areas. Costly in ammo, but not in U.S. lives. Attempts to keep the enemy off balance.

halazone tablets   Used to purify drinking water taken from streams and bomb craters.

HE   High-explosive shells.

heat tabs   Heating tablets, small blue chemical disks that burned slowly and gave off an intense, smokeless heat. Used to heat C rations and water. Useless for popping Jiffy Pop.

Ho Chi Minh trail   Not just one path through the jungle. A vast network of trails and roads running from southern North Vietnam, down through Laos and Cambodia, and into South Vietnam. It comprised the transportation system that supplied men and matériel to the NVA and VC.

hootch   Multilingual term for small house or bunker. Living area.

horn Radio or handset to a radio.

hot LZ A landing zone that was or would be under fire as the choppers set down.

HQ Headquarters.

Huey UH-1 helicopter. The workhorse of the Vietnam War. It carried troops to and from battle, food and supplies to the field, and generally did anything that required transportation.

humping or humpin' Carrying a heavy load. Also to work the jungle on a search-and-destroy mission.

IG Inspector general.

in country In Vietnam.

Indian country Areas in the jungle where hostile forces could be found. Same as bush, boonies, or boondocks.

infiltration To slip into and out of an area without being detected.

insert or insertion To be placed in a combat area, usually by helicopter.

Instant NCO Same as shake-and-bake sergeant. Someone who attended a special leadership school for NCOs at Fort Benning, Georgia, before they went to Vietnam. Although many Instant NCOs were fine people, some let the rank go to their head. The smart ones learned from the seasoned grunts, no matter what the rank.

Jungle penetrator A metal cylinder, usually painted yellow and used to pull wounded GIs out of the jungle canopy. It had foldout legs and was attached by a steel cable to a Dustoff or medevac chopper. Used when the helicopter could not land to pick up the hurt GI.

K-bar knife A type of military knife prized as an elite weapon and utility knife.

KIA Killed in action. Also called Line one.

kill zone An area that was constructed outside of permanent bases and fire support bases where the vegetation had been cleared so that there would be a clear zone of fire. On ambush, it was the area covered by claymore mines and small-arms fire. Any enemy caught in the kill zone was supposed to be dead meat.

Kit Carson scout Converted Communist VC or NVA who acted as guides and advisers for the U.S. units. A flip of the coin as to how good they were. Some had a grudge against their former political system and were extremely good soldiers, and some were less motivated.

Lambrettas   Vietnam motorcycles made into taxicabs with a covered platform on the back.

landline   A telephone system installed at permanent bases.

LAW   Light antitank weapon. Used against bunkers sometimes. It was a single-shot weapon and was fired from the shoulder the same way one would fire a bazooka.

lifer   A career soldier. As they said, "The Vietnam War isn't much of a war, but it's the only one we have."

Line one   Killed in action. Same as KIA.

lock and load   To chamber a round into a weapon.

log or **log bird**   Resupply or resupply by chopper.

LP   Listening post. A group of three men who would set up outside the company perimeter and act as an early warning of attack.

LRP   Long-range patrol. Small teams of men, usually six in number, sent out to observe enemy movement or do behind-the-lines operations.

LRRP   Long-range reconnaissance patrol dehydrated food. Better than C rations, but required extra water to fix. Light to carry.

LT   (pronounced ell-tee) Lieutenant.

LZ   Landing zone. In the field, it was a clearing or opening in the jungle. Some units called fire support bases LZs.

MARS   The ham radio link between the United States and Vietnam.

M-14 rifle   The infantry weapon used before the M-16. It was used, with a scope, as a sniper weapon in some units even after the general introduction of the M-16.

M-16 rifle   The plastic-handle assault rifle used by U.S. forces in RVN. It was lightweight so we could carry more bullets than with the M-14. It was 5.56mm and said to jam easily. Maintenance was important, especially keeping the side dust-cover shut.

M-60 machine gun   The basic machine gun carried by the infantry. Usually very dependable. Fired 7.62mm ammunition that weighed thirteen pounds per can. Used by Rambo in many of his movies. (Ever wonder where the people carrying Rambo's ammo are?)

M-79 grenade launcher   Shot 40mm grenades. Also shot canister rounds. Every unit had one man who carried one. Good for clearing enemy snipers out of trees.

magazine   The container for bullets that was fed into the bottom of the M-16. Contained twenty bullets, although most people put in only nineteen so the spring that pushed the bullets up into the rifle would not jam.

marking round   The first round shot by the artillery to indicate where the next high-explosive rounds would land. A way of marking a unit's location in relation to where the unit thought that they were on a map.

medevac   A helicopter that would extract the wounded and dead.

MIA   Missing in action.

monsoon   More rain than you ever want to see. Roughly April through October. Usually comes about 4:00 in the afternoon or when you have just finished cooking your C rations over your fire and want to settle down and eat in peace. Continues until you are soaking wet and have used every cussword you know. Returns at night to make sure that you are too wet and miserable to sleep comfortably.

morning reports   A numerical accounting of where each member of the company was that day.

MPC   Military payment certificates. Looked like Monopoly money and was created as a money system separate from U.S. greenback or Vietnamese piasters. Attempt to keep American currency out of Vietnamese hands.

Nam (the Nam)   Short for Vietnam.

NCO   Noncommissioned officer; rank E-4 (corporal) through E-9.

NDP   Night defensive position.

Number fucking 10,000   Nothing in the United States is this bad.

Number One   GI talk for good or the best.

Number Ten   GI talk for bad or worst.

NVA   North Vietnamese Army. Hard-core fighters from North Vietnam who came down the Ho Chi Minh trail to fight American imperialist pigs.

OCS   Officers candidate school. Required a three-year enlistment and then you were a semiofficer and a gentleman. Better than ROTC and nothing like West Point training for the career soldier.

OP   Observation post (don't volunteer). Three or four individuals go outside the defense perimeter to act as an early warning for the main body of troops.

P-38   Army can opener.

PFC Private first class.

piasters Vietnamese currency.

point or **point man** The first man in line. The first to walk into danger. A person to be admired.

POW Prisoner of war.

PRC-25 or **PRICK-25** The most common radio humped by an infantry unit.

PX Post exchange.

R & R Rest and Relaxation. Time-outs from the war that lasted about six days. Men who were married or who had someone special would usually go to Hawaii. Single men sampled the delights of the Orient in Taipei, Bangkok, or Singapore. For round-eye women, soldiers went to Sydney, Australia.

Redleg Another name for artillery.

REMF Rear echelon motherfucker; what most infantry grunts wanted to be. A REMF-support personnel who served in a noncombatant role. It took seven REMFs to support one infantry soldier. I never appreciated that the REMFs played an important part in the war until I became one.

Re-up Reenlist.

RPG Communist-made rocket launcher, fired B-40 rockets and was used by both the VC and NVA. It was effective against armor, fixed emplacements, helicopters, patrol boats, and infantry soldiers.

RTO Radiotelephone operator.

rubber Rubber trees or rubber-tree plantations.

rucksack The backpack worn by grunts in the field. A person's rucksack was all he had in the world as he moved from place to place. It contained food, water, blanket and poncho, personal items, and munitions for war.

Saigon Tea girls Not really prostitutes. They provided company and companionship for stud U.S. soldiers. Watch your wallet. When you stopped buying tea, you became a Cheap Charlie.

sapper Sneaky devils. Especially trained VC or NVA who would infiltrate a permanent U.S. installation and, using various forms of explosives, cause as much damage as possible.

search-and-destroy mission A land tour of the Southeast Asian environment, carrying sixty to seventy pounds of equipment with the proposed military objective of finding the enemy and destroying him and his capacity to wage war.

selector switch A three-position switch on the left side of the

M-16 rifle that enabled the soldier to select safe, semiautomatic, or full automatic firing.

shit-burning detail   Mixing diesel fuel with human waste and burning both. This procedure required stirring and a strong stomach.

short   The way we measured time in Nam. Even with one day in country, you were short(er) than that FNG getting off the plane. A truly short person had fifty-nine days and wake-up left in country.

short-time   Sex with a Vietnamese female. Paid or unpaid. Good short-time was said to be when the female moved her hips too.

short-timer   Someone who was getting really close to the end of their tour of duty.

sitrep   Situation report; regularly scheduled radio transmissions between units in the field and command-and-control personnel to check to see if the unit is okay. Also a check between the unit's CP and the various platoons and squads to see that whoever is on guard is alert.

skid or **skid of a helicopter**   The runner under the helicopter.

SKS   Communist-made semiautomatic assault rifle. Replaced whenever possible by the AK-47, which, among other features, could fire on automatic.

slick   Another name for a helicopter.

smoke or **smoke grenade**   A hand grenade that issued various colors of smoke when the pin was pulled. Used to mark friendly positions.

solly or **so solly**   Slang for sorry.

SOP   Standard operating procedure.

SOS   Shit on a shingle, i.e., creamed chipped beef on toast, a fixture on army breakfast menus worldwide and beloved of lifers everywhere.

stand-down   When a unit returned from the field for rest and recovery.

starlight scope   A night-vision device to amplify any available light source, such as the stars and moon, so that someone using it can see at night.

Stars and Stripes   The U.S. military newspaper.

tarmac   The side of an airstrip or helicopter landing pad.

tracer bullet   Ammunition containing a chemical composition to mark the flight of projectiles by a trail of smoke and fire. American tracer bullets were red, and VC and NVA were green.

triple-canopy jungle　Very thick jungle with dense overhead foliage.

turcott　A not so nice word for shit.

Uncle Ho　Nickname for Ho Chi Minh, the leader of North Vietnam.

VC, Viet Cong, or **Victor Charlie**　Slang name for South Vietnamese who during the day were sympathetic to their government and at night changed sides and fought U.S. troops. Wore black PJs.

wait-a-minute vine　Any one of a million types of vines that covered the jungle floor and caused one to trip or fall.

WIA　Wounded in action, also called a Line two.

World or **the World**　The United States, USA, home.

WP or **willie peter**　White phosphorus round that burned with an intense heat.

XO　Executive officer.

zapped　Killed in combat.

zipperhead　Politically incorrect term for Vietnamese.

DON'T MISS THE MOST AUTHENTIC
THRILLER OF THE DECADE!

REMOTE CONTROL
by Andy McNab

A former member of the Special Air Service crack elite
force, Andy McNab has seen action on all five conti-
nents. In January 1991, he commanded the eight-man
SAS squad that went behind Iraqi lines to destroy
Saddam's scuds. McNab eventually became the British
army's most highly decorated serving soldier and
remains closely involved with intelligence communi-
ties on both sides of the Atlantic.

Now, in his explosive fiction debut, he has drawn on
his seventeen years of active service to create a thriller
of high-stakes intrigue and relentless action. With
chillingly authentic operational detail never before
seen in thrillers, REMOTE CONTROL is a novel so
real and suspenseful it sets a new standard for the
genre.

Available in hardcover in May 1999 from Ballantine Books
at a special introductory price of $19.95.

THE ONLY WAR WE HAD
A Platoon Leader's Journal of Vietnam

by Michael Lee Lanning

During his tour in Vietnam with the 199th Light Infantry Brigade, Lt. Michael Lee Lanning and his men slogged through booby-trapped rice paddies and hacked their way through triple-canopy forest in pursuit of elusive Viet Cong and North Vietnamese Army regulars. Lanning's entire year in Vietnam was spent in the field, and he saw a lot of combat, as an infantry platoon leader, as a reconnaissance platoon leader, and as a first-lieutenant company commander.

In this book, based on the journal he kept in Nam, Lanning writes of his experiences—and of the terror, boredom, rage, and excitement he shared with countless other American soldiers.

Published by Ivy Books.
Available in bookstores everywhere.